Being Korean, Becoming Japanese?

Being Korean, Becoming Japanese?

Nationhood, Citizenship, and Resistance in Japan

Hwaji Shin

University of Hawai'i Press
Honolulu

© 2024 University of Hawai'i Press
All rights reserved
Printed in the United States of America

First printed, 2024

Library of Congress Cataloging-in-Publication Data

Names: Shin, Hwaji, author.
Title: Being Korean, becoming Japanese? : nationhood, citizenship, and resistance in Japan / Hwaji Shin.
Description: Honolulu : University of Hawai'i, [2024] | Includes bibliographical references and index.
Identifiers: LCCN 2023055174 (print) | LCCN 2023055175 (ebook) | ISBN 9780824896140 (hardcover) | ISBN 9780824898427 (trade paperback) | ISBN 9780824898366 (kindle edition) | ISBN 9780824898359 (epub) | ISBN 9780824898342 (pdf)
Subjects: LCSH: Koreans—Japan--Social conditions. | Koreans—Legal status, laws, etc. —Japan—History. | Nationalism—Japan. | Japan—Ethnic relations—Government policy.
Classification: LCC DS831.K6 S5493 2024 (print) | LCC DS831.K6 (ebook) | DDC 305.8957/052--dc23/eng/20240315
LC record available at https://lccn.loc.gov/2023055174
LC ebook record available at https://lccn.loc.gov/2023055175

This book is freely available in an open access edition thanks to the generous support of Center for Japanese Studies at the University of Michigan.

Cover design by Soyeon Jung; photographs courtesy of the author.
The cover is inspired by the art of Korean bojagi patchwork.

University of Hawai'i Press books are printed on acid-free paper and meet the guidelines for permanence and durability of the Council on Library Resources.

For my son, Oliver

Contents

Preface	ix
Acknowledgments	xiii
A Note on Names	xix
Chapter 1. Introduction: A Pendulum-Swing Pattern of Change	1
Chapter 2. Pan-Asian Empire	34
Chapter 3. The Birth of a Homogeneous Nation-State	78
Chapter 4. The Fight for Social Justice and Human Rights	127
Chapter 5. Conclusion: Toward Diverse and Inclusive Japan	176
Notes	211
Bibliography	225
Index	253

Preface

"You will see a world I have never imagined."

I distinctly remember these words of my late grandfather. As he sat on a hospital bed, he was in awe to learn about the near end of the USSR on the evening news. I was not sure why he would care about such a remote event abroad. I was much more concerned about his deteriorating health as he lost his battle to cancer. Shortly after this conversation, his life came to end, and so did the USSR.

His life and mine were starkly different. My grandfather came to Japan as a child labor migrant from Korea after it was colonized by Japan. To support his family after his own father's untimely death, he started working full time in various forms of manual labor at rice cake factories, coal mines, and construction sites, instead of attending school. When he was twenty years old, he began to acquire the skills to work in manufacturing factories. He eventually started his own small factory near Korea Town in Osaka to produce nuts and bolts for airplanes. As a child, I was not allowed to see him at work as he said it was dangerous because of all the heavy equipment. But I later learned from my mother that our grandfather did not want his grandchildren to see him working in such filthy conditions, covered with metal dust and oil. His business slowly died out in the late twentieth century as computerized machines in China were able to mass produce those parts more cheaply and quickly.

I grew up directly witnessing the struggles of colonial migrants in Japan. Like many Koreans of their generations, my grandparents and parents grew up poor, and none of them could afford to attend college. Our grandmothers were illiterate, so I would have to accompany them as their translator whenever they needed to travel via public transportation or visit their doctors' offices. All of them worked very hard despite limited opportunities and blunt racism so that my siblings and I could receive education, with the hope that this would help us overcome the structural barriers that marginalized many Koreans like us. Thanks to them, I went to college, not only in Japan but also in the United States. I became a first-generation college graduate and the first in my family to earn a PhD.

My academic achievement is often misinterpreted as meaning that racism in Japan was no longer an issue for my generation. But the truth is that no matter how hard we worked, we were never able to escape from racism and discrimination in Japan. I was subject to racially motivated bullying at school. My parents told me to use a Japanese name to remain inconspicuous at Japanese public schools, but they also instructed me not to hide our identity if anyone asked. This contradictory instruction made perfect sense to me: I should not feel ashamed of who I am, but I shouldn't expose myself to the danger of ethnoracial hatred and violence, either. I had to live in an intricate balance of resilience and vulnerability.

This book is about the trajectories of historical transformations of nationhood, immigration, and the Japanese national self-image. But underneath such a large historical process, there is also the historical transformation of the lives of ordinary people, including my family, who witnessed and survived a turbulent twentieth century in Far East Asia. People's lives were interrupted and many families were displaced and separated as conflicts and violence rampaged in front of their eyes during the past century. Their defiance, defeat, sorrow, joy, despair, and hope were the fuel of the engine that drove Far East Asia throughout the last century. I wanted to capture these dynamic emotions and share this story with the rest of world, not only as a sociologist but also as someone who has firsthand knowledge of the legacy of colonialism and generational trauma.

However, publishing this book was nothing but easy. I tried to publish this book fifteen years ago, shortly after I completed my PhD, but I faced many rejections from academic publishers. Some editors bluntly told me then that there was little interest in and thus no market for this type of book or subject, while others simply ignored my queries. Meanwhile, I saw other scholars with little to no direct experience of the trauma suffered by descendants of colonial migrants in Japan publishing their own scholarly narratives about our experiences. I eventually developed the same false consciousness that plagued many minority scholars like myself: I began to believe I was simply not good

Preface

enough to write a book. Thus, I hid my work like an old scar with shame and tried to convince myself to move on to another project.

In 2020, I was supposed to temporarily relocate to Ann Arbor, Michigan, so I could begin my tenure as a Toyota Visiting Professor at the Center for Japanese Studies (CJS) at the University of Michigan. During such a coveted research fellowship, I planned to embark on a new research project that had nothing to do with Koreans in Japan. However, the pandemic changed everything for me and my family; it led to my husband's job loss, my son's yearlong school closure, and Japan's border restrictions, preventing me from doing field research in Japan for a new project. I ended up doing this fellowship remotely from San Francisco. Like many female academics with school-age children, I was prepared to accept that the academic year of 2020–2021 would be the least productive time span of my career.

However, I ended up writing the entire book manuscript during this supposedly lost year. Being cooped up at home with my husband and son, I had a chance to reckon with what was transpiring in the world around me. The world had changed from fifteen years ago, when I first attempted to publish this book. As evident in the success of Min Jin Lee's best-selling novel, *Pachinko,* and its TV adaptation by Apple TV, for which I served as a historical content and cultural sensitivity consultant, people around the globe are interested in and moved by the historical narratives of Koreans in Japan. After all, our world has continued to be plagued with the repeated symbolic and physical violence of xenophobia, racism, and sexism. People continue to irrationally opt for dis- and misinformation rather than scientific data presented by scholars, and to harbor hatred against those they regard as "different." History indeed repeats itself; democracy is once again in peril, exposing how toxic racism and xenophobia continue to pose a real threat to people at the margins of society. These are the same topics examined in this book, but in a different historical and geopolitical context.

At the same time, however, we also have witnessed an undying passion for justice and democracy prevailing around the world. Many people, including my students, marched on the streets after George Floyd's death to call for justice for the African American community as well as to protest against rising anti-Asian hatred and violence. Witnessing the display of their fierce courage, all the ideas that I had written and stored away over the years rushed through my mind. It was in this context that I agreed to give a webinar on the project that I was about to abandon at the University of Michigan in September 2020. After the talk, I received numerous emails from members of the audience, including Asian Americans who had family connections with Koreans in Japan. They thanked me for filling the void of their family history and for my authentic and candid narrative. After I read these strangers' feedback, the project that I had hidden like an old scar suddenly felt like a battle scar I should display with pride. Perhaps the world not only wants but needs someone like me to write this kind of book after all, I thought.

My remaining challenge, then, was that I didn't know how I would pull off writing the book while juggling competing demands at home in the midst of a global pandemic. To make the matter worse, my own university's administration issued a building closure policy as a pandemic-related cost-saving measure, preventing me from freely accessing vital archival data stored in my office on campus in San Francisco. The deck was stacked against me as I strove to write this book. Yet despite the challenges I faced, I managed to push this manuscript through, largely thanks to the supportive family, friends, and colleagues I list in the acknowledgments.

Acknowledgments

The first colleagues and dear friends I want to thank for their support are Allison Alexy and Reggie Jackson at the University of Michigan. As director of the Center for Japanese Studies (CJS) at the University of Michigan, Reggie warmly welcomed me and allowed me to exercise a level of academic freedom that I had never enjoyed before in my career. His commitment to antiracist pedagogy inspired me profoundly. Allison generously and patiently shared her expertise with me. Her keen intellect, compassion, and professionalism saved me on countless occasions. I often told her (and truly believed) that my late grandparents sent her as my guardian angel so I could finish this book against all odds. Writing a book for the first time was like learning how to swim in open water. Whenever I felt like I was drowning, Allison reminded me that the water was in fact so shallow that I could actually stand up myself. She embodies the definition of the strong, loyal, caring ally and confidante that every minority woman needs to survive the demanding and toxic academic world. I am proud to tell her, "My rocket is now launched, all thanks to you!"

Many scholars inspired me to explore the questions addressed in this book. I am particularly thankful for these area experts: Martin Albrow, Eammon Callan, David Jacobson, John Torpey, Kiyoteru Tsutsui, and Jane Yamashiro. I especially appreciate Kiyo at Stanford University, whom I first met at Stony Brook University when I was a graduate student. I had the privilege of sharing my dissertation work and insights as a Korean minority woman from Japan with him for our two collaborative projects, and he has always been supportive of my career development. If it weren't for his introduction, I would not have had a chance to work with Allison and Reggie, as well as with amazing staff members such as Yuri Fukazawa, Robin Griffin, Do-Hee Morsman, and Barbara Kinzer, who supported me during my fellowship at CJS. I am immensely grateful for the generous support of CJS's Toyota Visiting Professor program, which made this book digitally available.

This book wouldn't have been published if it weren't for Stephanie Chun, an acquisitions editor at the University of Hawai'i Press, who gave my manuscript fair and due consideration. Stephanie is a very skilled editor. I knew through her clear guidance, punctual communication, and supportive patience that my book was in very good hands. I also want to thank the anonymous reviewers who gave me thoughtful and extensive feedback on an earlier draft of the manuscript. Their comments and suggestions were extraordinarily helpful during the revision process. I am grateful to the University of Hawai'i Press editorial board, which accepted my book proposal. I am also incredibly thankful to my managing editor, Gianna Marsella, for her compassionate support during the production process.

My book is based on a huge volume of archival data, which took nearly twenty years to collect and analyze. My data collection was made possible thanks to the generous support of the Japan Fund at the Freeman Spogli Institute for International Studies at Stanford University and to both the Faculty Development Funds and the Jesuit Foundation at the University of San Francisco. I also relied on data that belongs to private collections of Korean and Japanese activists in Japan. Out of respect for their wish to protect their privacy, I will not mention the names of all the private collectors, but I am deeply grateful to them for entrusting me to be a custodian of their priceless historical evidence. My special thanks go to Buraku Kaihōdomei, the Korean Christian Center in Osaka, the Korean Christian Church in Japan, the Human Rights Center at Kansai University, Mindan, Mintōren, Tokkabi Kodomokai in Osaka, the History Museum of J-Koreans in Tokyo, and the Utoro Peace Memorial Museum in Kyoto. Many of them kindly allowed me access to their archival collections. So many librarians and archivists at public libraries in Japan, especially the National Diet Library in Tokyo, patiently helped me to locate the archives that I needed. In the United States, where I struggled to access Japanese-language sources, especially during the pandemic lockdown, Keiko Yokota-Carter at the Asia Library at the University of Michigan and Ih-hae Chang at the East Asian Library at Stanford University helped me tremendously.

The task of organizing and analyzing my massive collection of data in an orderly fashion presented a whole other level of challenge.

Acknowledgments xv

I would have been lost in the sea of archives if I had not met Professor Emeritus Mizuno Naoki at Kyoto University, who helped me to identify and analyze these archival data over the years. Hida Yūichi at Kobe Youth Christian Center also helped me to chronicle some key aspects of Korean activism in Japan. I benefited from the wisdom and knowledge of my friend and Korean history expert, Lee Sung-Yup at Bukkyō University. My graduate student research assistants at the University of San Francisco were incredibly helpful. Amanda Smith, Shun Savory, and Thuy Tran tirelessly digitized, cataloged, and coded voluminous historical data with me. Their assistance allowed me to analyze these voluminous data efficiently. I am grateful to Hannah Hutton, whose eagle eyes spotted numerous embarrassing typos in my manuscript. I also want to thank Mac Garcia and Ellen Tilton-Cantrell, who helped me polish my manuscript with their excellent developmental editing service. Thanks to their intelligent and meticulous guidance, I was able to overcome the linguistic bias in academia and to get over my imposter syndrome as a non-native English writer and first-time author.

I also want to acknowledge former dean of the College of Arts and Sciences Marcelo Camperi and former provost Jennifer Turpin at the University of San Francisco. Both of them eagerly supported me when I went through a challenging pregnancy and postpartum recovery—obstacles that could have easily derailed a female academic's career. Their committed support helped me to overcome these personal challenges in the middle of tenure and promotion applications and helped keep the door open for me to finish this book.

My special thanks go to the outstanding administrative staff members at Stony Brook, Wanda Vegas, Sharon Worksman, and Patricia Bremer, who always looked out for me during the time I was a graduate student. I also want to especially thank Amy Joseph and Jamie Andan, amazing administrative staff members and dear friends at the University of San Francisco, who supported me behind the scenes. I also acknowledge my friends Ih-hae Chang, Saburō Horikawa, Stephanie Sears, Matthew Sommer, Amy Traver, and Kären Wigen, who have extended their warm encouragement over the years. Their genuine friendship has been a true blessing to me and my family. I also thank John LaViolette, a kind, generous, and intelligent human being who helped protect my academic freedom and intellectual property.

I would not have become an author, teacher, and researcher if I had not met my devoted advisers and mentors: Hitoshi Okuda, Jeremy Hein, Helaine Minkus, Michael Schwartz, Daniel Levy, Jackie Smith, xvi *Acknowledgments*

and Javier Auyero. Jeremy was the reason I pursued my academic career in sociology. If he had not introduced me to the works of Chuck Tilly, my sociology hero, I would not have developed my undying interests in big structure, large process, and huge comparison. Javier took me to Chuck's contentious politics seminar at Columbia University, which was a valuable outlet for me to present my scholarly ideas to first-class scholars in New York City and the world, some of whom became my lifelong friends. In both Michael Schwartz and Daniel Levy, I found the best dissertation advisers one could ever ask for. Michael has the gift of seeing the best qualities in a student, even when the rest of the world fails to notice them. He frequently reminded me why this book was still worth pursuing, even when I couldn't see its worth or my own. Whenever he introduces me to his colleagues, he compliments me as if I am a world-famous rock star. To me and everyone else, he is the rock star, with the magical power of turning the ordinary into the extraordinary. Daniel is more than just a mentor. He frequently checked on me even after I graduated and continues to encourage me professionally and personally. What made him so special was not only his superb intellect and critical thinking but also his sincerity and genuineness, which was anchored in his best interests not just for my academic success but also my personal well-being. I always look up to him as my mentor and role model, and cherish him as my friend. Michael and Daniel's humanizing and devoted mentoring style is something I am committed to emulating when I mentor my own students.

My academic career would not have started if it weren't for dedicated mentorship and encouragement from Okuda Hitoshi sensei. He mentored me patiently from the time I was a clueless and helpless eighteen-year-old junior college student at Kansai Gaidai in Osaka. As a first-generation college student, I was untrained and unsophisticated. But Okuda sensei patiently trained me and helped me to turn my own shortcomings into strength. When I couldn't obtain opportunities in Japan, he told me that my stage was not just Japan but also the world, and he enthusiastically supported me as I worked to obtain a chance to study abroad in the United States. When the scholarship foundations in Japan refused to recognize my eligibility on the grounds that I am Korean, he encouraged me to push back and helped me to win my eligibility and the scholarship itself. He is a strong intellectual, relentless activist, and compassionate teacher, whom I admired and aspired to emulate. His encouragement always felt like a bright ray of hope to guide me through the dark, unpaved path I chose to walk.

Acknowledgments   xvii

Thanks to him, I had the privilege to conduct my first research on Koreans in Japan in the Nishinari district of Osaka, where I met my dear friend and *senpai* Tanigawa Masahiko, the director of the Buraku Liberation and Human Rights Research Institute. He taught me how to listen and reach to the real voices of ordinary people at the margins.

I owe everything else to my loving family. I was fortunate to have a large extended family by both blood and choice. I would not have come to the United States for education if I had not met my very special host family in New Jersey, James and Nancy Mallett, and their daughters, Kim, Kristine, Karin, and Kori, when I was a sixteen-year-old Lion's Club Youth Exchange Student from Japan. They were my first impression of Americans—open, kind, generous, and loving. Because they embraced me like their own, I always felt secure in the United States while I was miles away from my family in Japan. Had I not met them, I probably would not have chosen the United States as a place for my education and career. I am forever grateful for their love and support.

My best friend, Joshua Kim, believed in me through the ups and downs in my life. He is always the first person I go to with the best and worst news in my life. He knew I would write this book one day, even when I didn't even think it was possible. He calmed me down and lifted me up when I fell apart, which admittedly happened rather often! I leaned on his reassuring and cheering words—"It's going to be fine, Hwaji!"—countless times during this unpredictable journey. I am forever grateful for his love, support, generosity, intelligence, humor, and candor. He is my inspiration and family by choice—one of the best choices I have ever made in my life.

Nothing in my life came easily to me. I had to be relentless, tenacious, and stubborn to get what my peers took for granted, from academic scholarships to job opportunities. My resilience stems from my grandparents and parents, who taught me the virtue of honest hard work. Now that I am a mother, I understand how difficult it must have been to raise a rebellious and overly independent-minded daughter like me. They must have been so worried when they allowed their teenage daughter to leave for the United States alone. I am forever grateful for my parents' courage in letting me leave Japan alone so I would be set free from the curse of the colonial legacy that plagued all of us. My siblings are the most powerful and valuable allies in my life. My brother financially supported me at times so I could focus on my education, while my sisters looked after me and later my son so

xviii   *Acknowledgments*

that I could work on my research in Japan. They also served as my research assistants during my archival research and often sent the books for me from Japan. Without them, I could not do even half of what I have done in my life.

My loving husband, Scott, and our dear son, Oliver, are my indispensable and core support system and the most precious treasures in my life. Scott was my editor-in-chief, a fellow sociology and data nerd, very competent tech support, and the most patient, kind, forgiving, and loving partner. He made all the charts for this book. But his contribution to this book is more than just tech support. He is always the first person I share my ideas and writings with. He is the first victim who has to listen to my endless frustrations. He is the last person at the end of a long day to give me a warm embrace. His intelligent, constructive editorial feedback is invaluable in my journey as an author. He has seen me at my worst moments, but he manages to give me his undying devotion and love and to forgive my unforgivable mistakes. I don't know what I did to deserve him, but I know how lucky I am. Oliver is our best cocreation (besides this book). His cheeky smile and silly jokes made me laugh, especially when I felt the weight of the world on my shoulders. I forever cherish all the walks we did together on Great Highway Promenade, Ocean Beach, and Stern Groves in San Francisco, during the scary and lonely COVID-19 lockdown. Walking while holding his warm, tiny hand comforted my tired soul after long nights of writing. He always reminded me of the reason I chose to write this book. It will be years before he will read and understand it. One day, however, I hope that he will see in this book the same kind of love, resilience, and hope which my own parents and grandparents planted in me so I could live the kind of life beyond their imagination to the fullest extent. After all, this book was born from such powerful energy that I inherit from the people who survived the turbulent history captured in this book.

A Note on Names

This book follows the East Asian convention for Japanese, Chinese, and Korean names, with the surname first, followed by the given name, with a few exceptions. In romanizing Korean names, I did not always convert personal names into a single uniform style such as Revised Romanization, McCune-Reischauer Romanization, or Yale Romanization. Whenever it was possible to verify the spellings used by the individuals themselves, I used those spellings out of respect for their personal preference. For historic and well-known figures such as Korean activists, political leaders, and scholars, I used the spellings most conventionally used in English publications. If neither condition applied, then I used the Revised Romanization style.

Chapter One

INTRODUCTION
A Pendulum-Swing Pattern of Change

In 1932, on the streets of Tokyo, a Korean man named Park Chungeum celebrated his election victory with his supporters. He was a citizen of the Japanese Empire. He came to Japan from colonized Korea as a labor migrant and then became engaged in politics in Japan. Exercising his full suffrage in Japan as a citizen of Japanese Empire, he became the first Korean elected member of the House of Representatives in Japan. He enjoyed two terms as an elected official and worked side by side with Japanese lawmakers and political activists. Park Chungeum lived in Japan until his death in 1973.

In 1948, in Kobe, another Korean man, named Park Jubeom, was arrested and imprisoned. Like Park Chungeum, he came to Japan as a labor migrant during the colonial period and became a local political activist. When the Japanese government unilaterally revoked citizenship from Koreans living in Japan after Japan lost the war and its colonies, he became stateless and held no citizenship status recognized by any sovereign state. Despite the precariousness of this situation, Park Jubeom and his fellow Koreans organized mass protests on the streets of Kobe and Osaka when the Japanese government abruptly ordered the closure of all Korean ethnic schools and urged Koreans to send their children to Japanese schools instead. Park Jubeom was accused of disturbing the social order, was arrested, and died shortly after his medical release from prison in 1949.

In 1974, in Yokohama, a young Korean man named Park Jongseok joined with Japanese supporters to celebrate his landmark legal victory against one of Japan's largest global corporations, Hitachi Inc.

His parents came to Japan as colonial labor migrants from Korea, just as Park Chungeum and Park Jubeom did. But Park Jongseok was born and raised in Japan and has used a Japanese name, Arai Shōji, throughout his life. The use of a Japanese name was and remains a common practice among Koreans in Japan and is but one legacy of Japanese colonial assimilation policy. Park Jongseok is a Special Permanent Resident Alien of Japan and holds citizenship from South Korea—a country he has never lived in. Soon after his high school graduation, Park Jongseok applied for a job at Hitachi using his Japanese name. Although he successfully received a job offer, Hitachi rescinded the employment opportunity after they learned of his Korean identity. Park Jongseok filed a lawsuit against Hitachi for job discrimination, and the lower court of Yokohama city decided on his behalf. Park Jongseok worked for Hitachi, using his Korean name, until his retirement in 2011.

These three Korean men happened to share the same surname. Although they all fought for political and social causes in Japan, their similarities end there. At the junctures mentioned above, each of these men held a different legal status in Japan; this legal status determined the specific rights, if any, granted to each. In 1932, Park Chungeum was a citizen of the Japanese Empire and could therefore exercise his suffrage and enjoy political stature as an elected member of the Japanese national government. By 1948, however, Koreans in Japan had been turned into stateless aliens whose rights were neither recognized nor protected by any sovereign state in the aftermath of World War II. Park Jongseok is a Special Permanent Resident of Japan who holds South Korean citizenship. Despite his noncitizen status in Japan, he successfully fought one of major global corporations to have his rights recognized.

The stories of these three Parks provide an important glimpse into the intertwined and shifting histories of nationhood, citizenship, and migration in Japan. Over a period of less than half a century, the legal status of Koreans in Japan was drastically transformed: from Japanese citizens to stateless people, and then to Special Permanent Resident Aliens. These changes fundamentally impacted their livelihoods and life chances. At the same time, Japan's nationhood and migration policies underwent drastic changes, as Japan shifted from a pan-Asian empire that permitted migration from its colonies to a nation-state imagined as homogeneous that rejected immigrants and refugees and then to a global nation-state that, once again, imported labor immigrants to fill labor vacuums as Japan's population declined. These multiple transformations, which occurred in rapid succession over the course of the twentieth century, present an important opportunity for scholars to investigate how these changes came about and how such changes can happen in any society. This book offers exactly such an investigation.

What triggers the transformations of nationhood, of citizenship, and of migration policies in societies? And what kinds of relationships exist between nation, citizenship, and migration policies? *Being Korean, Becoming Japanese?* explores these two questions by tracing nearly one hundred years of historical transformations of nationhood, citizenship, and migration policies in Japan. This book challenges the persistent popular belief that Japan's collective sense of homogeneous nationhood is responsible for the exclusive citizenship and migration policies practiced in Japan. I argue that the relationship between nationhood, citizenship, and migration policies in Japan is neither causal nor static, as popularly assumed. Instead, the nature of the relationship between them has always been fluid, malleable, and historically contingent. As such, the relationship appears to be different depending on the specific historical contexts in which we examine it. In other words, nationhood, citizenship, and migration policy appear to be closely coupled at particular historical points, and decoupled at other points.[1]

To understand the contingent and shifting nature of this relationship, we need to identify both endogenous and exogenous factors that influence these transformations. Then we need to examine their impact simultaneously, emphasizing their relationship to each other. Specifically, we need to trace three sets of factors across a flow of history: (1) the larger policy currents of the state and elites; (2) efforts by nonstate actors, and especially marginalized groups, to organize around citizenship and migration issues; and (3) the placement of the nation-state within world society. The term "world society" refers to a concept by sociologist John Meyer (2010), which views the world as consisting of states, institutions, and social actors that valorize globalized cultural norms. Examinations like the one I undertake here must be sensitive to the different ways these sets of factors interact with one another under different historical circumstances. This book shows how a sociohistorical analysis of these transformations helps explain the nature of the relationship between nationhood, citizenship, and migration in any society.

My analysis travels through the course of the twentieth and early twenty-first centuries. During this journey, snapshots of numerous key events provide information that is analytically important for addressing this question: What prompts a society to choose and embrace a certain type of nationhood, a specific self-image, and particular citizenship and migration policies? In analyzing these snapshots, we will see how the relationship between nationhood, citizenship, and migration is contingent on the properties of the political and cultural fields during a given period in history. Additionally, previous choices pertaining to national self-image and to citizenship and migration policies unexpectedly limit subsequent options for constructing self-image and policy. Thus, nationhood and citizenship cannot be constructed in a way that is entirely free from past imaginaries; at the same time, they are also not the direct result of an unbroken continuity of past practices. Instead, they are always circumscribed by the past itself.

This book uses the Japanese case to demonstrate that nationhood, citizenship, and migration policies are not just the invention of a select group of powerful elites or lawmakers. The policy repertoire of the state was simultaneously shaped by those who became the target of those policies and who became marginalized throughout society. This book shines a special light on such marginalized people—namely, Koreans in Japan, whose legal status shifted in parallel to the transformation of Japan's collective sense of nationhood. Although their voices were often suppressed, their persistent dissenting efforts shaped the making of nationhood, citizenship, and migration policies in Japan, even if these efforts inadvertently led to unfavorable outcomes for them.

Deciphering this mechanism allows us to understand why Japan's nationhood, citizenship, and migration policies followed a dialectical, pendulum-swing pattern of change—from inclusion to exclusion to inclusion or from decoupling to coupling to decoupling—in the twentieth and early twenty-first centuries. While laws, policies, and a sense of nationhood oscillate in such a pendulum-swing pattern, the Japanese government continues to oppress and exploit its migrant population, creating a durable structure of ethno-racial inequality. By analyzing not only the text of laws and policies but also the ways these laws and policies were practiced and applied to marginalize migrants, my sociohistorical analysis shows how this dual process—shifts in nationhood, laws, and policies, on the one hand, and persistent ethno-racial oppression, on the other—manifested itself in twentieth- and twenty-first-century Japanese society.

The Hegemonic Influence of Japan's Mythical Homogeneity

For those who are unfamiliar with Japanese history, it may seem odd to explore these questions in the context of Japan, given its perceived lack of diversity. Japan does have a smaller population of foreign-born residents, immigrants, and refugees on its soil than most other nations do. Data from the United Nations Department of Economic and Social Affairs shows that only 2 percent of the total population in Japan consists of foreign citizens—a figure nearly six times less than that of the United States (15.3 percent) and more than eight times less than that of Germany (18.8 percent) (UN Department of Economic and Social Affairs, Population Division 2020).[2] Yet if we fixate on these statistics, we fail to recognize the very important sociological and historical reality of ethno-racial diversity, which has significantly influenced Japan's culture and society. To accept these statistics as an accurate depiction of human diversity in Japan would ignore the fact that the Japanese census does not even ask a question about one's ethnic and racial background or identity.

Japan is not and has never been a homogeneous nation, nor has it been free from racial and ethnic conflicts. Japan has various minority populations: the indigenous Ainu; Korean and Taiwanese colonial migrants and their descendants; the Burakumin, who were believed to be descendants of social outcast groups from the ancient and feudal periods; and Okinawans, who were formerly known as Ryūkyūans, in the southern islands. Japan has a long history of social marginalization and of both symbolic and physical violence against these groups, which has already been well documented by scholars inside and outside Japan.[3] Despite the persisting hegemonic myth and façade of homogeneity, Japan's immigrant population from Latin America and Asian countries such as Brazil, China, Korea, the Philippines, and Vietnam has been increasing since the 1990s.

A relentless effort to challenge the hegemonic ethos of Japanese homogeneity emerged in the 1980s and continues among intellectuals and grassroots activists.[4] However, despite these efforts to expose the reality of diversity, the notion of Japan's homogeneity continues to exert hegemonic influence over popular discourse on national self-image, citizenship policies, and migrant integration in contemporary Japan. Scholars and activists' efforts to challenge this hegemonic ethos have been confronted with fierce resistance from rapidly growing right-wing groups' discontent about the extension of citizenship rights and privileges to Koreans and other non-Japanese residents (Fackler 2010; Shibuichi 2015). Their hate speech and provocative street demonstrations have triggered many racist and xenophobic incidents in recent decades, resulting in the birth of the Hate Speech Act of 2016.

Japan's myth of homogeneity has often been cited to explain why the Japanese state has adopted exclusive citizenship and migration policies, as well as the persistent racism against the ethno-racial minorities in Japan. Due to this myth, cultural assimilation, and/or their relative phenotypical proximity to Japanese people, minorities in Japan are often described as "invisible" or "hidden" in scholarly and public discourse (Hicks 1997; Kristof 1995; Wagatsuma and De Vos 1966). But if we accept this hegemonic myth and treat these minorities as "invisible," we will miss a valuable insight that these minorities' experience could provide us. Despite the popular perception of their invisibility, minorities in Japan have fiercely resisted this hegemonic myth of homogeneity and, throughout Japan's modern history, have refused to be invisible or silenced. Koreans in Japan are among the dissenters whose resistance has found its way into larger policy debates. This book will chronicle their trajectory of resistance from the twentieth century through the twenty-first. As the subsequent chapters will show, this trajectory shows that the nexus between nationhood, citizenship, and migration policies is far more discursive, malleable, and fluid than commonly imagined. It also helps us understand why we must scrutinize the exogenous and endogenous factors that prompt a society to embrace particular types of national self-image, citizenship, and migration policies, and it helps us to see the circumstances under which these elements are related or not related.

KEY CONCEPTS DEFINED: NATIONHOOD, CITIZENSHIP, RIGHTS, AND MIGRATION

Nationhood is defined as the manifestation of a collective self-image and self-understanding among people who believe themselves to belong to a larger common community. This community is united by a shared cultural heritage, destiny, memory, and/or territory. As scholars of nation and nationalism have articulated, nationhood is a socially constructed category, and its construction is engineered by powerful elites (Anderson 1983; Gellner 1983; Hobsbawm 1990). This book argues that the construction of nation is also influenced by marginalized individuals. They are often pushed to the margin of a national community, but they nevertheless challenge the elite's construction of nationhood and compete for the representation of such a ubiquitous yet supposedly distinctive collective entity. Throughout the book, a variety of terms—"national self-image," "national self-understanding," "collective sense of nationhood," and "national boundaries"—are used to specify how nationhood has been imagined, constructed, and practiced by various state, nonstate, and subaltern actors, and consequently transformed in a society. These terms should be considered as operationalized forms of the same concept, namely nationhood.

Citizenship, another key concept, is also understood as multi-dimensional. The first dimension of citizenship is its legality: as a legal status, citizenship is associated with a certain set of civic, political, and social duties and rights. The second aspect of citizenship deals with its agency: citizenship is a manifestation of individual free will, an ability to take part in exercising rights and duties and contributing to a cohesive society and its rule of law. The third dimension considers citizenship a type of membership and a source of specific identity. Sociologically, citizenship is also understood as an institutionalized form of social closure that establishes the boundaries of inclusion and exclusion in political communities (Brubaker 1996; Parkin 1979, 44).

The state—a centralized political apparatus recognized as legitimate by the people whom it governs—plays a major role in instituting the rules of citizenship and the ways nationhood is imagined, organized, and institutionalized (Brass 1985; Gellner 1983; Hobsbawm 1990; Hobsbawm and Ranger 1983). This book elaborates on who these elites were and what exactly they did. State actors were not monolithic. While the words of top policymakers have received the most scholarly attention, my work also sheds light on relatively unknown local bureaucrats, especially at the municipal level, who directly dealt with noncitizens on a day-to-day basis. Their words and practices give us important insights about how policies designed by elite policymakers in the central government are actually implemented at the local level.

The third key concept, rights, are regarded as ability, entitlement, and privilege. They are not only guaranteed and codified by states in domestic and/or international laws but also are claimed by individuals and/or groups. The basis of rights could be either particular cultural or political entities such as nationhood or universal personhood. Human rights are based on the latter. This book recognizes that the concept of rights and human rights transforms significantly over the course of history. This concept responds to different social forces, such as nationalism and globalization, that trigger change in people's normative and subjective understanding of their rights, as historians such as Micheline Ishay (2008) and Lynn Hunt (2008) have articulated. Thus, rights and human rights are understood as socially constructed and as subject to change over time in this book.[5]

Migration is the fourth key concept of this book. Generally speaking, migration refers to the movement of people from one geographical location to another. As such, we could conceive of at least three different types of migration. The first is the internal or domestic movement of people within the territory of a sovereign state: for example, the Great Migration among African Americans leaving the South for the North in the United States. A second type is international migration, or "immigration," which refers to the movement of people from one country to another. Finally, colonial migration refers to the movement of colonized populations from one colonial province to another within the territory of an empire. My work pays special attention to the third type, colonial migrants, although I do refer to the second type as well when relevant.

All three types of migration warrant scholarly attention, as they generate a long-lasting impact on the economy, politics, and culture of a society. Today immigration receives the most political and scholarly attention. Many studies on immigration policies are based on binary categories: citizens with full sets of citizenship rights and noncitizens/immigrants without such rights. My book problematizes this persistent and pervasive binary division in the social scientific studies of citizenship and nationhood. The following section explains why we must confront this binary and move forward with a new approach.

Beyond the Citizen/Immigrant Binary

Sociologist Julian Go (2016, 83–91) identified a problematic tendency among sociologists to artificially binarize social relations in his thought-provoking analysis of postcolonial thought and social theory. Go (2016, 83) called this tendency "analytic bifurcation" and attributed it both to persistent Eurocentrism in sociological inquiries and to the "occlusion of empire from sociological accounts." He argued that empire is often mistakenly treated as an inevitable outcome of modernity in social science scholarship; thus, it has not received due consider-

Introduction 9

ation in sociological inquiries. When the occlusion of empire goes hand in hand with analytic bifurcation, Go claims that they together repress colonial agency and consequently minimize—if not erase—the contribution and influence of colonized people in the historical process.

The same tendency can be found in the sociological inquiries of citizenship and nationhood, where a key social relation was almost always centered around the binarized social relation between citizens and noncitizens vis-à-vis immigrants. This binary approach indeed obscures the lasting colonial legacy in citizenship and migration policies in the former empires. To adequately understand the colonial impact and legacy in today's citizenship and immigration policies and practices around the world, we must transcend the pervasive and artificial binary classification. To this end, we need a third concept of migrants, specifically *colonial migrants,* who had been classified as a constituent of a sovereign imperial nation but effectively treated as "outsiders" or "others."

Colonial migrants are defined and treated as subjects of the imperial state, but they do not necessarily enjoy a full set of rights, including suffrage or free movement within the territory of the empire. British colonial subjects exemplify this point. Historian Kathleen Paul's extensive archival research demonstrates how the postwar British government introduced regulatory changes to discourage British subjects of color from coming to the United Kingdom, while encouraging the emigration of White aliens from Central and Eastern Europe, to address the postwar labor shortage (Paul 1997). Paul shows that the British government had separate policies for four different types of migrant groups, including (1) British stock from overseas, such as the United States, Canada, and Australia; (2) White European aliens from Central and Eastern Europe; (3) Irish migrants who were neither subjects nor aliens; and (4) people of color from its colonies. Postwar Britain prioritized the second category, namely White nonsubjects, partly due to policymakers' racial preferences. Paul's work exposed the hierarchy defined by race, gender, and social class hidden behind the system of formal legal equality. She convincingly argued that racism influenced the concept of nationhood and citizenship in the modern United Kingdom.

The case of postwar Britain reminds us of facts that are often taken for granted: citizens and migrants are neither monolithic nor homogeneous, and the states do not treat them as such. Colonial migrants were neither citizens nor immigrants. Rather, they existed in between.

They were direct products of empire and thus embodied the colonial legacy. However, they are often referenced as simply a "minority" or "diaspora." Such a broad reference may address one dimension of their experience and status. Yet such labels fail to capture the complex history and fluid reality of the coloniality embedded in their existence and experience. Put differently, recognizing them merely as a diaspora, noncitizens, aliens/foreigners, outsiders, or a minority disregards the fact that they would not have been displaced and minoritized had it not been for the colonial invasion of their homeland and exploitation by a foreign empire.

Being Korean, Becoming Japanese? argues that conceptualizing these people as "colonial migrants" is analytically both fertile and necessary. For one, this conceptualization forces us to directly confront and acknowledge the impact of colonialism and its legacy in today's world, which will be discussed in depth in chapter 5. For another, it enables us to unearth the history of the state's fluid treatment of these people, especially at the time when the empire transitioned and became a nation-state, as chapter 3 demonstrates. The state's evolving treatment of these people yields important insights into the malleable nexus between nationhood, citizenship, and migration. In particular, it allows us to compare and contrast the similarities and differences in how boundaries of nationhood are transformed, defined, and institutionalized in empire and nation-states.

Furthermore, because the existence and identity of colonial migrants cannot be separated from the colonial past, analyzing their experiences shows how the colonial past, and the unresolved issues arising from it, continues to exert influence over the public discourse about current migrants. This point is particularly relevant today, as scholarly and public discourse increasingly engage in the politics of decolonization, generational trauma, and restorative justice. As many minoritized and colonized populations around the globe began to call for restorative justice, it became clear that the colonized populations and their descendants made lasting contributions to nation-building and citizenship making. As scholars, we should meet the moment by deciphering how the colonial past has continued to matter to our lives today and by tracing the ways that colonized people have contributed to society.

To this end, we must transcend the pervasive binary mode of analysis that places citizens in opposition to noncitizens—a mode that leads scholars to force Koreans in Japan into existing categories of

Introduction 11

"noncitizen" such as "immigrants," "foreigners," or "the diaspora." By focusing on colonial migrants in this book, I bring attention to the history of colonization that brought Koreans to Japan.[6] We must pay attention to the concrete ways in which the colonial legacy continues to impact the colonial migrants and their descendants, and to analyze how colonized people assert their influence over the nation and citizenship making. Chapters 3 and 4 in this book unpack these aspects. Rather than narrowly focusing on international migrants (or immigrants) and the policies about them, this book pays attention to colonial migrants who had been classified as being both inside and outside the nation and examine how their experiences informed the policies created for newly arrived migrants in the subsequent postcolonial period. The following section explains why Koreans in Japan are a fitting case for this endeavor.

THE KOREANS IN JAPAN AS KEY ACTORS

Koreans in Japan are colonial migrants who were displaced as a result of the Japanese colonization of Korea. Throughout the historical periods considered in this book, Koreans in Japan constantly resisted structural domination by the Japanese state. Their resistance ranges from organized collective action to individual disobedience. They played a key role in shaping the boundary of citizenship and nation.

In the process of building a nation-state and developing the concept of citizenship, state officials and powerful elites strive to exert control over the populations they govern. At the heart of this effort is delineating who has access to full and equal citizenship and who does not. Hence, despite its universal tone, citizenship often involves systematic exclusion, and this exclusion usually takes place along preexisting categorical boundaries such as race, ethnicity, age, gender, class, national origin, religion, and so on (Parkin 1979; Tilly 1998). Those who are excluded from accessing full and equal citizenship often—but not always—challenge the structure of exclusion and the dominant groups who guard it. Thus, the contentious relationship between the included and the excluded often plays a significant role in altering the boundaries of citizenship and the meaning of national belonging in a society (Marx 1997).

However, the literature focusing on this aspect of citizenship rarely considers the role of claim-making by noncitizens. Instead, scholars often focus on marginalized citizens who have full legal status but whose ability to exercise and enjoy their civil rights is circumvented by discrimination and socioeconomic structural inequality—for instance, African Americans. On the other hand, the literature on international migration is centered on the question of integration and incorporation rather than on claim-making by immigrants. This skewed portrait of immigrants has been called into question (Chung 2010; Koopmans et al. 2005; Milly 2014; Shipper 2008). In their seminal work based on cross-national comparison, Koopmans and colleagues (2005) underscore the critical role of long-term immigrants' claim-making in the public discourse on citizenship in five countries that were then in the European Union (Germany, France, Britain, Switzerland, and the Netherlands). Exploring the East Asian context, political scientists have also addressed the important role played by marginalized immigrants and their allies in grassroots activism at national and municipal levels (Chung 2010; Milly 2014; Shipper 2008). However, because their works focus on what transpired within national territorial boundaries, it does not center the impact of transnationalism and globalization. Sociologist Kiyoteru Tsutsui (2018) expanded the analytical scope of this exploration by considering the impact of global human rights on local social movements among minority groups in Japan.

This book builds on these works by centering the importance of claim-making among noncitizens, especially colonial migrants and their descendants. In previous scholarship that focuses on Koreans in Japan, the impact of the past—the colonial past in particular—was taken for granted or treated merely as background information, partly because of the aforementioned problem of the "occlusion of empire" in social scientific analysis (Go 2016). Korea was the largest colony for the Japanese Empire, and absorbing this population was a serious challenge for the rapidly emerging empire, which possessed neither abundant colonial experience nor economic and military power to compensate for that lack of experience. Historical records and previous studies by historians have shown that absorbing and managing the Korean population was a primary concern for Japanese policymakers in the first half of the twentieth century (Oguma 1995, 1998; Robinson 1988). Indeed, colonial experiences significantly shaped how Japanese and Koreans viewed one another, and their mutual perceptions consequently had a large impact on how Koreans were treated throughout and beyond the Japanese Empire. Hence, it is perhaps not an exaggeration that for much of the twentieth century, Koreans served

Introduction 13

as one of the most critical others in constructing Japanese collective self-image—but rarely does their claim-making receive due scholarly attention. Thus, it is imperative to pay attention to how Koreans responded to Japanese state policies, especially concerning their rights and obligations, as we consider the process of Japan constructing citizenship and nationhood.

To be clear, Koreans' responses to the state's exclusion and marginalization practices were anything but uniform, monolithic, and static. Some Koreans closely collaborated with Japanese policymakers, while others fiercely resisted Japanese colonialism. Many of them simply dealt with it as a part of their reality and focused on survival rather than committing themselves to either collaboration or resistance. Such variations notwithstanding, their reactions to the Japanese state's policies were an important influence on how the state conceived of and put into practice citizenship and migration laws. This book traces the relationship between Koreans' varying reactions and Japan's migration and citizenship laws in the twentieth century.

My book starts its analysis with the colonial period and articulates how practices during this period circumvented the Korean subaltern's subsequent dissent efforts. Furthermore, focusing on Koreans in Japan who were imperial citizens but who later transformed into noncitizens, while continuously resisting the states' policies, provides a unique comparative opportunity to understand under what circumstances citizens and noncitizens could (or could not) exert their influence in the process of making nationhood, citizenship, and migration policies. It also helps us transcend the aforementioned issue of analytical bifurcation that has masked the long-lasting impact and contribution that these Koreans made to Japan's history of building nationhood and citizenship.

THEORIES OF NATIONHOOD, CITIZENSHIP, AND MIGRATION

A sense of nationhood and policies on migration and citizenship are often presumed to be closely coupled, suggesting, for instance, that a country with an exclusive sense of nationhood would choose exclusive citizenship and migration policies, and vice versa. This assumption persists even though scholars in recent decades have challenged this assumed link and presented a far more complicated model of the relationship. For the latter half of the twentieth century, Benedict Anderson (1983), Reinhard Bendix (1964), and Eric Hobsbawm (1990) and many other scholars of nationhood and citizenship across disciplines engaged in a common question: What triggers and/or constrains the transformation of nationhood and citizenship in societies?[7] Answers to this question vary from one scholar and discipline to another, yet prevailing classical theories of both nationalism and citizenship share a few problematic premises.

One such premise is the belief that all forms of nationalism and citizenship can be classified into a dichotomous categorization: (1) the Eastern model, based on jus sanguinis, and (2) the Western model, based on jus soli (Kohn [1944] 2005). Later generations of scholars have proven that, in practice, these two models of nationhood and citizenship are neither as fundamentally opposed nor as mutually exclusive as they are in principle (Kuzio 2002; Shulman 2002; Soysal 1994; Yack 1996; Zubrzycki 2001). This dichotomous model also ignores the fact that people imagine their nationhood in far more discursive and malleable terms (Calhoun 1997; Croucher 2003; Lamont 1995). The reevaluation of these dichotomies has led to questions about another problematic premise: the intimate or even causal connection between the nation and citizenship. The concept of citizenship predates modernity, but because the modern concept of citizenship developed in parallel to the territorially delineated nation-state formation, nationhood and citizenship are often viewed as being closely related. Because they have been informed by dichotomous models, earlier scholarly works on nationalism and citizenship have largely drawn a strong association between nationhood and citizenship (Brubaker 1992; Dumont 1994; Ignatieff 1993; Kohn [1944] 2005).[8]

This dichotomous model popularized a linear and unidirectional transformation of nationhood and citizenship: one that expects types of nationhood and citizenship to move away from the ethnic, exclusive, and nonliberal Eastern model toward a more secular, inclusive, and liberal Western model. This popular understanding is anchored in the presumed connection between a regime type and citizenship-immigration policies, suggesting that the global diffusion of democratic values gradually leads societies to embrace democratic regimes and to replace exclusive citizenship and immigration policies with more inclusive, liberal ones. Citing the incorporation of guest workers and illegal immigrants into host societies without formal citizenship, scholars have argued that the ideas about citizenship as well as the institution of citizenship in Europe and North America are gradually being reconfigured into what Yasemin Soysal (1994) calls "postnational membership," a new conceptualization of citizenship and membership that is rooted in universal personhood rather than particular nationhood (see Sassen 1998).[9]

However, as witnessed by the resurgence of ethnic nationalism and fragmentation in multiethnic regions across the globe in the last century, departure from an authoritarian regime does not automatically cultivate a path to liberal democracy or ethno-racial harmony. Nor does liberal democracy lead to an inclusive model of citizenship and nondiscriminatory migration policies (FitzGerald and Cook-Martín 2014; Mann 2005; Ngai 2004). In fact, the rise of liberal democracy has often been accompanied by the question of differentiation and claims of distinctive identities rather than a drive toward inclusion (Benhabib 1996; Mann 2005). Critical race theorists such as Charles Mills (2017) have demonstrated the intertwined relationship between liberalism and racism and challenged the notion that liberalism is a hallmark of social justice and equitable inclusion.

If neither nationalism nor regime structure fully explains why a society will choose a certain mode of citizenship and migration policies, then what else can account for this choice? Many studies have looked for an answer to this question by focusing separately on what is either outside or inside national boundaries. One of the most persistent endogenous factors examined by scholars has been the impact of the emergent capitalist system. Early scholars of citizenship regarded an emergent capitalist society as a primary facilitator of the birth of modern citizenship (Bendix 1964; Giddens 1982; Marshall 1950; Moore 1966). They agreed that "theories of citizenship should be based on an exploration of the sometimes contentious, sometimes cooperative, sometimes legitimating dyadic relationship between the state and the capitalist economy" (Somers 1993, 588).

Around the 1990s, many scholars of citizenship began to challenge T. H. Marshall's minimization of struggles in the formation of formal citizenship. These post-Marshallian scholars included other endogenous dynamics in their analytical scope, such as the relationship between the state and associational practices of civil societies (Beiner 1995; Habermas 1995; Ikegami 1995; Kymlicka and Norman 2000; Marx 1997; Somers 1993). They redefined citizenship as an "instituted process" that involves contentious negotiations and conflicts between the agents of the state and members of socially constructed categories such as gender, class, ethnicity, race, and national origin (Hanagan 1997; Marx 1997; Somers 1993; Polanyi 1957; Thompson 1963).

16 *Chapter 1*

Other scholars focused on the source of struggles outside the national boundaries (Albrow 1997). Noting that national sovereignty is increasingly circumscribed by transnational norms and nonstate actors, they argued that the nation-state, in a global age of political and moral interdependencies, has become exposed to increasing challenges from transnational migration, globalized norms of human rights, and international pressure for democratization.[10] Meyer, Boli, and colleagues (1997), in particular, argued that the global spread of Western cultural norms has produced a vast array of institutional similarities. In line with this idea, prominent citizenship scholars assert that although ethnic migration may occur sporadically, the trend toward adopting nondiscriminatory and multicultural membership is by now a definitive phenomenon among Western liberal states (Joppke 2005a).

Building on these works, sociologists David Scott FitzGerald and David Cook-Martín (2014) made an ambitious attempt to untangle the relationship between liberal democracy and exclusive immigration policies. Reviewing racial and ethnic selection in immigration and naturalization laws across six countries in North and South America between the eighteenth and twenty-first centuries, FitzGerald and Cook-Martín (2014, 9) demonstrated that liberal democracy did not lead a society to abandon overtly racist immigration policies; rather, what led societies to abandon such practices was the pressure from horizontal and vertical institutional relationships. They described how the relationship between liberal democracy and racist immigration policies have "elective affinity" or "a relationship that is nondeterministic and probabilistic and that involves choices by those it links" (FitzGerald and Cook-Martín 2014, 7). While acknowledging that we don't live in a postracist society, they suggest that the resurgence of overtly racist immigration policies is unlikely in today's world: "If the point of reference is historical experience, there is no question that the trajectory of immigration policy has moved away from ethnic selection for many decades" (FitzGerald and Cook-Martín 2014, 347).

Their critically acclaimed sociohistorical analysis nevertheless received some constructive critiques. For one, their definition of racist immigration laws, based on ethnic selection and racial restrictions in naturalization law, is too narrow "to hang the argument that liberal democracy and racism are not inherently linked but rather share an elective affinity" (Fox 2015, 1288). Fox cautions that it may be premature to argue that "the relationship between liberalism and racist immigration policy was fundamentally severed in 1965" and expressed concerns that FitzGerald and Cook-Martín (2014) unintentionally downplayed "the significant ways that race continues to shape the adoption and implementation of immigration and immigrant integration policies today" (Fox 2015, 1289). FitzGerald and Cook-Martín (2014, 1320) responded to this critique by underscoring their point that "the historical fact that immigration policy has become far less racialized over time does not mean that any of these countries reached a post-racial nirvana." It may be a historical fact that immigration policy has become less racialized, but this is neither satisfactory nor comforting to those who wish to implement immigration policies with still less racism. Moreover, the resurgence of racist, bigoted, and xenophobic policies a few years after their book was published makes Fox's critique rather prophetic and suggests that it warrants further attention.

PERSISTENT OPPRESSION AND THE PENDULUM-SWING PATTERN OF CHANGE

A few years after Fitzgerald and Cook-Martín's influential work was published, the forty-fifth US president, Donald J. Trump, signed a series of executive orders for immigration policies that directly targeted specific ethno-racial groups. While the language in these orders is not as explicit as in the Chinese Exclusion Acts or Jim Crow laws, it is not hard to notice the racist intention embedded in such orders. This is not to say these Trump-era policies invalidated FitzGerald and Cook-Martín's analysis. Nevertheless, what has transpired in the United States and elsewhere in the past several years prompts us to revisit the question "What triggers the transformation of citizenship and immigration policies?" and propels us to investigate how we can explain the pendulum-swing pattern of change in these policies.

FitzGerald and Cook-Martín (2014) legitimately argued that the transformation of immigration (and citizenship) policies should be analyzed in the context of *both* endogenous and exogenous factors and that such an analysis must pay attention to how these two types of factors interact. Past practices indeed influence subsequent policy repertoire. Regime type or structure also plays little role in contouring migration and citizenship policies in Japan. Although many aspects of their approach resonate with this book, my main purpose is neither to replicate nor to rebut their arguments.

Being Korean, Becoming Japanese? argues that the continuing significance of ethno-raciality in making and applying citizenship and immigration policies hardly declined throughout the twentieth and early twenty-first centuries; instead, its significance was temporarily suppressed, but surged again as it morphed into different forms under specific conditions. Put differently, despite their repeated revisions, immigration and citizenship policies continue to marginalize targeted populations and consequently to facilitate and reproduce familiar forms of durable ethno-racial inequality. This remains the case even as its targets, forms, and outcomes shift across historical periods and cultural contexts.

My analysis does not narrowly focus on specific aspects of immigration and citizenship policies such as ethnic quotas or selection and racial restriction, or the specific text of these policies. Instead, it broadens its scope by examining how these policies and laws are applied and enacted toward targeted populations, in addition to how they are written. As we see in the United States, Japan, and elsewhere, the language used in laws and policies may be ethno-racially neutral, but the removal of ethno-racially explicit languages or codes hardly eradicates the racist intentions of the architects from these laws (Crenshaw et al. 2019). Restrictive voter identification laws in the United States are a notable contemporary example: such laws do not use explicitly racist language, but the outcomes will in fact disproportionately discriminate against minoritized voters. Societal conditions and the ways in which these policies and laws are applied matter just as much as the language and codes of the laws and policies. Whether or not the significance of ethno-racial inequality and oppression persists largely depends on the contexts and manners in which they are applied and practiced. In the Japanese context, even if postwar citizenship and immigration laws do not specifically mention race or ethnicity, they were applied and enacted against remaining colonial migrants in Japan, thus facilitating further ethno-racial inequality.

Rather than exclusively focusing on immigrants, this book centers colonial migrants who exist unsteadily between the binary of citizens and immigrants. Focusing on colonial migrants, perpetually betwixt and between, allows us to interrogate the ongoing colonial legacy of preserving ethno-racial inequality despite the imagined break between the two periods. Considering law and practices through the lens of colonial migrants enables us not only to consider who can enter the country and become a citizen but also to examine the actual extension of rights to long-term noncitizens. This broader approach has the

Introduction 19

potential to increase our understanding of why these policies in some societies follow a dialectical, pendulum-swing pattern of change.

Focusing on Japan also allows us to address the skewed geopolitical concentration in the fields of nationalism, citizenship, and migration. While increasing numbers of scholars today have produced high-quality research on issues of nationhood, citizenship, and migration by focusing on non-Western regions, the vast majority of the existing literature still focuses on the West, a region that witnessed a significant increase in transnational migration flow amid public support for multicultural ideals. While citizenship and the nation-state are ubiquitous in the modern world, their development process is deeply embedded in local geopolitical conditions, economy, culture, and history, producing different outlooks across the globe with regard to nationhood and citizenship (Cesarini and Fulbrook 1996). On the other hand, we also witness emerging tensions between global human rights and national social rights in various industrial countries, suggesting that globalization renders a certain degree of institutional isomorphism of citizenship across the globe today (Jacobson 1996; Soysal 1994; Tsutsui 2018). Thus, it is important for us to synthesize the diverse and rich theoretical knowledge that is available and to apply it to an appropriate empirical case, which will allow us to evaluate this accumulated knowledge for its explanatory power beyond these well-studied cases.

Some scholars began this effort by directly or comparatively focusing on non-Western cases, including some cases in Asian contexts (Chung 2010; Janoski 1998, 2010; Kim 2016; Kondō 2001; Kymlicka and He 2005). Anthropologist Takeyuki Tsuda (2003, 2006), political scientist Erin Chung (2010), and sociologist Jaeeun Kim (2016) are among those social scientists whose work has significantly expanded geographical and theoretical horizons on the question of transborder membership, citizenship, and nationhood. This book complements their endeavors by examining the impact of colonialism during the postcolonial periods through rich historical data from Japan. It also argues that what we should debate and explore is not so much whether or not nation and citizenship are coupled but, rather, under what circumstances they are coupled or decoupled. This book demonstrates specific conditions under which the connections between nationality and citizenship are made and unmade through an analysis of experiences in Japanese society.

20   *Chapter 1*

The Japanese case is informative and illustrative because Japan's nationhood, citizenship, and migration policies have drastically shifted, corresponding to varying geopolitical contexts, changing demographic compositions, and contentious responses to immigrant populations in Japan. Imperial Japan advocated pan-Asianism as an ideological tool to gain control over their multiethnic empire and did not overtly institutionalize ethno-racial differences between the colonizer and the colonized in its citizenship laws. However, in everyday life, Koreans were routinely discriminated against by people in Japan. The severity of this racism was brutally illustrated by the massacre of Koreans following the Great Kanto Earthquake in 1923 (Kang 2003; Yamada 2003). During the same colonial period, the Japanese imperial regime allowed its colonial subjects to enjoy some civil rights, including even suffrage in some cases. After the democratization of Japan starting in 1945, we might have expected ethno-racial liberalization for colonial migrants after their colonies were emancipated; instead, policies shifted to the legal exclusion of the colonial migrants remaining in Japan. The new democratic government revoked not only Japanese citizenship but also various social and political privileges from the colonial migrants and their offspring who were born in Japan and had lived there all their lives. In parallel to the institutionalized exclusion of colonial migrants and their descendants, postwar Japanese intellectuals from both political sides developed and nurtured an opposite type of self-image, namely, a construct of a "homogeneous nation." This concept of a homogeneous nation penetrated through various structures of postwar Japanese society, masking the colonial legacy in the policies and attitudes toward colonial migrants and their descendants. The concept eventually was used to justify exclusive citizenship and immigration policies and practices, allowing durable oppression against non-Japanese peoples to persist in postwar Japan.

Since the 1980s, this postwar image of Japan as a homogeneous nation, as well as its exclusive citizenship and migration policies, has been increasingly contested by supranational institutions (e.g., the UN), by Japan's former colonies (i.e., South/North Korea, Taiwan, and China), and by domestic minority groups. Japanese economic expansion has once again created ongoing interaction with its Asian neighbors. This time, it has generated two contradictory impacts on nationalism: a rise of neoconservative nationalism and blunt racism, on the one hand, and the questioning of Japanese bigotries and extension of citizenship rights to long-term noncitizen residents, on the other. Japan's multiethnic past and its pendulum-swing pattern of change in policies toward Koreans in Japan offer an unparalleled window through which to reexamine some of the prevailing premises and to investigate the existing framework on which the literature of nationhood, citizenship, and migration rest.

Japan's twentieth-century history includes differences in regime type (empire versus nation-state), demographic and geographical characteristics (a large territory with a multiethnic population versus a small territory with a relatively homogeneous population versus a small territory with global reach), economic structures (a semi-peripheral economy versus a core economy), and geopolitical contexts (imperialism versus the Cold War versus globalization). Japan's internal politics, like other parts of the global community, are infused with contentious dynamics between state and nonstate actors, particularly colonial migrants and other minority groups. In fact, the Japanese case contains all the key factors—both endogenous and exogenous—that have been present in the European and North American cases, yet have produced a contrasting trajectory pattern.

All these facts from the Japanese case suggest that the same variables can interact in different manners under different geopolitical and cultural contexts. As such, the Japanese case allows us to refine our understandings of the mechanisms that produced different trajectories. Because the transformation of nationhood, citizenship, and migration policies in twentieth-century Japan took place in parallel with the transitions of regime type, economic structure, and the emergence of a new ideology and norms, we can divide the history of twentieth-century Japan into three contrasting contexts for this analytical purpose. The first is the imperial context, which began with Japan's conquest of Taiwan and Korea in the 1890s, when an imperial regime responded to Japan's military and economic position within the world society with policies that combined brutal territorial expansion with an assimilationist approach to ethnic minorities. The second is the Cold War context (1945–1970s), which involved the simultaneous development of parliamentary democracy and strict ethnic exclusion under the strong influence of Cold War politics. The third is the global context (1970s–present), which features a renewed clash between the forces of assimilation and exclusion as the globalized concept of human rights penetrated Japanese society and combined with internal and external protests to force yet another redefinition of Japan's national self-understanding and the ways that citizenship and migration policies are being applied to the non-Japanese population.

Regime type is referred to in this book as a type of government or the set of rules and norms that regulates the repeated, strong interactions among political actors (Tilly 2006, 19). It is an important concept, and thus is considered in this book, but it is not the main focus of the book's analysis. In fact, the findings from Japan's experience suggests that regime type alone does not explain the malleable, fluid, and contingent nature of transformations of nationhood, citizenship, and migration policies.

Furthermore, this book complements existing works emphasizing how national sovereignty is increasingly circumscribed by transnational norms and nonstate actors (Albrow 1997; Guidry, Kennedy, and Zald 2000; McAdam 1998; Meyer, Boli et al. 1997; Meyer, Frank et al. 1997). In this view, the nation-state in a global age of political and moral interdependencies has become more exposed to exogenous pressure, driven by waves of globalizing processes in economic, cultural, and political fields.[11] The global integration of markets, transnational communities of immigrants, and intergovernmental institutions are just a few examples of the effects of globalizing processes. Although the global context shares economic and geographical characteristics with the Cold War context, there are distinctive features in the global context that justifies this periodization. Among them are an increase in trade, investment, and travel relations between Japan and its former colonies. These developments have unfolded against the backdrop of a globally sanctioned normative repertoire of demands for reparations from the era of colonial conquest. In addition, the declining population in Japan has created a need for labor immigrants from nonindustrial countries that did not exist in the Cold War context, bringing Japanese national self-understanding into sharp relief.

This dynamic social history of Japanese nationhood, citizenship, and migration allows us to further specify the actual mechanisms by which political, cultural, and economic fields within and outside national boundaries influence the contentious relationships between state and nonstate actors. And this history allows us to see how these contentious relationships have led to differing attitudes on the part of policymakers, differing modes of citizenship, and various imaginations of national self-understanding. Moreover, the constant presence of Korean social movements that have contested Japanese national self-

Introduction 23

image, citizenship, and migration policies allows us to examine the function and significance of the conceptualization of otherness in the construction of national self-understanding. By focusing on both the policy-formation process and the history of resistance, we can illuminate the factors that determine the impact of subaltern resistance on national self-image, citizenship restrictions, and migration policies.[12] The contentious and varying history of Japanese nationhood and citizenship development allows us to examine the validity of existing theories formulated on the basis of Western experiences. In particular, this historical analysis allows us to further elaborate on the relational approach to the studies of nationalism proposed by Rogers Brubaker (1996, 2004), who argues that we need to examine nationalism as a contingent event and practice rather than as a static category.

DATA AND METHODOLOGY

Being Korean, Becoming Japanese? belongs to the genre of historical and political sociology and focuses on nationalism, citizenship, migration, and race and ethnicity. It was inspired by work on citizenship and globalization by important sociologists, including but not limited to David Jacobson (1996), Anthony Marx (1997), and Yasemin Soysal (1994, 1997).[13] Furthermore, this work intersects with Japanese and Asian studies, because it was also inspired by the seminal works of historians and anthropologists such as Harumi Befu (2001), Takashi Fujitani (2013), Tessa Morris-Suzuki (1998), and Sonia Ryang (2000), to name just a few.

This is the first work of historical sociology published in English on this subject written by someone who has firsthand experience of the marginalization in Japanese society depicted in this book—a direct descendant of colonial labor migrants from Korea who also lived through the turmoil of Japan's colonialism and the Cold War. A narrative presented by someone who has directly witnessed and experienced the history is not necessarily superior to one created by those who do not share these histories. But it should also not be regarded as less objective or more biased. Max Weber's (1949) binary distinction between value and fact became a standard in social scientific methodology, and sociologists are trained to adhere to the principle of objectivity. In the real world, we are exposed to different sets of values and biases depending on our own positionalities in our social worlds. Scholars who have experienced the same or similar challenges as the subjects they study will have to deal with the challenge of pursuing objective analysis differently than those who have not, and vice versa. This book is based on the conviction that the field of sociology and academia in general, which has been predominantly represented by scholars who have never directly experienced the social problems and oppressions they study, will progress more readily if we respect one another's different challenges in achieving objective analysis.

This book is based on the analysis of historical archives and secondary literatures on the topic of nationalism, citizenship, and migration. The archival data used in this book includes but is not limited to parliamentary debates; writings published in periodicals, newsletters, pamphlets, leaflets, newspapers and other media publications; memoirs and private diaries; and missives and websites among key ideologues, scholars, policymakers, jurists, journalists and activists. Over the years, I have frequently traveled to the National Diet Library in Tokyo and to other public and university libraries in Japan to collect archival data. I also relied on digital data, including the National Parliamentary Transcription Data at the National Diet Library and the National Archives of Japan. I used the Kobe University Law School Library as well as the library at Kansai University's Human Rights Research Institute to collect the data concerning migration laws and court cases. These sites are invaluable sources of data regarding state and judicial matters.

The dissonant voices of subaltern actors are not as well archived as voices of the state and judicial actors. Even if they are archived, they are not always available at central locations such as public or national libraries. Instead, they are often held in smaller collections, most of which are privately owned by minority organizations or individual activists. To access these vital data, I personally reached out to the activists and scholars in Japan who study this subject as well as to numerous Korean organizations when possible. They are concentrated in Osaka, Kobe, and Kyoto (the areas with the largest Korean populations in Japan). I requested their cooperation to locate and review such documents as flyers, newsletters, letters, journals, and diaries. To establish trust and credibility with these activists and scholars, I attended various workshops and meetings organized by them, introducing myself and sharing my family background as a descendant of Korean colonial migrants. In some cases, disclosing my own family background was important and helpful to earn deeper trust and understanding from the activists. Given that this topic of study is heavily politicized

Introduction

and polarized, many activists are rightfully wary of scholars and might have experienced extractive research requests in the past. The data they shared with me serve as an important window to see what actors thought and what they actually did. Such data allows us to do what sociologist Kathleen Blee (2012, 12) advised: to track "between these layers—between what is done/said and what is not done/unsaid," and by so doing to "see what activists collectively regard as possible, authorized, and imaginable."

It is important to note that not every piece of archival data specified page numbers or the exact date and year of publication. Thus, the inclusion of publication years and dates for in-text citation is not always possible or feasible. In those cases, explanations are provided in the endnotes. Approximate dates were estimated contextually and inferred from other historical sources, so that the archival data could be properly analyzed whenever possible. Furthermore, some activists shared archival data with me on the condition of anonymity. Given rising threats and violence targeting Koreans in Japan and those who support them, it was ethically important to honor and respect their wishes; thus, their identities are deliberately omitted in this book.

Whenever it was possible and appropriate, I have also relied on secondary literature, including published works by historians and other social scientists who researched topics relevant to this project. I directly communicated with the researchers whose work I relied on to gain a deeper understanding of their ideas, interpretations, and the types of data that they used to produce such work. While collecting data in the massive sea of archives is no easy task, organizing and analyzing it in a systematic manner is no less challenging. I spent a significant amount of time organizing and analyzing the data I collected. Existing works on historical sociology are useful for formulating conceptual and analytical logics in research design, but they rarely explain in detail how one should organize and analyze the primary archival data in qualitative historical research. To analyze the data in an organized and systematic way, I created a spreadsheet to record the data in chronological order and sort it by key factors, including the actors involved. I categorized the data according to state or nonstate actors as well as exogenous and endogenous events, including but not limited to international and domestic conflicts, natural disasters, international treaties, economic incidents, and lawsuits.

The shifts in intellectual and political discourses on nationalism, migration, and citizenship policies, and the minority movements that animate and respond to them, occur in gradual as well as abrupt and discontinuous ways. Even though the changes that lead to these shifts may occur over long periods of time and may represent the accumulation of incremental changes, they appear as historically specific, time-delineated incidents. To track the impact of subtle shifts in the discourses and policy changes, it is imperative to identify analytically significant events in each period that crystallize developing dynamics. Thus, I added a column of these significant analytical events in my spreadsheet. I used this chronology of key events and changes in citizenship and migration policies as an analytical map to trace how varying historical contexts and specific historical incidents impacted discourses among intellectuals, policymakers, and minority groups, and how such shifts in discourse ultimately affected the policymaking process. This sheet allows me to understand what key events and contexts are considered important among state and nonstate actors, and how state and nonstate actors responded to them. Organizing voluminous archival data nested with key variables in this manner enabled me to see the bigger picture and identify systematic patterns, while allowing me to remain cognizant of my own biases.

The writings on methodological nationalism also inspired me to transcend the nation-state model of analysis (Wimmer and Glick Schiller 2003). As the world was divided into territorially delineated imagined communities vis-à-vis nation-states in the twentieth century, scholars began to rely on the nation-state as a naturally demarcated, politically and culturally stable unit of their analysis, a practice now known as "methodological nationalism." Methodological nationalism can be found in various aspects of scholarly endeavors, but its impact was perhaps the most profound in the studies of nationalism, migration, and citizenship. Rather than taking the territorial and legal boundaries of nationhood for granted, my book analyzes the forces that influence the actors' imagination and practice of making such boundaries. To this end, I found John Meyer's (2010) theories and concepts of world culture and world society particularly useful, as they view the world as a society consisting of institutions and relationships, and understand individuals, states, and supranational organizations as social actors who interact and together contour globalized cultural norms. The archival data that records the thoughts and emotions of these key actors help decipher how these boundaries are imagined and translated into practices.

Naming and Classifying

Naming and classifying the subjects of studies is arguably one of the most important responsibilities of scholars, not just for the sake of analytical clarity but also because the choices of terms used to explain and describe groups, collective behaviors, and other social phenomena contribute to the construction and reproduction of a social reality. American psychologist Jerome Bruner once wrote, "We organize our experience and our memory of human happenings mainly in the form of narrative—stories, excuses, myths, reasons for doing and not doing, and so on" (Bruner 1991, 4). The words used in narratives affect the perception and construction of social reality. As we learned from the series of events in the wake of George Floyd's murder in May 2020 and the insurrection at Capitol Hill on January 6, 2021, in the United States, the kinds of words that policymakers, media, and law enforcement use to describe and frame the collective actions in those incidents influence the ways people understand the significance and nature of such events, as well as their consequences.

In this book, I refer to people who self-identified as "Koreans" (Chōsenjin or Kankokujin) and who have been classified and marginalized by Japanese people and state agencies as "Koreans in Japan." I will also add clarifying language as needed, including but not limited to "colonial migrants and their descendants," "North or South Koreans," and "minority." I intentionally avoid using the popular term "Zainichi" or "Zainichi Korean"—which literally means "Resident Koreans in Japan" or "Koreans living in Japan." However, my choice to avoid the term should not be mistaken as a denunciation of "Zainichi" as an identity or label. Nor should it be understood as implying that my choice is better than others. I respect the choice made by other scholars, especially John Lie and Sonia Ryang (2008), and their efforts to promote awareness about Zainichi as a diasporic identity.

I also understand the pragmatism behind the choice by some scholars to use a single term to avoid confusion and cumbersome connotations. It is certainly convenient to bundle all these people with complex self-identifications and legal statuses into a single category and to give them a unified, general classification label. Doing so, however, comes with risks and costs. As those who use terms like "Zainichi" acknowledge, such a simplified term hardly captures the reality of complex self-identification and the diverse existence and experiences of the population in question (Chapman 2008). Nor does it reflect the varying labels used by the Japanese state against these peoples throughout different circumstances in its history. Thus, it obscures the heterogeneity existing within this overarching term. Just as Koreans' reaction and action toward Japan's policies were heterogeneous, so are the ways in which they identify themselves in the territory of Japan. The complicated ways that Koreans understand their identities reflect the tumultuous treatments they received from the state and its agencies, who unilaterally categorized them with various labels—often against the will of these people—in order to control and exclude as they deemed fit.

Scholars previously identified these two dynamics in identity constructions. Rogers Brubaker and Fredrick Cooper (2000), Yen Le Espiritu (1992), Richard Jenkins (1996), and Mara Loveman (1999) demonstrated that how society perceives a group—"external categorization"—and how a group understands itself—"internal self-identification"—are not necessarily the same; they may not even overlap. In fact, more frequently than not, there is divergence between them, which often leads to contentiousness between those who hold authority to unilaterally classify and categorize others and those who do not have the same level of authority or ability to assert their own self-understanding against top-down, unilateral, and external categorization (Brubaker 2004; Brubaker and Cooper 2000; Jenkins 1996; Loveman 1999, 2014). To understand the nature of the relationship between a society's collective national self-understanding and its citizenship and migration policies, we must pay careful attention to the nature of the relationship between "external categorization" and "internal self-identification" (Jenkins 1996, 80–89). Using a simplified and overarching label or the label endorsed by the state would hinder our effort to articulate this intricate relationship.

For a similar reason, I also avoid using hyphenated identification labels such as "Korean-Japanese" or "Japanese-Koreans" in this book, which are sometimes used in Anglophone media to identify Koreans in Japan. Such hyphenated identification reflects neither the reality of the way Koreans in Japan are labeled and understood by the Japanese state nor the way many of them identify themselves. The hyphenated identification label is commonly used in a society like the United States, where marginalized populations were recognized for their birthrights to American citizenship based on their jus soli citizenship law. In other words, they are fully recognized for their "legal" citizenship status in the societies where they were born even if their ability to exercise the legally recognized rights to the fullest extent may be constrained to varying degrees due to socioeconomic and political inequality. However, under Japanese citizenship law, based on the principle of jus sanguinis, Koreans in Japan are not recognized as having birthright citizenship. As the following chapters demonstrate, Koreans in Japanese territory were forced to adopt the legal status of Japanese imperial citizens by the Japanese rulers and became Japanese imperial subjects after 1910 when their sovereign country became Japan's colony. Their legal status as Japanese citizens was unilaterally revoked in 1952 by the Japanese postwar state, and they became aliens in Japan overnight. Their homeland was divided into two separate sovereign states, North and South Koreas, which required them to declare their allegiance to a country that did not exist when they had migrated to the Japanese mainland. Given these historical realities, hyphenated identification labels fall short in describing the intricate conditions surrounding their identity and legal status.

This book also refers to and regards Koreans in Japan as "colonial migrants." As an earlier section in this chapter articulated, conceptualizing Koreans in Japan and their descendants as colonial migrants is theoretically important. Recognizing them as "colonial migrants" rather than "foreigners," "noncitizens," "a diaspora," and "a minority" forces us to be sensitive to the historical fact that they would not have become minoritized, a diaspora, or noncitizens had their ancestral land not been colonized by Japan. Thus, it also allows us to examine the impact of colonialism and its legacy, to which Koreans in Japan were subject.

My terminology and classification also resonate with other scholars' empirical findings on this matter (Miyazaki 1973a; Mizuno 2001; Oguma 1995, 1998; Yamawaki [1999] 2003). Neither the prewar nor the postwar Japanese state explicitly classified and labeled Koreans in its territory as immigrants or even migrants (*imin*), nor did it call its policies to control these populations immigration or migration policy (*imin seisaku*).[14] In fact, in the Japanese language, the distinction between "immigration" and "migration" is not always as clear as in English. *Being Korean, Becoming Japanese?* nevertheless underscores the analytical importance of understanding these people as "migrants," even if the state did not use such a classification or label, because it directly reflects their lived experience. As demonstrated in previous historical studies as well as in historical archives such as parliamentary debates, newspapers, news magazines, newsletters, and pamphlets circulated among minority activists, Koreans were treated and controlled as migrants (*imin*) (Miyazaki 1973a, 1973b; Mizuno 2001; Oguma 1995, 1998; Yamawaki [1999] 2003). During the imperial period, the Japanese government did not refer to its effort to control colonial migrants as "migration laws" because it wanted to downplay its colonial ambition and to sustain its ethnic amalgamation ideology. Thus, if we avoid such classifying labels simply because the state intentionally avoided using them, we commit ourselves to reproducing the Japanese colonial state's intention and interests, and consequently to distort our objective understanding.

This book uses the term "ethno-racial" and the concept of ethno-raciality to describe how the boundary between Koreans and Japanese is constructed. Despite similar physical appearance and relative cultural proximity, Koreans and Japanese imagined each other as ethnically and racially different. Japanese state actors and intellectuals locally developed the definition of race and ethnicity to imagine the boundaries between Japanese and non-Japanese. There is a pervasive and commonsense tendency among North Americans to artificially separate the concept of race from that of ethnicity. In this commonsense understanding and practice, race is regarded as being based on visible phenotypic differences such as skin color, while ethnicity is rooted in cultural practices and customs such as language and religion. If we were to apply these definitions, Japanese and Koreans supposedly belong to the same "Asian" race; thus, it may seem odd or even inappropriate to use the concept of "race" to describe the boundary and relation between two. In fact, this is the logic that the Japanese postwar state frequently cited to claim that there has been no "racial" issues or "racism" in Japanese society, referring to its demographic homogeneity, especially when confronted at the United Nations and asked to address discrimination against its minority populations. I concur with sociologist Mara Loveman's (1999, 894) assertion that there is a North American bias to treat race and ethnicity as analytically distinct and elevate them to the status of sociological concepts.

Applying such US-centric definitions of race and ethnicity for cases outside the United States is analytically futile and problematic, because it ignores the very fact that these categories are deeply embedded in local geopolitical conditions and that, as such, their meanings shift across space and time. As historical evidence demonstrates, race and ethnicity exist in the intersection or continuum rather than a distinctive separation. This point was best articulated by anthropologist

Introduction 31

Richard Jenkins (1994, 209): "'Racial' differentiation and racism should perhaps best be viewed as historically specific forms of the general—perhaps even universal—social phenomenon of ethnicity." This is certainly the case in the social and historical context of Japan.

Finally, words matter. They are powerful tools for creating and re-creating narratives, which in turn constitute the construction of social reality. Scholars who study collective behaviors and social phenomena must be cognizant in selecting the terms and concepts in our analyses. Our terms and concepts should reflect empirical reality; we should resist the temptation to employ a broader term merely for pragmatic purposes, or to uncritically apply concepts simply because they are commonly used as "official labels" by states. State policies, which reflect the intention and interest of lawmakers, often powerfully contribute to the construction of social reality. We must instead call into question the legitimacy and intention behind labels and examine their meanings. Doing so allows us to further refine our analytical understanding.

THE STRUCTURE OF THIS BOOK

This book consists of five chapters, including this introduction, offering a chronological analysis of how the experiences of Koreans in Japan enable us to reconsider nationalism, citizenship, and resistance. Chapter 2, "Pan-Asian Empire," examines the imperial context (1890s–1945). Analyzing the impact of Western imperialism on Japanese perceptions of themselves, of Westerners, and of their colonial subjects, this chapter discusses how imperial Japan developed the concept of the hybrid nation and adopted inclusive citizenship and migration policies, despite its imperial monarchy. It also analyzes the role of intellectuals in developing the multiethnic conception of nationhood in the Japanese Empire. This chapter focuses on Koreans' responses to these policies during the colonial period and on how their responses triggered change, prompting state actors to redraw and reformulate their policies regarding citizenship and migration.

Chapter 3, "The Birth of a Homogeneous Nation-State," focuses on the postwar and Cold War contexts (1945–1970s). The first part of this chapter pays close attention to the occupation period, when the previously conflicting interests of Japan and the United States were suddenly merged as the two states faced their common obstacle, namely, the remaining Korean population in Japan, who were increasingly inclined to communist ideology. The second part of this chapter addresses how the division of Korea and Cold War tensions impacted the relationship between the states of Japan, the United States, and North and South Korea, and how this political climate influenced the solidarity and collective sense of self among Koreans. This chapter contrasts the process of citizenship and migration policymaking in the Cold War context with this process in the imperial context, and assesses how the different geopolitical contexts and different positions of states within world society affect the outcomes as well as the relationship between nationhood and citizenship.

Chapter 4, "The Fight for Social Justice and Human Rights," examines the time period beginning in the 1970s, when the reinvigorated social movement among second- and third-generation Koreans and the emerging globalized norm of human rights created renewed pressure on the Japanese state to revise its migration and citizenship policies to meet the demands of immigrants. As explained earlier in this chapter, this book refers to the decades from the 1970s to the present as the global context, because of the period's distinctive features. These features—frequent economic and cultural transactions, a declining population and labor shortage that prompted the import of immigrant labor, and a globally embraced notion of human rights and restorative justice for the colonial past—did not exist in the previous historical contexts examined in chapters 2 and 3, and all of them brought the Japanese mono-ethno-racial self-image into sharp relief. Chapter 4 also focuses on the impact of supranational institutions, particularly the United Nations, and of Japan's former colonial countries, who are now important economic partners, on the Japanese state's policymaking process. This chapter then compares these recent developments in citizenship and migration policies in Japan with the dynamics in the two previous contexts. It closes by analyzing how the concept and practice of nationhood, citizenship, and migration were transformed under the context of three distinctive regime structures and geopolitics.

The final chapter analyzes what has been transpiring from the late twentieth century to the early twenty-first and discusses how the colonial past and globalization impacts the current discourse and policies regarding citizenship and immigration in Japan. Rather than assuming that the legacy of colonialism continues in a linear, unbroken fashion, this chapter shows the disjunctures in this legacy. The chapter also demonstrates how a newly imagined concept and practice of nationhood, citizenship, and migration has emerged in the interplay between forces of colonial legacy and globalization. This chapter compares the parallels and divergences found in the three specific historical contexts and addresses what these findings can tell us about the making and remaking of concepts of nationhood, citizenship and migration in our societies. It also reckons with the role that the Koreans in Japan play for the future of nationhood, citizenship, and migration in twenty-first-century Japan.

Chapter Two

PAN-ASIAN EMPIRE

> Koreans have Japanese citizenship as a result of the Annexation by Japan, but it is important to note that Koreans and Japanese are not at all the same. Koreans have Japanese citizenship [but that citizenship is meaningful] only in relation to other countries.
>
> —*Yamada Saburō, "Heigō go ni okeru kankokujin no kokuseki mondai"*

As a latecomer to imperialism, the Meiji Japanese state had a set of unique advantages and disadvantages. Historical records reveal that Japan's belated transformation into a modern nation-state and its late participation in imperial expansionism critically shaped its colonial policies, especially those regarding citizenship and migration, in the early twentieth century.[1] Japan was in a position to observe and learn from its Western predecessors' experiences, including their mistakes and successes. Yet it also had to establish its colonial empire in a relatively short period of time in a White-dominated world. The Japanese Empire's citizenship and migration policies were often contradictory and inconsistent. Unlike European empires, which emphasized their racial superiority to their colonies, the Japanese Empire advocated "racial affinity" between itself and its colonies, which was manifested in its "pan-Asian ideology." Japanese policymakers also developed an inclusive and expansive conceptualization of nationhood (i.e., as a pan-Asian empire) and extended Japanese citizenship to the entire colonized population, regardless of gender, class, age, religion, race, or ethnicity. These policies give the impression that inclusive nationhood triggered inclusive citizenship and that there was a causal relationship between nationhood and citizenship.

However, a closer examination of the way in which citizenship rights were extended to Koreans complicates this connection. The extension of citizenship status hardly meant an egalitarian treatment of colonial citizens. Contrary to its inclusive legal definition of citizenship, the Japanese state drew a distinction between mainland Japan (*naichi*), which I will refer to henceforth as "the metropole," and the colonies (*gaichi*) and maintained a hierarchical relationship with its colonized populations.[2] This distinction was maintained through a separate family registry system called *koseki*. Colonized populations such as the Korean and Taiwanese peoples were, in practice, routinely discriminated against in daily life. Despite establishing an inclusive legal definition of citizenship, the Japanese Empire did not actively impose cultural assimilation policies toward its colonies in its early phase of colonial rule. It was more than ten years after the colonization of Korea that the Japanese state started inflicting its cultural assimilation policy on the colonized population.

This inclusive legal definition of citizenship, without the immediate practice of cultural assimilation, seems to be in contrast with European empires' practices toward their colonies, which Japanese policymakers attempted to emulate. In other European empires of the nineteenth and twentieth centuries, particularly the British and French Empires, "colonized persons were designated as subjects, not citizens. They had duties but few rights" (Conklin 1998, 419). French empires, for example, granted citizenship status only to those who acquired fluency in the French language and converted to Christianity, suggesting that an extension of citizenship status and rights was contingent on attaining a sufficient level of cultural assimilation. However, in the case of Japan, the colonized populations—regardless of their cultural assimilation or socioeconomic status—held the same Japanese citizenship status as the Japanese, enjoyed a certain degree of freedom to travel to and work in the metropole, and were even granted suffrage in some limited cases (Kiyomiya 1944, 39–40). Through such policies, Imperial Japan advocated for unity among Asian nations in order to fight against their common threat: Western imperialism, which was anchored in the belief of Whites' racial superiority over non-Whites.

This chapter both identifies the forces that triggered the disparity between the principle and practice of citizenship and deciphers the

36 *Chapter 2*

mechanism by which those forces interacted. Analyzing these forces and the mechanism of their interaction helps us understand the nature of the relationship between citizenship and nationhood and how they develop in our societies. As we will see below, in the case of Imperial Japan, this disparity was not an accidental by-product of colonial history. Instead, it was by deliberate design, a result of the state's efforts to reconcile its competing political and economic interests, which were rooted in the particular historical and geopolitical contexts of the late nineteenth and early twentieth centuries. A series of historical records suggests that distinctive material, cultural, and political conditions in the late nineteenth and early twentieth centuries both in and outside Japan played a critical role in shaping not only the content of citizenship and migration policies the state created but also the way the state practiced such policies. The same archival data indicates the limits of the state's ability to translate the principle of citizenship into actual practice, in part due to persistent dissent and resistance by nonstate actors. Official documentation recording the voices of policymakers in the Japanese Empire demonstrates the vital impact that the resistance of Koreans had on the transformation of Japanese prewar citizenship and migration policies. All of these facts signal a far more complex relationship between citizenship and nationhood. The task at hand is to untangle this complexity by simultaneously paying attention to the state and nonstate relationship; to the material, cultural, and political conditions at the local level; and to power dynamics among states within the early twentieth-century world society.

In this chapter, I explain how the disparity between the principle and the practice of citizenship in the context of Japanese Empire was deliberately developed by lawmakers in order to conceal Japan's imperialist motives from both its colonies and Western powers. Yet this deliberate disparity had an unexpected consequence: it solidified a collective anticolonial sentiment among previously disconnected people in colonial Korea. This dissent effort subsequently forced the state to revise its policies and eventually contributed to the disintegration of the Japanese Empire in the mid-twentieth century.

Japan's Challenges: Modernization under Duress

Since the nineteenth century, East Asia was under the pressure of what Peter Duus (1995) called "informal imperialism" by the West. Western countries did not extend their domination by directly governing the local population with force. Instead, they pressured weak East Asian states to trade with them under unequal treaties. By seeking leaseholds and concessions, European imperialists attempted to secure their exclusive rights to raw materials, markets, and naval stations in China, Korea, and Japan. After the arrival of Commodore Matthew Perry and his four black ships in 1854, Japan was thrown into a world dominated by Western imperialism. Against its will, Japan signed unfair trade and diplomatic treaties with the United States in 1854 and then with the Netherlands, Russia, Britain, and France in 1858. All of these treaties exclusively favored the demands and interests of Western imperialists. For example, Western countries set an unfair trading tax in their own interest and justified their extraterritoriality on the grounds that the laws of Japan were too "uncivilized" for Westerners to submit themselves to. These unfair agreements with Western countries were considered a national humiliation and disgrace by the leaders of Meiji Japan, as they symbolically placed Japan in a subordinate position to Western powers in world society.

However, Western dominance also provided a model for the agents of the modernization project of nineteenth-century Japan, including politicians, bureaucrats, military generals, jurists, and intellectuals. Given the successful example of colonial domination provided by the Western countries, Meiji Japan's policymakers concluded that the acquisition of overseas possessions and the building of a modern army and navy were essential steps toward revising these unfair treaties with Western powers (Dickinson 1999). The revision of these unfair treaties was a path for Japan to earn its status as a first-class civilized nation that deserved respect and equal treatment by Western powers. To this end, the Japanese government rigorously studied Western models of jurisdiction, international laws, imperialism, and colonial governance and attempted to learn the secrets of Western wealth, strength, and power by sending envoys to Western countries and/or hiring foreign advisers from European nations.

Learning from the experience of the Western powers and emulating their models might have been the only advantage that Japan enjoyed as a novice to the global game of imperialism. Japan also faced numerous challenges and dilemmas that other Western countries did not have to consider in their process of modernizing their nations. Unlike Western countries, Japan had to industrialize and modernize its economy, jurisdiction, and military under the great threat of Western imperialism. Furthermore, unlike Western countries that achieved their dominant status over the course of several centuries, Japan had to catch up to Western modernization in haste. The Meiji leadership was acutely aware of the possibility that Japan would fall prey to Western imperialism and follow the same fate as India and other Asian countries that fell into the hands of Western powers, unless it achieved parity in the eyes of Western countries.

Under such ominous conditions, Japan nevertheless succeeded in modernizing its military power in a relatively short period of time. Its victories in wars with China (1894–1895) and later with Russia (1904–1905) attest to such success. However, the victory in the Sino-Japanese War was also bittersweet, because the so-called Triple Intervention by Russia, France, and Germany forced Japan to relinquish the Liaodong Peninsula, which Japan had made China cede, along with Taiwan and a war indemnity of 200 million taels. This Triple Intervention indicated that Western empires didn't fully recognize Japan as a powerful and sovereign country, even if Japan's military power had become strong enough to defeat Asia's sleeping tiger, China. This bitter lesson eventually led Japan to wage another war with Russia in 1905 (Okamoto 1970).

Victories in two wars with countries much larger than itself gave Japan a much-needed boost of confidence. More importantly, these wars also brought coveted new territories—Taiwan and Korea—both of which became critical for Japan's national defense as well as for economic resources. However, the expansion into Taiwan and Korea also presented Japanese lawmakers with a new dilemma. They sought to distinguish themselves from the people whom they were about to govern, while also distinguishing themselves from the Western colonial powers with whom they were competing for regional dominance. This project was made more difficult because Japan had not yet established itself as an advanced industrial society. In terms of fiscal and military power, Japan was relatively closer to those countries it was about to colonize than to Western powers. Furthermore, without obvious differences in phenotypes, culture, economy, military power, and level of civilization between the Japanese and the colonized population, Japan struggled to justify its dominance and faced defiant resistance from the colonized population (Oguma 1995, 1998).

Japanese citizenship and migration policy is one of the critical windows through which to observe the dilemmas and interests of Japanese policymakers in the nineteenth and early twentieth centuries,

Pan-Asian Empire   39

because this policy was designed specifically to resolve their dilemmas and reconcile their conflicting interests. The following section examines this intricate system of drawing and maintaining the boundaries of empire through citizenship and migration policy and shows how it later became an obstacle to the Japanese Empire maintaining its integrity. As the subsequent chapter will show, these actions and policies also impacted the postwar Japanese state's repertoire of citizenship and migration policies in the aftermath of World War II.

JAPANESE CITIZENSHIP DEFINED

The first Japanese citizenship law was enacted in 1899 when the first modern constitution was compiled. After the Meiji Restoration, Japanese policymakers made efforts to modernize their legal codes to the standard of countries in Europe and North Americas (Kashiwazaki 1998; Kojima 1988). This effort was made in part because the absence of both a modern constitution and legal system was cited by Western powers as a reason for the unfair treaties. Thus, drafters were very conscious of the compatibility of their new citizenship law with those of their European and North American counterparts (Endō 2010). The drafters of the citizenship law were also concerned about its compatibility with the existing family registry, or *koseki* (family registry) law, in Japan.

Koseki, or family registry, is the family-based system of population registry that was originally imported from China in the sixth century and reinforced during the feudal period. Premodern forms of *koseki* were used to control Japan's population, mostly for the purposes of taxation, social order, and military draft (Endō 2017).[3] *Koseki* records information on births, deaths, marriages, adoptions, permanent addresses, and even criminal convictions within each registered household. The Meiji state's lawmakers modernized this family registry to construct a unified modern nation-state. The new Meiji family registry served as a mechanism not just to make the population legible and controllable but also to transform and reconstruct the basis of national unity and collective sense of nationhood. In the transitional process from feudal system to modern imperial nation-state, leaders of the Meiji state sought to reestablish national unity. They constructed nationhood as a larger extension of the existing paternalistic family or household system (*ie*), in which the father is regarded as the head of the household and the rest of the members of the household belong to the father's blood lineage. At the level of the nation, the emperor was the symbolic father, and his subjects belonged to his "unbroken mythic blood lineage." Although the emperor never retained practical political power in modern Japan, his symbolic role in uniting modern Japan through the *koseki* family registry system was undeniable.

The development of the concept of citizenship and its institutionalization in Japan also took place in parallel to Japan's efforts to expand its territory. Consequently, Japanese lawmakers had to take into consideration the legal definition and treatment of these newly acquired territories and the population when they codified the boundaries and definition of the Japanese nation. The full development of colonial policies regarding citizenship and migration took place during Japan's colonization of its second colony, Korea—the main subject of this book. However, before proceeding to an empirical discussion about the case of Korea, it is important to discuss how the consequences of the Sino-Japanese War—specifically, Japan's acquisition of Taiwan—influenced embryonic forms of citizenship in Japan.

Initial citizenship policies for the colonies reflected suggestions made by Henry W. Denison, an American legal adviser to the Japanese foreign ministry (Itō [1936] 1970).[4] He first served as a vice consul in Yokohama and was later appointed a legal adviser by the Japanese government. He remained a prominent figure in Japan's foreign affairs until 1880. Denison suggested that citizenship should be understood not only as a symbol of national belonging but also as the collection of rights and duties held by a member of the nation-state. In his view, if one's national belonging was defined as "Japanese," then it was only logical and inevitable to recognize that person's full civil rights as a Japanese citizen. In other words, to Denison, nationhood and citizenship were inseparable and should be closely "coupled." Therefore, if Taiwanese people were to be given Japanese citizenship and defined as "Japanese," they should be recognized as having rights and duties equal to those of any Japanese citizen.

Initially, the Japanese colonial government practiced policies organized around Denison's conceptualization of citizenship; they did not believe that simply because Taiwan became a territory of Japan, Taiwanese citizenship would automatically change from Chinese to Japanese. To extend Japanese citizenship to the Taiwanese, the Japanese government required that they present a certification that proved that they were residents of Taiwan; without such a certification, they would not receive protection from the Japanese government. At the same time, the government also ordered the colonial police department to survey each Taiwanese household (to learn who and how many people lived in each household as family members) in order to establish a family registry system. According to historian Asano Toyomi (2000), this survey was done because the government intended to extend its citizenship by family unit rather than individually, as in mainland Japan. That is, if a male head of household was given Japanese citizenship, his family members would be given Japanese citizenship automatically. On the other hand, if he did not have any family members, he would be considered unfit for Japanese citizenship status and consequently deported to mainland China. Considering that anti-Japanese insurgents were the most likely to claim to have no family members, the government attempted to systematically identify those insurgents through the family registry survey and to withhold Japanese citizenship from them.

However, the Japanese authorities faced numerous challenges. One major obstacle was that family structures among native Taiwanese people were far more heterogeneous than Japanese officials expected.[5] Many households had quite a few non–family members residing together, such as a householder's mistress and her siblings, and so on. Thus, the diverse structures of Taiwanese families made it difficult for the Japanese authorities to establish a rigorous family registry system that they could use to smoothly extend Japanese citizenship to the local population.

In this context, lawmakers began to revise their strategies in extending Japanese citizenship to the Taiwanese. Concurrently, Denison's concept of citizenship was challenged by Dr. Yamada Saburō, a prominent jurist from Tokyo University who had played an influential role in defining Japanese legal systems, particularly citizenship laws.[6] Yamada introduced a fluid conceptualization of citizenship that decoupled national belonging and rights. He claimed that these two were separable: there existed national belonging, on the one hand, and rights and duties, on the other (Yamada 1895). This conceptualization sharply contrasted with Denison's more rigid conception, which viewed national belonging and citizenship rights/duties as an inseparable unit. The concept and practice of citizenship on the acquisition of new territories was heavily debated in law journals among prominent jurists in Japan. Yamada Saburō (1896, 787–788) argues against Denison's conceptualization of citizenship in the following passage (although he does not use Denison's name): "A Westerner, Mr. So-and-So

42   *Chapter 2*

[Henry Denison], conflates the status of citizenship with the privileges of citizens. Hence, he argues that those who are not recognized as having such privilege are not regarded as Japanese [citizens]. If so, then [the Taiwanese] will be Chinese citizens living in our national territory. Since the ancient times, no victorious country . . . has never practiced such a thing."[7]

Yamada's conceptualization of citizenship became increasingly popular among lawmakers, in part because it saved significant transactional costs and time in processing the extension of citizenship to the colonized population (Asano 2000). If national belonging and rights and duties were separable and decoupled, then the government need not be concerned about to whom they were extending their citizenship status. In other words, the state could simply extend its citizenship status, instead of having to check and assess which of the more than 2 million inhabitants of Taiwan were deserving of and eligible for Japanese citizenship. Moreover, if the Taiwanese did not wish to have their national belonging defined as Japanese, they could simply decline Japanese citizenship themselves by submitting a petition to refuse or renounce their Japanese citizenship. This conceptualization neatly fit the interests of the Japanese imperial state, enabling it to label the colonized population as "de jure Japanese" without recognizing or protecting their civil rights, and to control and exclude them as "de facto aliens" whenever this was deemed necessary.

TRAPPING KOREANS WITHIN CITIZENSHIP

Taiwan was in many ways an "experimental laboratory" for Japanese colonialists, one where they tested and developed various colonial policies that could serve as a blueprint for Japan's future colonies (Myers and Peattie 1984, 84). However, it was in Japan's next colony, Korea, that this conceptualization was further developed, elaborated, codified, and institutionalized into a series of more exclusive and exploitative policies that concretized the symbolic distinction between de jure and de facto Japanese. This distinction manifested in citizenship policies and in migration and cultural assimilation policies implemented in colonial Korea.

Although the Japanese government allowed the Taiwanese to choose between Japanese and Chinese citizenship within a two-year grace period, they did not allow such an option for Koreans. Instead, they unilaterally extended Japanese citizenship to all Koreans, regardless of age, gender, ethnic origin, religion, level of cultural assimilation, and even country of residence. Literally overnight, all Koreans, including those residing abroad, were defined as Japanese citizens and became subjects of Japanese imperial sovereignty. Unlike the Taiwanese, Koreans were not allowed to renounce Japanese citizenship and were prohibited from becoming naturalized citizens in other countries. When Japan's modern citizenship law was first enacted in 1899, there was no mention of a process by which to renounce Japanese citizenship. Thus, there was no legal procedure whereby one could remove his or her Japanese citizenship. However, in 1916 and then again in 1923, the Japanese government modified its law and specified a legal procedure for citizenship renouncement. This change was intended to allow Japanese immigrants living overseas to renounce their citizenship upon their naturalization in other countries.[8] This was clearly an effort to update Japan's law to the standards of other European and North American countries. Nevertheless, this modification was never applied to Koreans, because the Japanese government classified its colonies under a separate jurisdiction in which not every mainland law was executed or practiced (Asano and Matsuda 2004). Citizenship legislation was not executed in the colonies. Japanese policymakers were aware that denying Koreans the ability to renounce their Japanese citizenship was not an exemplary practice of a "modern nation." We can see this awareness in a recommendation made by jurist Yamada to Terauchi Masatake, who was governor-general of Korea at the time. Noting that no other country "entirely prohibited becoming naturalized citizens of another country," Yamada suggested that "even in Korea, [Japan would] eventually need to allow them to become naturalized citizens of another country."[9]

Japanese policymakers realized that confining Koreans within the legal boundary of Japanese citizenship could potentially harm Japan's reputation as "a civilized modern nation."[10] Since they were attempting to achieve this reputation by modernizing Japan's legal system and infrastructure to reach the same standard as those of Western countries, they preferred avoiding any practices that appeared to drastically deviate from Western standards. Yet Japanese policymakers also had significant political and military interests that motivated them not to allow Koreans to renounce their Japanese citizenship. A government report from 1915 suggests that the government would not execute the same Japanese citizenship law in Korea. Instead, the government maintained Korea's old common law on naturalization (which prohibited

Koreans from becoming naturalized in another country), because the Japanese authorities realized that they would lose their ability to control Koreans if they were to become citizens of other nations:

> And as for the naturalization for Koreans, there has been traditionally no law in Korea that allows Koreans to become naturalized in another country. . . . The reason we decided to maintain this Korean common law is there are quite a few Koreans living in the United States and Russia who are attempting to collaborate among themselves to plot against the Japanese. Thus, if these Koreans become naturalized in those countries and come back to Korea as foreign nationals who have different sets of rights and privileges, it would be very difficult for us to control them. In short, it is the best policy for us to not allow any Koreans to become naturalized in another country at all.[11]

The Japanese government was particularly concerned about those Koreans in the Gando region—a part of Manchuria and a border region between Russia, China, and northern Korea (Mizuno 2001).[12] Ownership of the Gando region was unclear at that time; there were a large number of Korean settlers, but they were highly acculturated into the local Chinese culture. Some of them were recorded under the Chinese resident registry system. In 1906, though, Japan sent its military troops and declared ownership over this region, and tensions between China (the Qing dynasty) and Japan arose rapidly. Nevertheless, in 1909, through the Gando Convention, Japan affirmed the territorial rights of China over the Gando region. The large number of Korean settlers in the Gando region were considered "Japanese citizens" and remained under significant influence by Japan. These Korean settlers in the Gando region were critical of the Japanese authorities who exerted influence over the border region between Korea, Russia, and China. The Gando region was increasingly becoming a strategic base for anticolonial Korean partisan fighters. Because this was the region where the largest army of anti-Japanese combatants—including the first North Korean leader, Kim Il-sung—organized its force against the Japanese colonial army, the Japanese government's apprehension was not entirely abstract or imagined. To suppress the potential threat posed by naturalized Koreans abroad, the government did not want to recognize Koreans' rights to abandon Japanese citizenship and become naturalized in another country, especially China or Russia.

Defining all Koreans as Japanese citizens might have served a national security purpose and allowed Japan to assert ownership of its colonized population and territory, but extending Japanese citizenship status to all Koreans before acculturating them posed another problem for agents of the Japanese colonial government. Acquiring Korea and Taiwan was critical for national defense, to counteract fears of invasion by the West. Yet managing two large colonies was an enormous economic burden on Japan, whose economic and military ability was still relatively feeble. This concern was widely addressed in various newspapers and magazines, including an article from the popular Japanese newspaper *Yorozu Chōhō* (August 29, 1910): "Because the annexation of Korea brings happiness to Koreans, it is not only welcomed by Koreans, but is proudly recognized as Japanese graciousness in the world. However, this graciousness would increase our burden and sacrifices . . . [and] could pose a negative impact on our economy."

When the Japanese state acquired Taiwan, they faced vehement resistance from the local population, which reminded policymakers in Japan of the military, economic, and human resources required to control the local population at such a scale. The same situation was expected in Korea, which was much larger than Taiwan both in terms of geographical land and population. Although the Japanese government needed to define the colonized population as Japanese to assert ownership and control of the population and territory, they also wanted to be able to easily distinguish the colonized population from the population that was ethno-racially Japanese in order to control them in case of rebellion. To put it differently, the Japanese imperial state needed and wanted to keep its colonized population "legible" and thus controllable (Scott 1998). Exploiting the colonized population without costly rebellion appeared key to Japan's successful colonial governance. A critical question remained for agents of Japanese colonialism: how could they exploit the colonized population while also nurturing a sense of loyalty toward the Japanese emperor? Finding strategies to meet these conflicting interests became a core part of the agenda of Japanese lawmakers throughout colonial Korea and Taiwan.

Creating an Internalized Other

The Japanese government needed a systematic yet discreet way to maintain the distinction between the colonizers and the colonized so that they would not have to expose their imperialist tendencies to either the colonized populations or Western powers. The solution they found for this intricate dilemma was to utilize their local family system, the *koseki* system, as a means to maintain a hierarchical distinction between the colonizers and the colonized.[13] This solution ended up creating a lasting legacy of colonialism in the postwar legal classification of the same population that remained on Japanese soil after the empire's dissolution.

Once again, the jurist Yamada Saburō played a critical role in offering a solution for this dilemma. In his replies to Terauchi Masatake's inquiry concerning the legal treatment of Koreans, he suggested using citizenship to sustain the integrity of empire and to take advantage of the local *koseki* system to maintain hierarchical distinction between Japanese and non-Japanese within the empire. Korea also has its own family registry system, but its organizing format is different from that of the Japanese family registry system, reflecting Koreans' distinctive cultural concept of kinship. Yamada argued that the population registry under the Korean dynasty was inadequate and incomplete and thus that it was necessary to establish a more rigorous family registry system in Korea that would be comparable to the one utilized in mainland Japan. However, he cautioned against merging the Korean family registry and the Japanese family registry:

> Nowadays, we often debate whether or not Koreans living in the mainland should be considered "*naichi-jin*" [mainland Japanese]. By definition, Koreans are not foreigners; they are indeed citizens of the Japanese Empire. Unless there is a regulation specifying otherwise, in theory, Koreans could move to the mainland, become registered as residents of local cities in the mainland, enjoy suffrage, and have military duties as Japanese citizens. . . . However, if there is a political necessity to maintain a distinction between Koreans [*gaichi-jin*] and Japanese [*naichi-jin*]—to prevent Koreans from migrating to the mainland, to prevent them from becoming *naichi-jin* even after their migration to and residence in the mainland, or to establish a requirement of naturalization to become mainlanders as if they were foreign nationals—it is acutely necessary to establish a family registry law that articulates the necessary requirements and eligibilities for Koreans to become members of the mainland. Otherwise, Koreans could be automatically recognized as mainlanders simply by physically moving to the mainland.[14]

In his replies to Terauchi, Yamada also expressed concern about being unable to legally distinguish Koreans from Japanese due to the absence of a law that would prohibit Koreans from becoming a part of the Japanese registry system.

Most of Yamada's recommendations were eventually incorporated into the actual family registry policy, except for one point. While Yamada recommended that the government should create a new act as a part of the existing family registry law that would clearly prohibit Koreans from becoming a part of the Japanese family registry system, the Japanese government avoided creating an explicit law establishing such a prohibition. Here as with citizenship law, the Japanese government achieved the same goal (i.e., prohibiting Koreans from becoming a part of the Japanese registry) by not extending its own family registry law to its colonies. In other words, the Japanese government continued to keep the traditional Korean family registry that was practiced during the Yi dynasty, and it maintained separate family registry laws between the colonies and mainland Japan. In 1922, the colonial government announced the family registry law as "colonial law" to further specify the practice of the family registry in Korea, but this law was technically distinguished from the mainland law.[15] Because Japan established separate jurisdictions for the colonies and the metropole, there was no legal procedure for Koreans or Japanese to transfer or merge their registries.[16]

The Japanese government's choice appears somewhat irrational, especially when we consider other options that they could have chosen. There were at least two other ways to handle this situation: they could have established a unified jurisdiction for the entire empire, or they could have simply established a law prohibiting Koreans from becoming a part of the Japanese family registry system, as Yamada Saburō suggested. Historical records and existing historical research suggest that Japan's usage of complex and separate legal systems between the mainland and colonies was in fact based on some strategic rationales—that is, to protect Japan's interests and reputation in the international community while avoiding Western criticism of its colonialism (Asano and Matsuda 2004; Mizuno 2001). Policymakers in early twentieth-century Japan were keenly aware of the possibility that Western powers, if given the opportunity, might prevent Japan from expanding toward its neighboring Asian countries. Masking its colonial intentions was a compulsory strategy for Japan as a means to

48 *Chapter 2*

avoid giving the Western powers any excuses to interfere in its policies. A sense of apprehension was vividly expressed in the diplomatic reports written by the bureaucrats of the Foreign Ministry before and after Japan's participation in the League of Nations Codification Conference (or Hague Conference) in 1930. In the following report, Japanese bureaucrats refer to the possibility that Japan might be accused of not having civilized citizenship laws for Koreans who technically had Japanese citizenship (Schlichtmann 2003): "Although it is not our wish to recognize the same rights [as Japanese] for Koreans, it is also necessary to recognize their rights, in order to maintain our governance over the colonies. At this [international] conference, we must be extra-cautious about this point" (Gaimushō 1930a).[17]

The Hague Conference, organized by the League of Nations, was the first intergovernment conference that aimed to codify international law. Delegates from forty-seven governments, including Japan's, participated in the conference to codify law concerning three main subjects: territorial waters, nationality, and states' responsibility for damage to the person or property of foreigners in their territory. Due to competing interests, the conference was unable to establish agreed-upon conventions regarding territorial water or state responsibility. According to the UN's own account, "the only international instruments which resulted from its work were on the topic of nationality" (UN International Law Commission 2017).

Japanese diplomats and bureaucrats were afraid that their discriminatory practice in the application of citizenship law to Koreans would be exposed and criticized at the Hague Conference (Mizuno 2001). Anticipating possible criticism of Japan's legal treatment of Koreans, the Japanese government prepared to state at the conference that it was considering conditionally allowing Koreans to renounce Japanese citizenship in the future. The government sent a telegraph to one of its main delegates, the Japanese ambassador to Germany, Nagaoka Harukazu, to remind him that he should mention the Korean issue "only if necessary." The government gave him the following instructions: "We [the Japanese government] hope that you would consider the Korean issue and adequately proceed without creating any potentially difficult situations for Japan in the future" (Gaimushō 1930b, 629). However, the European and North American nations never problematized this point. The Hague Conference largely held that each state would specify the conditions concerning citizenship and how to handle dual citizenship. This was to the Japanese state's great relief, vividly captured in a postconference report by a Japanese official: "Now, the [citizenship] issue of Koreans is no longer our concern" (Gaimushō 1930b, 635).

Imperial Japan's seemingly contradictory citizenship practices—unconditionally extending Japanese citizenship to the whole colonized population while maintaining a distinction between Koreans and Japanese through the *koseki* system—were a result of the state's effort to reconcile its competing interests. Extending Japanese citizenship without allowing for its renouncement enabled the Japanese state to expand its boundaries and establish a new national self-image as a pan-ethnic empire. This extension was combined with the creation of an internal boundary between colonized and colonizers by maintaining a separate family registration system (*koseki*) and jurisdiction between colonies and metropole. This internal distinction allowed Japanese authorities to keep the Korean population legible and thus controllable. This intricate and discreet system of drawing and maintaining external and internal boundaries for the Japanese Empire would be revisited and revised extensively throughout the colonial era.

THE LIMITS OF EMULATION

Distinguishing Koreans from Japanese and not allowing them to renounce Japanese citizenship was hardly an effective way to tame anticolonial sentiment or to nurture loyalty for the Japanese ruler among the colonized population in the long run. The Japanese government's colonial policy prior to 1919 was called *budan tōchi* (military governance), which later transitioned to *bunka tōchi* (cultural governance). But despite its military governance, the Japanese government did not "forcefully" assimilate Koreans into Japanese culture until the 1930s. As Japanese historian Komagome Takeshi claims, *dōka seisaku* (assimilation policy) or *kōminka seisaku* (Japanization policy) has been overused as an analytical concept in studies of Japanese colonialism. He writes, "This 'inflation' of usage of *dōka* (assimilation) as an analytical concept made it more difficult for us to understand the nature of Japanese colonial policies and conceptualization of the colonies" (Komagome 1996, 12). More recent work by historians such as Mark Caprio (2009), Todd Henry (2014), Sakamoto Shinichi (1997), and Mizuno Naoki (2004a, 2004b) has revealed that Japanese colonial policies were complex and hardly monolithic or uniform. The Japanese colonial policies were characterized by moments of drastic transformation, while assimilation practices were uneven and incomplete. The historical records of the political and intellectual discourse of colonialism at the beginning of Japan's colonial conquest attest to this point.

In search of effective colonial policies, Japanese policymakers assiduously observed and learned from the techniques of Western imperial powers. After the acquisition of Taiwan, officials in the Japanese government hired European advisers with in-depth knowledge of their countries' colonial policies, and Japanese policymakers eagerly studied the positive and negative outcomes of European colonial policies and experiences. By the time Japan annexed Korea, a strong liberal movement known as Taishō Democracy had taken hold.[18] This movement, named after the reign title of the emperor Taishō, was characterized by flourishing party politics and by an embrace of Western liberal democratic ideals and the French-inspired concept of human rights. Within this context, in 1922 the largest minoritized group, Burakumin, created an organization named Zenkoku Suiheisha (National Levelers Association) with the goal of eradicating discrimination against Buraku-identified individuals. Taishō Democracy not only inspired marginalized populations but also prompted policymakers to incorporate Western ideals into their politics.

While searching for effective colonial strategies, two European models, in particular, caught the attention of Japanese policymakers. One was the British model, which encouraged alliances between colonizers and local elite groups in order to facilitate control over the local population while minimizing cultural assimilation. A key virtue of this plan, according to the policymakers' British adviser, William M. H. Kirkwood, was that restricting access to education prevented Indigenous people from being fully exposed to enlightened philosophical ideals such as human rights and civil liberty. Because such enlightened beliefs often served as a moral basis against colonialism, a limited access to modern education could avert rebellions against the colonial government.

Kirkwood criticized the Japanese government's decision to provide free education to the native population in Taiwan. Although his recommendations did not explicitly reference this point, it is not difficult to imagine that his criticism was based on problems that British colonialists were dealing with at that time. The British empire was facing a resistance movement led by local elites who had received higher

Pan-Asian Empire

education in the metropole and who had been exposed to the ideas of human rights and anticolonial philosophy pervasive in late nineteenth-century Europe. Thus, Kirkwood cautioned that unless the Japanese government had a concrete plan to eventually integrate culturally assimilated elite groups from the colonies as lower- or higher-ranked officials in colonial governance, the Taiwanese who currently studied at Japanese schools would be extremely disappointed when they realized that their education did not pave the way for them to attain successful careers in the Japanese Empire. He also warned that those disappointed elites would eventually rebel against the Japanese government.[19]

However, the British model suggested by Kirkwood was based on an unquestionable gap in military power between the colonizers and the colonized. The British could forcefully control the local population and suppress any rebellion. Without abundant military resources, Japanese policymakers could not adopt the unmodified British model (Oguma 1998). This deficiency in military power led Japanese policymakers to conclude that they must nurture a sense of "Japaneseness" and loyalty to the Japanese emperor through cultural assimilation. In this context, the French cultural assimilation model was considered.

The French colonial model, *mission civilisatrice,* was based on both the core beliefs of French republicanism (i.e., that all men were created equal and free) and the evolutionary aspiration of human progress (i.e., that human progress takes place in a unidirectional and linear fashion). From today's standpoint, democratic beliefs and colonial oppression may seem to be competing and irreconcilable concepts, but in the eyes of the nineteenth-century French colonialists, these neatly related concepts actually complemented each other (Pitts 2005). The evolutionary aspiration of social development situated the French in a superior position in terms of modern progress in technology, knowledge, military power, and culture. This sense of superiority allowed French colonizers to rationalize the colonization of non-European societies by arguing that it was a "humanitarian act" because they were guiding the "barbaric" populations in mastering the lifestyles, manners, beliefs, and language of a more "civilized" French culture (Cooper and Stoler 1997; Cox 2002; Daughton 2006). Although to a certain degree all the European empires felt a sense of superiority, French colonialists are often said to have regarded themselves as the most qualified nation to conduct this civilizing mission because they were supposedly the first European nation to overcome

52   *Chapter 2*

oppression and superstition to form a democratic government (Conklin 1997, 1998).

European colonizers further justified their civilizing mission by racializing visible cultural and physical appearances between themselves and the colonized population, but Japanese colonizers found such visible physical and cultural markers of differentiation between themselves and their colonies too scarce and obscure to rely on. A case in point is the list of physical characteristics of Koreans appearing in a confidential document titled "Materials concerning Korean Identification" that was distributed by the Department of Police in Japan to governors across Japan in 1913:[20]

- There is no difference between Koreans and Japanese in terms of their height. Many Koreans have good posture and few have stooped shoulders or bent backs.
- Korean facial characteristics are not different from Japanese. But many have straight, thin hair which grows downward. Their facial hairs tend to be thin, and many of their faces are so-called *nopperi gao* (smooth and blank faces) and they have little facial hair, such as a beard or mustache.
- Their eyes are cloudy and not sharp.
- There are some Koreans whose heads are slightly deformed due to a common Korean hairstyle (a ponytail style, commonly used after their rite of passage), and if you look carefully, you may be able to see the traces of where they used to part their hair in the middle when they were young. The backside of their heads tends to be flat due to the wooden pillows they use.
- Their teeth are white due to the salt they use to clean their teeth.
- Their feet tend to be small and thin because of their custom of wearing tight socks and shoes. Their middle toes are often the thinnest, and the backside of their feet have a straight line. The lower class use slippers; thus, their feet have bumps.
- They have a custom of decorating themselves. They particularly like hair accessories, and they tend to prefer decorative and shiny items.
- Those Koreans who are middle to upper class or Confucian scholars have a custom of keeping their little fingers' nails long.

This confidential document argued that due to the recent increase of Koreans adopting Japanese hairstyles and clothing, Koreans were starting to look much more like Japanese. For this reason, the Department of Police created a list of physical characteristics that local officials could use to identify Koreans. However, as we see in that list, titled "Materials concerning Korean Identification," the characteristics used by the Japanese authorities hardly proved any clear physical demarcations between Koreans and Japanese, because most of them applied to both Japanese and Koreans. Instead, the list demonstrates that although Japanese visually distinguished Koreans from themselves, they found it difficult to reify such distinctions because of the absence of clear visible phenotypical differences between the two groups.

Contrary to European colonists, Japanese intellectuals and policymakers could not assert their superiority over their colonies on the sole assertion that they were more civilized and developed and racially superior. They were aware that White imperialists considered Japan and its colonies—Taiwan and Korea—to be equally undercivilized, underdeveloped societies and to be part of the same inferior racial group. Even though Japanese leaders had developed a sense of superiority over their colonies and attempted to maintain a hierarchical relationship with the colonies, they knew that White imperialists would view their level of civilization and modernization as being closer to that of their colonies.

Moreover, by the time Japan acquired its own colonies in the late nineteenth century, French colonialists were already facing difficulties in maintaining their cultural assimilation policies due to resistance from their colonized population, and they took a pragmatic turn toward the principle of association. Therefore, some of the colonial specialists in Japan expressed skepticism against adopting the early nineteenth-century French-style assimilation policy (Oguma 1998). The scarcity of both materials and symbolic resources led Japanese policymakers to design their own colonial policy, incorporating some features from various European practices while emphasizing the racial and ethnic affinity among Asian nations.

ETHNO-RACIAL CONTRADICTION

Although lawmakers realized that a top-down assimilation policy such as the nineteenth-century French colonial strategy would invite strong resistance from the local population, the discourse on the treatment of the colonized population in the early phase of the colonial period nevertheless fixated on the idea of assimilation. Many theorists and

54   *Chapter 2*

specialists in colonialism in Japan argued that cultural assimilation was not only necessary but also relatively "easy," especially compared to assimilation projects by Western countries in their colonies in Africa and southern Asia, because Japan had ethno-racial proximity to its colonies. Colonial General of Korea Terauchi explained this perspective in his October 1915 statement: "The relationship between Japan and Korea is very different from the European colonial relationships. Not only are we geographically close to one another, we also share common interests and our cultures and customs have little difference. Therefore, under the same sovereignty, the amalgamation of these two cultures and nations is hardly an intricate matter."[21]

Many historians, anthropologists, and linguists produced academic theories that supported Terauchi's stance (Oguma 1995, 1998).[22] Although they may not all have agreed on technical details about ethnic and racial proximity between Korean and Japanese peoples, they claimed that both groups were originally from the same ethnicity and race (Oguma 1995). Ōkuma Shigenobu (1906, 67–71), one of the most prominent intellectuals and politicians, stated in the nation's leading magazine, *Taiyō*, that Koreans and Japanese shared the same roots and that as long as their politics improved, Koreans had the potential to become as modernized as the Japanese. These intellectuals also publicly claimed that Japan's relation to Korea was not colonialism but, rather, the restoration of their ancient shared roots and thus "annexation" (Kang 1984).

The ideas of *dōso dōshu* (same origin, same race) and *kunmin dōso* (imperial subjects sharing the same origin), buttressed by the concept of *isshi dōjin* (imperial impartiality and equal favor for all imperial citizens), characterized the early colonial discourse in Imperial Japan. The concept of *isshi dōjin* contains the moralistic ideal that all citizens who were subjects of the imperial sovereign received equal and impartial benevolence from the emperor. This concept was closely linked to a mythical belief that the Japanese emperor was head of the Japanese nation and race and that the entire Japanese population could be traced back to the imperial family who created the Japanese nation— the same idea used among the leaders of early Meiji state to unify the postfeudal Japanese population.

The idea of *isshi dōjin* was translated into a paternalistic and gradualist approach to the colonies, particularly in Japan's education policies. Education was a key vehicle for bringing forth successful assimilation among the colonized population. Hence, there were serious and intense debates among intellectuals and policymakers in Japan about colonial education in the early twentieth century. When Japan acquired Taiwan, the Japanese government attempted to establish state-funded Japanese schools that Taiwanese of all ages, classes, and sexes were encouraged and invited to attend. Although this move was criticized by foreign advisers such as William Kirkwood, Izawa Shūji, a Japanese policymaker in charge of the colonial education in Taiwan, enthusiastically recommended that the colonial governor establish the same level of state-funded education available in Japan for the whole colonized population. However, his plan was quickly diminished because of the financial constraints Japan was facing at that time. After the Sino-Japanese War, the Japanese state had amassed a large debt due to military expenses, and although acquisition of the colony should have compensated for long-term military spending, maintenance of that colony posed a huge financial burden. This left the colonial government with little budget with which to fund comprehensive state-operated free educational institutions for the entire colonized population. An effective assimilation strategy also required an abundance of Japanese experts with local knowledge who could successfully initiate cultural assimilation through education. However, these experts were scarce in Imperial Japan (Furukawa 2006; Komagome 1996; Sano 1993).

The situation was similar in Korea, if not worse. As in the case of Taiwan, there was a series of debates concerning the colonial education policy toward Koreans. One of the most debated issues was to what extent Japan should impose assimilation in order to transform Koreans into loyal subjects of the Japanese emperor. There was a large gap in the opinions of colonial policymakers and theorists in the colonies and those in the metropole (Komagome 1996, 96). Since 1890, the Japanese government had used the Kyōiku Chokugo (Imperial Rescript on Education) to cultivate an attitude of Japanese nationalism and transform its citizens into devout imperial nationals. To internalize their spirit of loyalty toward the emperor, for example, Japanese schoolchildren were required to memorize this script. Although an assimilation policy might have been regarded as an important colonial strategy in theory, most of the officials, particularly those in the colonies, believed the immediate implementation of assimilation was neither realistic nor feasible (Myers and Peattie 1984, 100). However, although the officials in the colonies were more skeptical and less willing than those in the metropole to introduce this script to the colonized population, the colonial government nevertheless implemented it as part of the mandatory curriculum of the colonial education system, suggesting an acute interest in nurturing a spirit of loyalty among the colonized population.

Paradoxically, however, the historical records on Japanese educational policies and practices in Korea and Taiwan also indicate that a project to transform the colonized population into pious imperial citizens was neither complete nor efficient. Although the imperial script was incorporated as a part of colonial education, the number of Koreans who were exposed to it remained too limited to nurture a sense of loyalty toward the emperor at a mass scale (Furukawa 2006; Komagome 1996; Sano 1993). Because these Japanese schools required a high level of Japanese-language proficiency, only a small number of elite Koreans learned Japanese; the majority of Koreans were prevented from attending such schools and were thus deprived of opportunities to learn the Japanese language. As a result, the rate of Japanese-language acquisition among Koreans in the early colonial period remained low among the general public.

Once again, the discrepancy between the rhetoric of the colonial governance and the actual practices of the officials in the colonies was a reflection of their competing interests and of the dilemmas that derived from the position that Japan held within world society in the early twentieth century. As mentioned previously, early twentieth-century Japan lacked an abundant military force and desperately needed to transform the colonized population into loyal imperial citizens to prevent rebellion. Education was key to nurturing this sense of loyalty among the population, but there were not enough economic or human resources to implement such a vehicle in the colonies. In the absence of visible phenotypical characteristics and an unquestionable gap in the level of civilization status between themselves and their colonized population, Japanese policymakers were not able to confidently establish a rapid assimilation project in the colonies.

Instead of investing their limited resources in a rapid assimilation project, colonial policymakers chose a gradual approach. The result was the enactment of an incomprehensive and incomplete cultural assimilation policy. Although many policymakers and theorists of colonialism were alarmed by the ineffective application of assimilation in their colonies, government officials argued, or (to put it more accurately) "hoped," that the colonized population would gradually be assimilated and transformed into loyal imperial citizens. Such "hope" was not entirely irrational and abstract in the eyes of Japanese policymakers in the early twentieth century, especially given the many scholarly theories advocating the idea of the same ethno-racial origins among colonized and colonizers (Kang 1984; Oguma 1995).

The Japanese version of inclusive citizenship articulated a pan-ethnic conception of nationhood. In practice, however, the state enacted a gradual and ineffective cultural assimilation policy. The lack of abundant symbolic and material resources prevented Japanese policymakers from practicing a full-fledged assimilation policy in the colonies. The acute necessity of governing the colonies for economic and national security purposes without causing strong resistance from the local population did lead agents of Japanese colonialism to develop the rhetoric of racial affinity manifested in *isshi dōjin* (imperial impartiality and equal favor for all imperial citizens) and *kunmin dōso* (imperial subjects share the same ancestral origin) to justify their colonial acts. But ideas such as *isshi dōjin* and *kunmin dōso* never became a practical policy guideline; rather, they remained a dogmatic rhetorical device for early Japanese colonial policies (Peattie 1984). At the everyday level, the Japanese colonial government oppressed Koreans by restricting their freedom of speech, and if Koreans rebelled, the imperial police responded with force, vividly demonstrating the contradiction inherent in Japanese colonial policies.[23]

All of these facts indicate that political, material, and cultural conditions at the local level played a critical role in the state's policymaking. Furthermore, they also suggest the ways these conditions informed policymaking and how policy itself varied depending on global power dynamics. This point becomes more evident when we compare Japan's justification for its colonial practices and policies to that of its European counterparts. For example, while French colonialists justified their colonial acts as their *mission civilisatrice* to fortify the inferior races, Japanese colonialists rationalized theirs as a mission to construct a hybrid nation based on the idea of racial proximity manifested in the ideology of *isshi dōjin* and *kunmin dōso*.

This contrast between European and Japanese justifications may hardly seem startling: the two approaches reflect the same imperialist interests—greed, racism, and a quest for power—dressed in different cultural clothes. But though European colonialists were in a more favorable position than Japan in terms of the material and cultural superiority they exerted against their colonies, Japanese policymakers nevertheless found it necessary to seduce their masses and even themselves into supporting overseas expansionism. This suggests that regardless of the abundance or scarcity of materials and cultural resources, policymakers in these empires shared a common need to rationalize their colonial policies and practices.

This intricate interaction among three elements—the state's interests in rationalizing its colonialism; local cultural and economic conditions; and the political dynamics in world society—is what led Japanese policymakers to adopt the rhetoric of racial hybridity. Unlike European colonialists, who managed to reconcile competing interests and ideologies (colonialism and democracy versus universalism and assimilation) by perceiving the colonized as racially inferior, Japanese colonialists achieved the same goal by extending their citizenship as a gesture to show their faith in their rhetoric of racial affinity, though this was accompanied by an incomplete cultural assimilation policy. These facts offer an interesting insight into racial formation by the imperial state: in a context where relatively abundant material, symbolic, and military resources exist, the imperial state tends to emphasize racial differences between themselves and the colonized population to rationalize its colonial acts. In a context where such resources were scarce, the state resorted to racial proximity to achieve the same goal.

The reality of Japanese colonies, however, was by no means an ideal environment for any successful intercourse of two races to take place spontaneously or gradually. Although the colonists elaborately masked their colonial intentions at the policy level by tactfully manipulating citizenship law, their sense of superiority over the colonized population was obvious at the level of quotidian interactions in the colonies. The first colonial governor-general, Terauchi, tightly controlled the colony with the military police, intimidating the Korean public. Although the Japanese government did not legally prohibit interracial marriage between the colonized and the colonizers—because such a legal code would directly contradict their rhetoric of *isshi dōjin*—marriage between Korean and Japanese people was socially condemned among the Japanese, who had developed a strong sense of prejudice against Koreans and subsequently discouraged many Japanese citizens from marrying colonial people (Suzuki 1992). The number of intermarriages did gradually increase as colonial governance persisted and as the interaction between Koreans and Japanese peoples became more frequent, but this increase was not drastic enough to confirm that a successful amalgamation between two cultures and races was taking place.

Historian Mark Peattie writes that because Japanese government officials in the colonial empire "failed to come to grips with the contradictions inherent in Japanese attitudes toward colonialism, official policies supporting assimilation were reduced to this mechanical level and generally achieved results among colonized populations that were similarly limited and superficial" (Peattie 1984, 100). This is perhaps true for most of the Japanese governmental officials at that time. However, historical records concerning citizenship policymaking in early twentieth-century Japan also indicate that some of the Japanese policymakers—at least those who had a hand in crafting citizenship policies—were aware of the inherent contradiction in those policies, precisely because they were the ones who deliberately invented the discrepancy in order to reconcile their competing interests. But whether such a discrepancy was a deliberate design or resulted from an absence of self-consciousness, this disparity between the rhetoric of hybrid Asian unity and the actual practice of colonialism exposed the true color of colonialists and invoked collective resistance from Koreans ten years after the annexation of Korea.

PAN-ASIAN CITIZENSHIP UNDERMINED

On March 1, 1919, hundreds of thousands of Koreans across the peninsula joined in a well-organized demonstration to declare Korea's independence from Japanese colonial rule, a demonstration that was intended to be pacifist. Unlike the earlier nationalist movement, which was largely supported by cultural and political elites, the participants in the March First Movement came from highly diverse backgrounds in terms of gender, age, education, and occupation, and the movement spread across the Korean peninsula over the course of a few months (Kang 2005). The March First demonstration for independence from Japanese colonial rule—a day that many Japanese officials had feared since 1910—marked a watershed event in the history of modern Korea. Japanese policymakers had assumed that a gradualist approach in their colonial policies would prompt Koreans to harmoniously assimilate into Japanese culture little by little. They had assumed that the extension of Japanese citizenship to Koreans, the freedom for Koreans to travel to the metropole, and the absence of any clear legal prohibition of intermarriage between colonizers and colonized would mask Japan's colonialist intentions and facilitate the amalgamation of the

60   *Chapter 2*

two groups. However, such theories about ethno-racial harmony were proven wrong on this day.[24]

Before the March First Movement, many Korean ex-officials and anti-Japanese intellectuals protested in the press, and a guerrilla army called Uibyong (also known as "the Righteous Army"), led by the local Confucian elite and ex-soldiers of the disbanded Yi army and supported by the peasant population, fervidly attacked Japanese facilities and residences across Korea (Dudden 2005; Ichikawa 1983). The guerrilla resistance resulted in a series of bloody struggles with the Japanese imperial army and police force. Although Japan's modern army and imperial police eventually subdued the guerrilla force, the fact that such a vehement anticolonialist resistance was supported by a considerable number of local peasants indicates that colonization by Japan "unintentionally" triggered the transformation of the nationalist movement in Korea from an elite reformist movement into a more comprehensive popular independence movement. In other words, the contradictory Japanese attempts to construct a new national self-image as a pan-Asian empire and to establish a hierarchical relationship between the colonizers and the colonized brought together previously divergent and disconnected groups of Korean political elites and popular masses.

The Japanese colonial government was acutely aware of the danger of rising rebellion among Koreans and attempted to stifle it by providing support for Korean aristocratic elites (*yangban*). The colonial government began affiliating with collaborationist Korean officials, expanding their citizenship status to all Koreans, recognizing some of their civil rights, and gradually introducing Japanese culture to the colonized population through education systems as well as news publications.[25] In terms of colonial state building, economic reforms, and the imposition of Japanese laws, the Japanese were making strides in colonial Korea; this development included the rapid construction of an expansive railroad connecting a previously isolated Korea to the rest of the Eurasian continent (Cumings 1997; Shin and Robinson 1999). Railroad construction also hastened the commercialization of agriculture and allowed the rural population to move to urban centers where more jobs were created. Urbanization, industrialization, and increasing mass communication also stimulated the political consciousness among elites as well as the popular masses among Koreans (Robinson 1988).

Even though the Japanese government in the metropole extended Japanese citizenship status to Koreans and projected the rhetoric of *isshi dōjin* or *kunmin dōso* to underscore ethno-racial affinity between Japanese and Koreans and to promote Western-style modernization within the Korean peninsula, this rhetoric did not easily penetrate the minds of Koreans. The systematic discrimination and blunt prejudice against Koreans exercised by Japanese colonial officials and civilians at the quotidian level starkly contradicted the official rhetoric of hybrid empire, which held that Koreans and Japanese could amalgamate their cultures and national identities due to their cultural proximity and shared interests. Given that Korea had maintained sovereign power for centuries, and that colonized Koreans now had to contend with Japanese military and socioeconomic oppression and blunt racism in their everyday lives, mere de jure status as Japanese was not enough to facilitate a sense of belonging to the Japanese empire. Instead, through their experience of everyday colonial oppression and racism by Japanese colonialists, many Koreans experienced the inherent contradiction between their lived reality and Japanese colonial rhetoric. On the one hand, they were able to perceive the boundary of ethno-racially hybrid Japanese empire that Japanese imperialists attempted to promote and propagate in relation to their common threat—the Western other. On the other, they could also see a border being constructed within the imperial boundary that distinguished Koreans (the colonized other or de facto alien) from the Japanese colonizing "self." Their lived experiences of exclusion further facilitated and reinforced their collective self as Korean—a collective self that previously had been fragmented by the intersection of class and regional identity.

All of these empirical facts have an important theoretical implication for the development of collective self-identification. The case of the Japanese-Korean relationship during the colonial period shows that the development of collective self-identification among groups inevitably involved the simultaneous and dual processes of constructing multiple boundaries between self and other. One part of these processes was intentional, while another part was not. In the eyes of the Japanese colonialists, Koreans were simultaneously other and a part of self; that is, in relation to a larger category of external other (i.e., Western powers), Koreans were a part of the Japanese imperial self or "internal self" who must be incorporated and absorbed in order to protect the interests of the Japanese Empire and construct the Japanese pan-Asian national self-image. Hence, the Japanese state intentionally codified Koreans' official status as citizens and transformed them into de jure

Japanese. However, within the internal boundary of the Japanese Empire, Koreans were also categorized as other; they were not only perceived as but also treated as inferior. In other words, Koreans were both de jure Japanese and de facto others or non-Japanese.

This dual boundary-making mechanism also facilitated another set of boundary construction among people categorized as other. It is important to note that this function was not deliberately planned or designed. As the oral history of Koreans who lived through the colonial period indicates, in the absence of actual practices to reify their belonging as Japanese in everyday life, a sense of Japaneseness did not develop in the minds of Koreans, contrary to the expectation of Japanese policymakers (Kang 2001). Instead, everyday oppression triggered their keen collective sense of a Korean "self," based on shared and collective experiences of Japanese colonization as well as the collective memories of precolonial national sovereignty and culture among otherwise disconnected members of society.

The March First Movement not only exhibits the transformation of this internal dynamic of collective self-identification among Koreans under Japanese colonial rule but also demonstrates the importance of exogenous factors—namely, political ideologies outside the national community as well as political activism across national borders. Historical records and preceding studies on the March First Movement show that the transnational movement and penetration of transnational political ideologies were evident in early twentieth-century colonial Korea. They also played a critical role in facilitating the mass independence movement in 1919. Overseas political exiles in Shanghai, Tokyo, and San Francisco played a critical role in initiating the March First Movement. Largely inspired by both the Russian Revolution in 1917 and US president Woodrow Wilson's advocacy of ethnic self-determination, elite intelligentsia and religious leaders abroad prepared the anticolonial and independence movement. This activism abroad spurred various leaders across religious backgrounds in Seoul. Thirty-three religious leaders collaborated and released the declaration of Korean Independence in Pagoda Park in Seoul on March First, igniting a massive anti-imperialist demonstration across the entire Korean peninsula between March and May. Although an accurate accounting of the number of participants and casualties is unknown, estimates indicate that at least half a million Koreans participated during the 1,500 or so demonstrations, and that numerous demonstrators were killed, injured, and/or arrested by Japanese military forces.[26]

Pan-Asian Empire

Political scientist Anthony Marx (1997) claims in his comparative studies on citizenship, nationhood, and race in Brazil, the United States, and South Africa that a state's legal institutionalization of such categories, although discriminatory, has the unintended outcome of defining, legitimating, and provoking group identity and mobilization, forging struggles between state agents and emerging political actors for inclusion. In other words, the institutionalization of racial and ethnic boundaries solidifies categorical identities among those excluded from formal citizenship. This process also facilitates political mobilization against racial and ethnic discrimination, though the absence of institutionalized forms of racial differences leaves racial inequality unattended and inaccessible to state policy. While Korean resistance against the Japanese government in prewar Japan arose without any concrete de jure distinctions inscribed in laws, the resistance also supported Marx's underlying logic: extranational factors and the everyday reality of oppression can have the same effect as de jure exclusion in facilitating social movements among the marginalized groups.

Despite the absence of a legally institutionalized inferior status, Koreans—in both the Korean peninsula and mainland Japan—mobilized themselves to fight Japanese colonial oppression. What reinvigorated the political consciousness and nationalist mobilization among Koreans was the combined effect of international political ideologies, including Marxist socialism and the Wilsonian ideal of self-determination; the absence of strong, centralized governments in the political sphere in Far East Asia during the early twentieth century; and the everyday oppression that starkly contradicted the official rhetoric of Japanese colonial justification.

In China and Russia, where many Korean political elites were exiled, there was a series of political insurgencies against the existing traditional governments, which created a fluid and flexible political field where civil societies could flourish. Driven by Marxist ideologies, Russian and Chinese revolutionaries were trying to build their provisional government. In Russia, Lenin and Stalin were on their way to replacing the existing provisional government with the Soviet state. In China, communists and student activists, including the young Mao Zedong, were protesting against their government, which had failed to protect their political autonomy and interests at the Versailles Conference, subsequently leading to the outbreak of the May Fourth Movement in China in 1919. This restless political atmosphere—the demise of the feudal state and the rise of socialist-communist movements—at this particular historical juncture in Far East Asia generated an aura of hope for Korean political exiles in the first decade of the twentieth century. It also created a discursive political field where Korean political exiles could become exposed to radical ideologies pervasive at that time, find their allies, and form civil societies to mobilize people inside of the Japanese Empire against colonial oppression. While Marxian socialism allowed Koreans to find their transnational allies in Russia and China, the Wilsonian ideal of ethnic independence gave Western legitimacy to their claims against Japanese colonial practice.

The March First Movement expressed Koreans' desperate desire for independence and generated calls for intervention from the Allied Powers at the 1919 Versailles Peace Conference in Paris, where Japan was given a permanent seat in the League of Nations. Historian Frank Baldwin (1979) demonstrated that Korean activists at that time believed international support for their claim was critical to their success. However, no such help arrived from either the Allied Powers at Versailles or the Washington Disarmament Conference the following year. The independence of a small Asian nation in the Far East was not a significant concern to many Western countries preoccupied with war reparations after World War I. In spite of the dissent Koreans expressed through nonviolent demonstrations and marches, the lack of interest in their claims among Western societies allowed the Japanese colonial government to quickly and brutally suppress the Korean mobilization with fierce military and police force.

Even after the failure of the March First Movement, Korean communities in the United States, Manchuria, and the Soviet Far East continued to support political activities with the goal of Korean independence. But their nationalist activity overseas remained fragmented due to their conflicting ideologies. Although they failed to achieve their immediate goal, the fact that Koreans mobilized at such a large scale shocked the Japanese political leadership and precipitated a major revision in its colonial policies, particularly its citizenship and migration policies. Joining the League of Nations at Versailles and gaining greater control over China, Japan was at a pivotal movement in its effort to achieve the status of a first-class nation in world society. Any criticism from the West for its brutal treatment of Koreans had to be avoided. Watching the crisis in Korea with great concern, Hara Takashi, the nineteenth Japanese prime minister, placed a new colonial administration in Korea. Rather than *budan tōchi* (military governance) in the colonies, Hara's administration appointed a much softer colonial policy, *bunka tōchi* (cultural governance). The Japanese government decided to take a pragmatic turn to induce more comprehensive cultural assimilation among Koreans by softening its colonial practices. Although these initiatives were closely monitored by the authorities, the colonial government permitted Korean-owned news publications, created government-sponsored organizations with the aim of facilitating affinity between Koreans and Japanese, expanded education (particularly Japanese-language education), and started hiring a small number of Koreans to work in government jobs. In so doing, the government aimed to regain control over its colonies and maintain the integrity of its imperial boundaries.

MIGRATION CONTROL

The Japanese economy craved more workers and cheaper labor as World War I created economic opportunities for Japan. Colonial labor from the peninsula was especially attractive to many businesses in the metropole given its proximity and exploitability. According to the Japanese government's prewar statistics, the number of Koreans residing in Japan increased significantly in the ten years after the annexation of Korea. This was the largest number of non-Japanese migrants that Japan had ever experienced at that time. However, this strong influx of Korean labor migrants continued even after the Japanese economy entered into a recession. During the economic recession, Korean labor and Japanese workers had to compete for scarce employment opportunities, which drastically increased hostility toward Koreans among the already prejudiced and frustrated Japanese population (Iwamura 1972).[27]

The massacre of Koreans in Japan in the aftermath of the Great Kantō Earthquake in 1923 was yet more proof that the Japanese early colonial policy of ethno-racial affinity was dysfunctional and failing to achieve its intended outcome. In the chaos following the magnitude 8.3 earthquake in Tokyo, thousands of Koreans were killed by the Japanese police force and by civilians who falsely blamed Koreans for arson, for poisoning the wells, and for robberies that took place after the quake, revealing that there was no sentiment of ethno-racial affinity or brotherhood/sisterhood emerging between Japanese and Koreans.[28] As this event made irrefutably clear, Koreans were, at best, disposable labor and, at worst, an unwanted threat to many Japanese civilians at the quotidian level.

66 *Chapter 2*

Even though the mainland mass media minimized news coverage of Korea's March First Movement, the visible existence of poor and dislocated Korean labor migrants vividly revealed to people of the mainland the problems of colonial rule in Korea. Piles of Korean bodies killed by Japanese civilian militias after the Great Kantō Earthquake concretized the image of Japanese public hostility and rejection of the colonized population. The 1923 massacre of Koreans convinced Japanese policymakers that the problems in the colonies were spreading into the metropole, increasing public frustration about the government's colonial policies. Facing crises in both the metropole and the colony, the Japanese government needed to revise its colonial policies promptly.

However, there was significant disagreement among policymakers concerning colonial policy in the wake of such a large-scale resistance movement among Koreans. Some liberal intellectuals and policymakers, such as Yoshino Sakuzō, Mochiji Rokusaburō, Inoue Tetsujirō, and Hara Takashi, advocated for more rights for Koreans (Matsuo 1968; Oguma 1998). For example, they advocated permitting some of the local elites from the colony to serve as congressmen, allowing suffrage within the colonies. Other policymakers, such as Ōtsuka Tsunesaburō, argued that allowing any degree of political independence to already rebelling Koreans would be too risky (Imanishi 1999; Oguma 1998). Instead, they advocated for a forceful assimilation policy. Although policymakers' solutions varied, they shared a common agenda—protecting the interests of the metropole, and further exploiting the colonies, while minimizing the risk of future rebellions.

Migration policies during the colonial period were as incoherent, discursive, and ad hoc as the citizenship policies. Imperial Ordinance No. 352 (on the migration and business of foreigners who do not have freedom of movement due to treaties or customs) was first established in Japan in 1899, the same year that the citizenship law was enacted.[29] The subjects of this law were mainly European and American diplomats and merchants, as well as a small number of Chinese laborers. This law did not apply to Koreans, mainly because Koreans were already allowed to travel freely to Japan due to the Japan-Korea Treaty of 1876 (Yamawaki 1994, [1999] 2003). And because the annexation of Korea transformed the legal status of Koreans into that of Japanese citizens, the Japanese government did not (or, more accurately, could not) apply Imperial Ordinance No. 352 directly to Koreans, given their legal status as Japanese citizens. However, as a range of historical evidence from parliamentary debates, newspapers, news magazines, newsletters, and pamphlets circulated among minority activists suggests, Koreans' entries into and exits from the metropole were tightly monitored and controlled. These historical facts confirm how the existing binary categorical distinction between immigrants and citizens falls short when attempting to capture the complicated and deliberately fluid ways in which the Japanese government defined and treated Koreans in Japan during the colonial period. These colonial migrants were treated as both "immigrants" and "citizens." As with immigrants, Japanese authorities controlled and restricted their free movement between the metropole and colonies, but they were also deemed subjects of the Japanese Empire and bore all civil obligations, such as taxation, that came with this designation (Mizuno 1992).

Throughout the colonial period, the Japanese government controlled the influx of Korean labor from the colony to the metropole. Before 1919, the Japanese government allowed the collective entry of Korean labor through a government-authorized labor recruitment program. The program was not forcefully conscripted; it remained voluntary through recruitment authorized by the state. In 1919, the Japanese government introduced the travel certificate system (*ryokō shōmei seido*) to monitor and control Koreans' movement. However, after the March First Movement, the government established a new regulation that required Korean colonial migrants to obtain a travel certificate to travel between Japan and Korea. This was specifically aimed at differentiating Korean political activists from labor migrants. Realizing that the March First Movement was facilitated by the collaboration of overseas political exiles, the Japanese government aimed to destroy the network among Korean political activists in Korea, the metropole, and elsewhere (Mizuno 1999). However, this regulation was banned in 1922, due to demand from the business sector for cheaper labor from Korea. Following the Great Kantō Earthquake in 1923, the regulation was temporarily brought back; it stayed in effect for a nine-month period. It was reintroduced again in 1925 to bar colonial migrants who did not hold a specific employment destination in the metropole.

In 1927, the government introduced another regulation that required Koreans to obtain a family registry certificate from municipal police in Korea before departing for Japan. In 1929, a regulation was instituted requiring Koreans to obtain a reentry permit if they planned to go back to Korea and return to Japan to work again. These

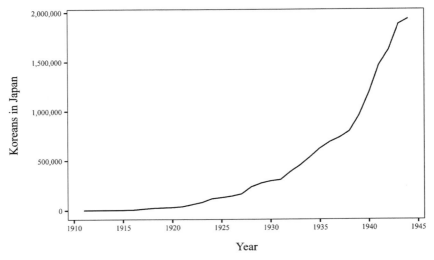

Figure 2.1. The population of Koreans in Japan, 1911–1944. From *Sūji ga Kataru Zainichi Kankoku Chōsenjin* (Morita 1996, 71).

regulations were all meant to discourage Koreans from traveling to the metropole and to minimize the number of unemployed Koreans in the metropole. Despite the Japanese government's control measures, however, the number of Korean colonial migrants to the metropole did not decline; rather, it steadily increased. As shown in figure 2.1, the number of Koreans in Japan rose continuously over the years. Proximity in physical appearance between Korean and Japanese made it even more difficult for the Japanese government to control unauthorized entries by Koreans.

The increase in the number of Korean colonial migrants to the metropole was closely related to the poor economic condition of the colony, but it was also an unexpected by-product of Japanese colonial policies that brought urbanization and industrialization to the colony and that established railroads and ship routes between Korea and Japan (Kimura and Komatsu 1998). All of this enhanced the mobility of Koreans within the empire. Furthermore, after the transition from military colonial rule to cultural rule, the Japanese government propagated the rhetoric of *naisen yūwa* (harmony between Japanese and Koreans) and encouraged the masses to learn the Japanese language and cultural customs by establishing associational clubs and organizations that directly aimed to facilitate amity between Koreans and the Japanese. These cultural policies aimed to increase ethno-racial affinity between Korean and Japanese peoples and to transform Koreans into loyal imperial citizens of Japan. At the same time, though, such cultural policies increased the literacy rate in Japanese among Koreans, which further motivated Koreans to head to Japan to seek employment opportunities. Meanwhile, the growing presence of such Koreans was triggering Japanese animosity, rather than amity, toward the colonized population.

By the end of the 1920s, it was clear to Japanese policymakers that the steady increase of Korean colonial migrants to the Japanese metropole was irreversible. According to archival documents that recorded the discussions at the Special Committee for Social Policy in July 1929, government officials decided to tightly control the entry of Korean laborers because they perceived that the increase of Korean labor migrants in Japan would worsen the Japanese unemployment problem (Nishinarita 1997). They believed the colonial government in Korea needed to cooperate with the Japanese government in the metropole to effectively control Korean migration to the metropole. But the government categorized this decision as "absolutely confidential" and did not publicize it (Mizuno 1999).

It was during this climate that Korean suffrage was considered in the Japanese metropole. The voter registration eligibility at that time was limited to wealthy adult Japanese males. In 1925, when Parliament considered the General Election Law to expand voter eligibility, they also debated whether Koreans living in the Japanese metropole should be eligible. If eligibility was extended, the number of Koreans who become eligible for suffrage was expected to increase greatly, reflecting the rapid increase of Koreans in Japan at that time. After careful deliberation, in 1925 the Japanese government eventually expanded suffrage eligibility to Korean males who had resided in Japan for more than one year.

The victory of Park Chungeum in the general election in 1932, mentioned at the start of this book's introduction, stemmed from this suffrage eligibility expansion.[30] Not many Koreans in prewar Japan met the suffrage eligibility. Park Chungeum was an outlier and a little-known figure in Japanese history (Oguma 1998, 362). But his life trajectory as a Korean activist and politician in Japan illustrates Japan's desperate attempt to promote ethno-racial affinity between Koreans and Japanese by manipulating the boundaries of citizenship. After the March First Movement in 1919 and the Kantō Massacre in 1923, the Japanese government made more deliberate efforts to

70 *Chapter 2*

promote ethno-racial affinity between Japanese and Koreans. One notable example of this effort was the establishment of the state-endorsed *Sōaikai* organization (Mutual Love or Brotherhood Association). Because this association was endorsed by the state, it collaborated with Japanese police forces closely to monitor Koreans, while remaining well connected to Japanese business leaders. To put it differently, this association was designed to offer job opportunities to colonial migrants from Korea while closely surveilling any anti-Japanese organizations among Koreans. It was in this context that Park Chungeum arrived in Japan as a young colonial labor migrant, greatly benefiting from the support of the *sōaikai*. Korean progressive activists often despised Korean collaborators with this association, such as Park Chungeum, and called them "Japan's police dogs" (Oguma 1998).

Park Chungeum was pessimistic about Korean independence and argued that assimilation was the only way for Koreans to achieve equity within the Japanese Empire. When he made his first speech as the first Korean elected official in the Japanese Parliament in June 1932, he passionately argued for allowing all colonial subjects in Korea to enjoy suffrage, for Korean participation in the Japanese military, for the removal of restrictions for colonial migrants to enter and work in the Japanese metropole, and for Korean migration to Manchuria. This agenda mirrored the concerns that Japanese lawmakers held toward Koreans at that time.

To maintain integrity in its colonial policy emphasizing affinity between the Koreans and Japanese, the Japanese government could not impose further migration control measures on Koreans who had Japanese citizenship status. At the same time, rising hostility among the Japanese public against Korean colonial migrants was once again putting the Japanese government's colonial policies in dangerous waters. The Japanese government needed a solution to decrease the continuous inflow of Koreans and to ease the hostility between Japanese and Korean populations. However, the Japanese government was not ready to embrace all parts of Park Chungeum's agenda. They centered on one component of his agenda: promoting Korean migration to Manchuria instead of Japan.

BOUNDARIES DISINTEGRATED

After the economic depression, a series of assassinations, military expansion, and various social conflicts in both the colonies and the metropole, a fascistic group dominated by the military seized power and hindered the budding Japanese liberal democratic labor movement that had developed in the 1920s (Gordon 1991). In an atmosphere of despair, Japan's newly established puppet state, Manchuria, served as a symbol of hope to many Japanese in various sectors (L. Young 1998). For political liberals, who were put under tight surveillance by military police at home, Manchuria appeared to be a better site for them to exercise their moral ideals. A depressed domestic economy also motivated many capitalists and industrialists to invest their money to expand industry in Manchuria rather than at home. The government also endorsed the movement to prompt poor farming families in rural villages in Japan to move to Manchuria to take part in agricultural production and support the Manchurian economy. Previous historical studies have well documented the impact and function of Japan's "informal empire in China" on the Japanese cultural, political, social, and economic order (Duus 1995; Young 1998).

The most comprehensive legal measure to control Korean migration to the Japanese metropole was established in the Japanese Parliament on October 31, 1934, shortly after Japan established Manchukuo following the Manchuria Incident. The Japanese government rationalized its migration control on the grounds that the increase of Korean population in the metropole had not only obstructed *naisen yūwa* (harmony between Japanese and Koreans) but also created a security concern in the metropole.[31] As Japan found another target of exploitation in Manchuria, it tried to divert the attention of the colonies and mainland from the existing problems in the colonies by emphasizing Manchuria's significance. While the Japanese government restricted the entry of Koreans to the metropole, it encouraged both Korean and Japanese peoples to move to Manchuria to support its economic development projects.

However, contrary to the intention of the Japanese government in the metropole, the subunit of the Imperial Japanese Army in the Kwantung region (a.k.a. the Kwantung or Kantō Army) in charge of controlling Manchuria initially restricted a strong influx of Korean migrants because it feared that increasing arrival of Korean settlers would enhance the power of already-booming anti-Japanese militias in Manchuria. In 1937, the Japanese government in the metropole and the Kwantung Army came to an agreement to allow a maximum of 10,000 households of Korean migrants into Manchuria. By 1941, the number of Korean settlers in Manchuria had reached 1,007,813—a

72   Chapter 2

startling total, given that only 76,133 Japanese settlers remained in Manchuria (Mizuno 1999). This figure clearly demonstrates the Japanese government's serious efforts to export its "Korean problem" to Manchuria as a means to maintain the integrity of the Japanese Empire. Furthermore, if the Kwantung army had not expressed security concerns, the number of Korean settlers could have been much larger than it was, suggesting that security concerns about subaltern resistance played a role in the way that migration policy was practiced.

As Japan expanded its power toward Manchuria and later prepared for war against the United States, Japanese policymakers in the mainland rushed to push forward a forceful cultural assimilation policy (*kōminka undō*). Despite the opposition and warnings from colonial officials in Korea, the mainland authority, which was controlled by military officials, concluded that a military draft in Korea was a vital and necessary strategy to protect its empire from China and the United States (Fujitani 2013). To conduct a military draft from the Korean population, it was necessary to reinforce the cultural assimilation policy in an attempt to nurture a spirit of loyalty as Japanese imperial subjects among Koreans. As part of this effort, the Japanese colonial government enforced a family registry (*koseki*) reform in Korea to replace the traditional Korean family system with a Japanese system that traced all Japanese families as a part of the imperial family. As I mentioned earlier in this chapter, Korea had its own distinctive *koseki* or *hojeok* registry system based on its distinctive cultural sense of kinship, which is different from the Japanese counterpart. And as part of this reform, the Japanese government forced Koreans to invent and use Japanese names, in order to destroy the Koreans' sense of belonging to clans—a sense that was deeply embedded in their name system and that provided a strong foundation for their collective identification—and to replace this sense of belonging with a Japanese family-nation ideology (Miyata, Kim, and Yang 1992; Mizuno 2004b). In so doing, the Japanese government attempted to absorb Koreans into its Imperial Army in wars against China and, later, against the United States.

The main purpose for replacing the Korean family registry with a Japanese registry was to destroy the existing kinship system embedded in Korean culture, which also served as a strong foundation for Koreans' sense of self. The Japanese-style family registry is deeply rooted in the ideological belief of *kazoku kokka* (the family nation), where every Japanese family is a descendant of the Japanese imperial family. By imposing this Japanese-style registry, the government did not just force Koreans to adopt Japanese cultural names. Rather, it tried to destroy the Korean kinship system and replace that system with a family-state kinship based on national belonging and thus to create a cognitive foundation where Koreans would respect the Japanese emperor as their symbolic father. This was exactly what had been done to Japanese citizens when Meiji policymakers transformed feudal Japan into a modern nation-state in the nineteenth century. However, the Japanese authorities forbade Koreans to adopt names that sounded exactly like Japanese names, because they wanted to be able to continuously distinguish between Korean and Japanese peoples. Japanese authorities were not interested in turning all the Koreans into fully assimilated Japanese. Instead, they wanted Koreans to be loyal but to remain inferior, while still maintaining some degree of distinction that reinforced the hierarchical relationship between colonizer and colonized.

This policy did not yield the outcome that lawmakers wanted. Historical records discovered by historian Mizuno Naoki (2002) indicate that Koreans resiliently and tactfully resisted this policy. Recognizing that the Japanese registry system would destroy their kinship-based identity, which was supported by their naming culture, many Koreans posted advertisements in newspapers to call all their relatives across Korea to adopt the same Japanese last name in order to maintain their kin ties through shared family names. Hence, even if they had to invent Japanese names, they could still identify their families and relatives and could thus maintain the cultural identities rooted in their kinship system. In other cases, Koreans deliberately adopted insulting names to mock the system—for example, the name of the late Japanese general Itō Hirobumi, who was assassinated by a Korean political activist. The historical record demonstrates that because of this resistance, the number of Koreans who registered name changes remained relatively small, reflecting the struggle of Japanese authorities to put their policies in effect.

After entering a war with China in 1937, followed by a total war against the United States, Japan exhausted its manpower in the metropole and began forced labor conscription in Korea and China (Kim 1990, 2003; Nishinarita 2002; Yamada 1987; Yamada, Koshō, and Higuchi 2005). The exact number of Koreans forced to come to Japan as free labor remains contested to this day (Nishinarita 1997; Trewartha and Zelinsky 1955). Photographic evidence as well as oral histories of Korean survivors demonstrate the inhumane and brutal treatment

74 *Chapter 2*

of Korean laborers by Japanese (Hayashi, Park, and Takasaki 1990; Matsumoto 1996; Nozoe 1999; Saotome 2000). In the eyes of Koreans, the drafted or forced labor conscription was a clear expression of the Japanese sense of superiority toward the colonized population.[32] The Japanese brutality toward Koreans during the colonial period vividly remains in Korean national memory; it became central to a historical restorative justice movement, as the following chapter will discuss. At the same time, it also revealed the desperation of the colonizers, who were facing both a losing battle against the United States and the disintegration of their empire. In these desperate acts, both the external and internal boundaries of the Japanese hybrid empire were nakedly exposed, and on August 15, 1945, the boundaries that Japan had attempted to maintain for thirty-five years at last disintegrated and were laid bare for all to see.

DISCUSSION

History is always too intricate to be neatly compressed into a uniform explanation. The colonial history of Japanese citizenship and migration policies is no exception. Neither Japanese colonial policies and practices nor the resistance by Koreans was ever static, uniform, and monolithic. They were dynamic, malleable, contentious, and at times contradictory, as they were corresponding to restless changes in the context of dynamic geopolitics. The historical details of the development of citizenship and migration policies during the colonial period in Japan demonstrate the struggles and dilemmas that the Japanese policymakers faced in drawing the boundary of their empire. This chapter has identified three key forces that were consistently present throughout the Japanese imperial context and that were critical in shaping the policy decisions: subaltern resistance, the larger policy currents of the state and elites vis-à-vis policymaking process, and pressures stemming from the country's position within the larger world society. By tracing the dilemma faced by the Japanese lawmakers, this chapter attempted to understand the mechanism by which citizenship, migration, and national self-image developed in imperial Japan.

By examining the historical documents that record the voices and ideas expressed by elite policymakers, intellectuals, and the colonized population, we can see these three forces intricately interacting with one another and shaping both the content and practices of citizenship and migration policy in Imperial Japan. To be recognized as an imperial power, the Japanese state expanded the boundary of its national imagery by projecting a rhetoric of pan-Asian ethno-raciality and adopting an inclusive citizenship policy. However, as an economically and militarily semi-peripheral country, Japan could not afford to either blur or to clarify the boundaries between itself and its colonies. Thus, it took advantage of *koseki,* a traditional legal practice embedded in both Japanese and Korean cultures and inconspicuous to Western powers, to maintain an internal boundary between Japan and its colonized population. While the boundary maintained by *koseki* might be barely discernible to Western eyes, its impact was felt immensely among the colonizers and colonized in their everyday lives.

These same historical details also demonstrated that there is no simplistic association between regime type and mode of citizenship. Imperial Japan extended its citizenship status to its colonized population before making any efforts to acculturate them, simply defining the colonized populations as Japanese and granting them suffrage, labor, and residential rights. This choice did not reflect its regime structure; rather, it reflected Japan's relatively weak economic and military position, as well as the ambition of Japanese officials to be recognized as a part of the modern world. Despite this official policy, for over twenty years of colonization, Japan did not strongly enforce cultural assimilation in its colonies. Even when the regime moved toward fascistic authoritarianism in the 1930s, Japan did not reverse these policies. Despite receiving citizenship status, Korean colonial subjects mobilized against the Japanese rulers.

These facts suggest two important theoretical implications. First, norms and ideologies derived from outside national boundaries have a strong impact on the rise of political mobilization among oppressed groups, even in the absence of legally supported forms of discrimination. Second, it is not the principle of citizenship but the practice of citizenship that matters to the formation of collective self-identification within a marginalized group. It was this disparity between the principle and actual practice of citizenship in which the marginalized group acutely felt and understood their subordinate position within the boundaries of the pan-ethnic Japanese Empire. Through this disparity, Koreans reconstructed their boundary of self-identification as Korean, rather than recognizing themselves as Japanese, despite an inclusive definition of their citizenship status imposed from above.

This historical dynamic between the Japanese colonizers and the Korean colonized population also informs us of an intriguing mechanism of multiple boundary formation. First, it shows that the development of collective self-identification involves multiple boundary formations. Specifically, Imperial Japan constructed an external boundary of a pan-Asian self to construct the West as Asia's common threat and, thus, their other. This external boundary formation coincided with the construction of an internal boundary of a superior colonizing self in relation to the inferior colonized others. As the historical details presented earlier demonstrate, this dual boundary formation was a result of conscious efforts among the Japanese to reconcile competing political and economic interests that were largely rooted in their position as a less powerful nation within world society in the twentieth century. Japanese policymakers also expected that the external boundary of pan-Asian collective self-identification would gradually prompt racial affinity among the colonized and colonizers and, consequently, that such a racial affinity would dilute the internal boundary between the colonizers and the colonized.

However, as this chapter has shown, such a spontaneous dilution of internal boundaries did not occur in Imperial Japan. Instead, the case of Korean-Japanese relations shows that this dual boundary formation by a dominant group also facilitated another multiple boundary formation among the subordinate group. The Japanese internal boundary construction triggered the transformation of a collective self-identification among marginalized Koreans. And this transformation of collective self-identification among the subordinate population was translated into collective action against Japanese colonialism in Korea. As a result, the Japanese authorities were forced to maintain this internal boundary, which later became an obstacle to absorbing Koreans into Japan's military power. This fact suggests the intricate connections between dominant categorization and subordinate self-identification as well as the intentional and contingent nature of collective identification formation among groups in a society.

In sum, the empirical evidence examined in this chapter demonstrates that it is neither the law nor national self-image that governs the practices of agents, nor the agents that determine how nationhood or laws are codified and practiced in a society. Instead, what determine the contents of law as well as the ways in which law is practiced is the intricate interaction among various nonstate and state agents with different (and at times conflicting) interests, sharply influenced by the dynamics in world society. The way nationhood is imagined, codified in law, and then practiced in a society is highly dependent on the convoluted interaction among these three forces—the larger currents of policymakers, nonstate resistance, and the position of the country within world society. In the following chapters, we will see how the same set of forces also operated in two later periods but produced a different collective national self-image and a different set of citizenship and migration policies.

Chapter Three

THE BIRTH OF A HOMOGENEOUS NATION-STATE

Toward the end of the Pacific War, the territory of Imperial Japan appeared to have expanded massively. It included the following lands, albeit briefly: Taiwan; Korea; Manchuria; part of the Aleutian Islands; the Netherlands' East Indies; French Indochina; the British possessions of Burma, Malaya, and Hong Kong; and America's Philippines (Dower 1999).[1] Simply looking at the map, it would have seemed that Japan's efforts to build and expand its empire were coming to bear fruit. In reality, however, the coprosperity sphere of the Japanese Empire was a castle in the air. Inside the empire, one could hardly find any coprosperity: colonial populations were severely exploited and marginalized as disposable labor, manpower and material resources were exhausted, and many people were starving and deprived of basic needs. Imperial Japan's dream of establishing a pan-Asian empire was not only a pipe dream, but a horrible nightmare for many Japanese civilians as well as for colonial populations.

The terrible wake-up call that led to the end of this nightmare arrived at 8:15 a.m. in Hiroshima, on August 6, 1945. As if one was not enough, another atomic bomb was dropped at 11:02 a.m. in Nagasaki three days later. These two atomic bombs in Hiroshima and Nagasaki ended the lives of many residents in Japan, including Korean residents,[2] and marked the end of the Japanese imperial era. The defeat of the Japanese Empire in the Asia-Pacific War in 1945 also meant the emancipation of Korea, Taiwan, and other territories from Japanese colonial rule. The colonial populations of the Japanese Empire celebrated the defeat of their colonial rulers. Some Koreans in Japan celebrated on the main streets in Tokyo and Osaka to cheer for their emancipation, expecting the United States and other Western allied nations to come and protect them as liberated people (*Chōsen Minshū Shinbun* 1994).

The end of empire also brought significant shifts to various institutional arrangements, including citizenship and migration laws (Hiraga 1951). The boundaries of Japanese nationhood, citizenship, and migration were about to be reimagined and rearranged under a newly established democratic regime in the geopolitical context of the Cold War. The resistance of the remaining Koreans in postwar Japan continued as it had in the colonial period, but the goals of the movement shifted as the geopolitical context and socioeconomic conditions changed. To put it differently, the remaining Koreans were forced to reimagine the world, their home, and their sense of belonging under circumstances that none of them chose.

Between 1945 and 1952, Japan was occupied by the Supreme Commander for the Allied Powers (SCAP), US General Douglas MacArthur (Schaller 1997). The United States' General Headquarters (GHQ) were established to oversee the reconstruction of postwar Japan. Officially, the Allied Powers in Japan involved other nations besides the United States, including Australia, Britain, China, France, New Zealand, and the Soviet Union (Schaller 1985). However, unlike in Germany—which was partitioned into four occupation zones and tightly controlled by the Allied Control Council, whose members were the United States, Britain, France, and the Soviet Union—the occupation of Japan was dominated by the United States, which decisively influenced all the aspects of occupation, including the drafting of Japan's postwar democratic constitution. The US-led GHQ set about reforming various institutional and legal structures, including citizenship and laws concerning international migration. The goals of the occupational government of the Allied Powers included but were not limited to (1) replacing the fascist regime with one based on democratic popular sovereignty; (2) demilitarizing the country to bring peace; and (3) creating a new constitution and legal systems that would protect civil rights and respect for individual liberty and human rights (Dower 1999).

In contrast with the occupation of postwar Germany, the United States preserved some of the existing government structures in Japan and retained some of Japan's prewar bureaucrats and lawmakers in order to achieve the above-mentioned goals. Hence, the Japanese government was allowed to have a limited degree of flexibility and autonomy in implementing the postwar policies. Existing historical studies on the postwar Japanese reconstruction suggest that Japanese lawmakers and bureaucrats negotiated as much as possible with SCAP to exert their interests in drafting the new constitution and other laws in Japan (Koseki 1997; Takemae 2003). Migration policies, particularly the regulations concerning the treatment and status of the remaining colonial migrants, reflected the sometimes competing and sometimes shared political interests of the Japanese and the US government, as seen later in this chapter.

Only in the past few decades have scholars begun paying serious attention to the issues of Korean colonial migrants during Japan's postwar period (Augustine 2017; Morris-Suzuki 2006).[3] This relative void in historical studies has given the impression that the issue of Koreans in Japan was insignificant to both the Japanese and US authorities, who were major players in reconstructing the political structure in postwar East Asia at this critical juncture of the twentieth century. But the problem of the Korean minority was hardly negligible to the US or Japanese authorities in the postwar period. Edwin Reischauer, who served as the expert on Japan for the US Army Intelligence Service during World War II and who was the US ambassador to Japan between 1961 and 1966, wrote the foreword for Edward Wagner's 1951 monograph *The Korean Minority in Japan*. In this foreword, Reischauer (1951, 1) described the Korean minority in Japan thus:

> The Koreans in postwar Japan have created many annoying complications for the American occupation forces, and the seemingly insoluble problem of their presence in Japan as an unassimilable minority will continue to cause bitterness between certain elements among the Japanese and Korean people, if not between their respective governments. . . . The Koreans in Japan, meanwhile, have remained a source of irritation and embarrassment to American groups in Japan and to the United Nations forces in Korea.

Wagner's monograph was one of the first English publications focused directly on the issue of the Korean minority in Japan in the postwar period. Both Wagner's and Reischauer's writings clearly signaled that the Korean minority was indeed an attention-worthy problem for the United States and for Japanese authorities in the postwar period—so much so that the presence and resistance of this minority altered the ways in which the boundaries of nationhood, citizenship, and migration were defined and then institutionalized in postwar Japanese society.

Nonstate subaltern actors, such as Korean colonial migrants and their descendants, played a crucial role in the creation of postwar Japanese nationhood, citizenship, and migration policies that is ill understood. Koreans—not only through their mere existence but also through their resistance—influenced the ways that lawmakers created a set of new laws on citizenship and international migration in the unsettling geopolitical context of the Cold War. And this set of postwar policies and laws paved the way for how subsequent flows of transnational migrants were viewed and controlled in contemporary Japanese society. Deciphering what transpired between the state and Korean colonial migrants during this tumultuous period is key to understanding the connections and disconnections between Japan's colonialism and the migration policies and legal systems that exploit many migrants and long-term noncitizen residents in Japanese society today.

Postwar Japanese intellectuals also unmade, remade, and helped institutionalize a new self-image of their nation as Japan tried to transition from an expansive pan-Asian empire to an emerging democratic nation-state. Cold War politics, the return of conservative politicians, and the looming shadow of American influence on Japan and greater Northeast Asia unexpectedly led postwar intellectuals from both ends of the ideological and political spectrum to embrace a similar sense of nationhood—of Japan as an ethno-racially homogeneous nation. Lawmakers then used this new sense of homogeneous nationhood to further justify exclusionary policies meant to marginalize the remaining colonial migrants and their descendants and further limit new flows of international migrants and refugees.

By scrutinizing how this set of exogenous forces impacted the endogenous relationship between the state and nonstate actors—Korean colonial migrants, their allies, and intellectuals—in the postwar period, this chapter unpacks the dynamics of the relationship among nationhood, citizenship, and migration that was being reconfigured in postwar Japan. Specifically, it unpacks the intertwined interests of various actors and shows that the concept and practice of citizenship and migration policies are neither simply a direct reflection of an exclusive sense of nationhood nor a result of the democratized regime structure. Instead, they are products of historical contingency, constrained by material, political, and normative conditions at a given geopolitical and historical period. As in the previous period, the relationship between nationhood, citizenship, and migration remained fluid and malleable. However, in this period, we observe how the legacy of colonialism continuously asserted its influence over the ways colonial migrants were perceived and treated, despite a clear break between these two periods.

This chapter first focuses on the initial period of American occupation, immediately after the end of World War II, when the interests of Japanese lawmakers, the American occupational authority, and liberated Koreans in Japan became formulated and concretized, corresponding to the rapidly shifting political climate in world society. Then it explores how these conflicting interests eventually influenced each group's perception of one another and how such perceptions were then translated into actual attitudes and practices toward one another. More specifically, this chapter scrutinizes how Cold War political interests led both Japanese and American authorities, who were erstwhile enemies, to share a similar view of Koreans in Japan as sources of communist ideology and hence as obstacles or "annoying complications," as Reischauer put it, to the postwar reconstruction of Japan.

By tracing the process through which these actors' perceptions of one another were being transformed under the growing tensions of the Cold War from the late 1940s to the early 1950s, we will see how the United States' Cold War political interests reversed the course of the Allied Powers' intervention. That is, the US occupation policy was supposed to redefine Japanese nationhood from an ethno-racial nationalistic conception to a more civic and democratic conception, protecting the interests of the emancipated colonial population and other foreign residents in Japan. Yet the Cold War climate merged the interests of US and Japanese authorities on the issue of handling the former colonial population and subsequently allowed grounds for the birth of a homogeneous ethnic conception of nationhood and exclusive citizenship and migration policies.

Second, this chapter demonstrates how the Cold War also impacted Koreans' perception of self, nationhood, and citizenship. It also discusses how Cold War politics and the changes in their perception impacted Koreans' resistance to the authorities. Specifically, we observe how this exclusionary treatment by American and Japanese authorities fostered frustration and dissatisfaction among Koreans, who viewed themselves as "liberated people" deserving protection from the Allied Powers and emancipation from Japanese oppression.

Such dissatisfaction triggered a series of collective actions among Koreans, including support for communist ideology. New states in Korea, namely the North and South Korean governments, and their international relationships with Japan and the United States in the Cold War context significantly impacted the ways that Koreans in Japan identified themselves.

This chapter also pays attention to the postwar intellectual discourse that gave birth to a new national self-image, based on a homogeneous conception of Japanese nationhood. This renewed collective perception of nationhood emerged among Japanese intellectuals and lawmakers against the backdrop of the devastating defeat of the nation, the everlasting presence of the United States, the return of conservative politicians to the Cabinet, and mounting Cold War tensions in East Asia and the rest of the world. Their contrition over the nation's dark military past and desire to democratize postwar Japanese society in the shadow of US global imperialism led these intellectuals and lawmakers—despite differences in their disciplinary approaches and political positions—to collectively negate the hybrid idea of nationhood previously used to justify their imperial expansion and to instead celebrate a concept of homogeneous ethnic nationhood.

By tracing the trajectory of intellectual discourse in postwar Japan, we see how this newly constructed sense of Japan's nationhood was not a direct cause of the state's postwar exclusive citizenship and immigration policies but, rather, was used as a justification for them. The decision by postwar Japanese policymakers to strip citizenship status and rights from the remaining colonial migrants and their descendants was largely influenced by the aforementioned exogenous and endogenous factors—Cold War politics, state actors' competing political interests, and subaltern responses. However, by the 1960s the conception of Japanese nationhood as homogeneous penetrated through various corners of postwar Japanese society, and policymakers began to use it to justify their exclusive citizenship and immigration policies. While this myth of homogeneity was not directly responsible for the genesis of postwar Japan's exclusive citizenship and immigration policies, it nevertheless produced the rationalization that the Japanese exclusion and rejection of non-Japanese populations was simply a by-product of its ethno-racial homogeneity and culture. It also effectively masked the institutionalization of colonial legacy through postwar citizenship and immigration policies in Japanese society. This new myth of homogeneity was coupled with existing exclusive policies

84   *Chapter 3*

against ethno-racialized minorities, leading to the spread of ethno-racial oppression across Japanese society.

In the Shadow of Colonialism, Defeat, and Cold War

By the end of World War II, there were nearly 2 million Korean migrants in Japan. Many of these migrants had been conscripted during the war and forced to work—many for free—in order to fill the labor vacuum created by the military draft of Japanese men. The majority of the colonial laborers endured inhumane labor conditions (Kim Y. 2003; Matsumoto 1996). Japanese officials anticipated that the defeat of Japan would trigger numerous revolts among these abused and oppressed colonial laborers. The Japanese concern over such a possibility was vividly expressed in a report submitted by the Security Division of the Police Department to the minister of internal affairs, dated August 26, 1945: "The most alarming issue would be conflicts between Koreans and Japanese—particularly collective riots by Koreans as well as collective attacks by Japanese against Korean workers at the labor sites. Fortunately, at this moment, we haven't yet witnessed any alarming conflicts" (Naimushō Keihokyoku Hoanka 1945, 33). Numerous revolts among colonial laborers in the mines and other manual labor sites across Japan indeed erupted soon after this report.

A huge influx of demobilized soldiers and colonial officials returning to Japan from Taiwan, Korea, and Manchuria intensified this situation. These returnees struggled to find homes or jobs and often faced mistreatment upon their return (Watt 2009). After four years of war, with the Japanese economy at rock bottom and unemployment extremely high, cheap Korean laborers competed against Japanese laborers, fueling more anti-Korean sentiment and escalating paranoia among the already distressed Japanese population. Commentary by Imperial Councilor Sekiya Teisaburō on December 14, 1945, in the Japanese parliamentary discussion of the treatment of Japanese returnees shows both his profound concern for his own people and his deep paranoia toward the growing anti-Japanese sentiment among liberated Koreans:

> Please allow me to read a letter from my friend [a Japanese returnee] that tells you in detail [about the conditions that Japanese returnees face] . . . "After [I had] lived in Korea for thirty-two years, the results of our

educational efforts disappeared like water bubbles, and Koreans after the war became victorious and hostile to Japanese. Especially after the US arrival, the police force fell into the hands of Koreans, and there was no police protection for Japanese." . . . Even if these Japanese folks came back home, there is no place for them to stay. Hence, we plead that the government and the public have sympathy for these returnees.[4]

Anticipating that growing anti-Japanese sentiment would soon be more prominently displayed by Koreans in Japan, the Japanese government at first attempted to deter the rise of explicit conflicts between Japanese and Koreans with more lenient tactics. Such tactics included avoiding overt mistreatment of Korean laborers and encouraging Koreans in Japan to return to their homeland, the Korean peninsula. In fact, the Japanese government announced the return policy for Koreans as early as September 1, 1945, two months earlier than SCAP announced its policy toward Koreans. Directors from various divisions, such as the Ministry of the Health (Kōseishō) and the Ministry of Internal Affairs (Naimushō), sent out an instructional note titled "Emergency Treatment of Collectively Imported Korean Laborers" that addressed specific orders in handling the Koreans' return to their homeland. For example, (1) nonconscripted laborers should be prioritized for returning home;[5] (2) the highest priority was to be given to construction workers and the lowest priority to miners; (3) continuing residency was permitted for skilled laborers at mines who wished to remain; (4) given that the government currently had very little capacity to send laborers back to Korea (less than one thousand people a day), laborers should expect the process to take a long time, and instructions should be given in order to prevent any disturbance; and (5) until the day of their return, employers should continue laborers' employment, and as for payment, employers should give laborers the necessary allowance, and the remaining salary should be put in savings under the employees' names. Also, (6) those nonconscripted laborers who were not currently employed should be given jobs through the local government, including jobs constructing roads and cleaning post-bombed and -burned areas. Finally, (7) as for other Korean residents in Japan who plan to return to Korea, the government should give them detailed orders in due course as to when their return would become possible, and until then, local officials should direct them to engage in their existing lives and wait patiently for further notices (Nishinarita 1997, 323–325).

86 *Chapter 3*

These instructions demonstrate that the Japanese government was willing to quickly dispose of Korean construction workers who were brought in, in some cases conscripted, from Korea during the war to work in military-related construction projects across Japan. With the end of the war, these laborers became unnecessary excess. On the other hand, Korean miners were encouraged to stay in Japan because the government regarded coal extracted from the mines as the main source of energy critical to Japan's postwar reconstruction. Furthermore, the government also gave high priority to the deportation of Korean political activists, who might incite revolts among laborers. These government orders in the early years of the postwar period reveal that the Japanese government did not have a specific or coherent plan on how to deal with other resident Koreans who had already settled and lived in Japan for a few decades by the end of the war.

Although Korean laborers who were deemed useful to the Japanese postwar economic recovery were encouraged to stay in Japan, the treatment of these remaining laborers did not improve materially even after the war, disappointing many Koreans. One example is the Utoro community in Kyoto, where many Korean laborers were brought to build the airfield. They lived in terrible conditions near the construction site but were abandoned and forgotten after the war. As the final chapter discusses, the Utoro later became a site for Koreans' fight for restorative justice and a target for an anti-Korean violence. The lack of improvement in living and working conditions after the emancipation of their homeland caused further distress for Korean workers, who were already very frustrated and exhausted. Their sentiments are reflected in the increasing numbers of revolts among Korean workers across various mines in Japan. This situation raised questions about the government's treatment of the remaining Koreans in Japan in the Diet. On December 14, 1945, at the eighty-ninth session of the Imperial Diet, when imperial councilor Sekiya Teisaburō questioned the government's policy of deporting Koreans involved in the revolts Minister of Commerce Ogasawara Sankurō replied as follows:

> To answer your question, immediately after the war, the government decided not to send Koreans and Chinese miners back to their homelands right away, but allowed them to work in our mines if they wished. However, as you know, we face the regrettable situation of miners' revolts, mainly among Chinese miners. Right now, we believe that it is the best strategy to send [these miners] back to their homeland. However, we do

not reject the Korean miners. Once the situation has settled down, we welcome Korean laborers to our mines if they wish to work for us.[6]

Koizumi Gorō, director of internal police affairs, further emphasized the importance of the repatriation project:

> I would also like to address the revolt of Koreans. . . . After the war, there were some Koreans who wished to go back to their home, while some wished to remain in Japan. . . . However, we could not send these Koreans back to their homeland as much and smoothly as we initially planned, and as a result, we now have observed more than fifty cases of collective violence, mainly among Koreans, by the end of November. And the number of Koreans involved in such cases is as many as seven to eight thousand. We regret that this negatively contributes to the maintenance of social stability in our society. But I believe the main cause of this situation is a mixture of different issues, such as the failure of our repatriation project, problems with retirement pensions, payment, food, and clothing distributions, or the accumulated frustration toward the discrimination that they previously faced.[7]

Parallel to this debate, the Japanese government adopted a paradoxical posture in defining the status of colonial migrants from Korea and Taiwan: it declared the emancipation of Korea and Taiwan from Japanese colonization while simultaneously promising that Koreans and Taiwanese who remained in Japan would continue to be *deemed Japanese citizens.*[8] This paradoxical posture reflects the Japanese government's initial lack of a concrete idea or sense of direction as to how to define the status of remaining colonial migrants. For example, at the government meeting on October 19, 1945, a representative of the Ministry of Agriculture and Forestry (Nōrinshō) asked, "Can we recognize Koreans and Taiwanese as foreigners?" (Nishinarita 1997). This inquiry received no specific answer, indicating the level of quandary that Japanese lawmakers experienced at that time.

The Japanese government began to mull over how to handle colonial migrants, especially on the issue of their suffrage in late 1945. In December 1945, as part of the postwar amendment to the election law, the Japanese government halted the suffrage of resident Koreans and Taiwanese in Japan. Historian Mizuno Naoki's research (1996, 1997) and existing archival documents suggest that in the process of amending the postwar election law, the Shidehara Cabinet initially

88 *Chapter 3*

considered continuously recognizing the suffrage of Korean and Taiwanese residents in postwar Japan because the government legally deemed them Japanese citizens, at least until the San Francisco Peace Treaty (Hida 1980; Ōnuma 2004). The outline that passed at the Cabinet Council on October 2, 1945, clearly states that Koreans and Taiwanese residing in the Japanese mainland are recognized with suffrage in Japan (Mizuno 1996).

Only two months after this outline was passed, however, the government reversed its position. A strong objection was raised within Parliament against colonial migrants' suffrage. One of the main objectors against the suffrage of colonial migrants was Kiyose Ichirō, an influential policymaker who served as the main defense lawyer for General Tōjō Hideki at the Tokyo Trial. Kiyose prepared and distributed to other Cabinet members a brief titled "On the Suffrage of Taiwanese and Koreans Living in Japan" in which he listed a series of reasons why their suffrage should no longer be recognized. Most of the reasons he cited were based on the fact that Korea and Taiwan were no longer part of Japan and that it was hence contradictory to acknowledge their suffrage in Japan. But one of his cited reasons, shown below, suggests that his objection derived from his belief that the existence of Koreans was an obstacle to Japan's peaceful postwar reconstruction: "In our country, we did not have any ethnic split, and we have never had an ethnically partitioned election before. . . . What if this [ethnic split] and political issues are conflated? That would be chilling. Those who would advocate for the abolition of the Imperial System would be most likely the ones whose national belonging is with Korea but their residency is in Japan."[9]

Kiyose held an influential position in the political arena at that time, and his blunt bias against Koreans in Japan and strong objection seems to have had a substantial impact on other lawmakers; indeed, his view eventually became a dominant position within Parliament. By December of the same year, the government reversed its initial position and decided to rescind suffrage for Koreans and Taiwanese on the grounds that they eventually would lose their Japanese citizenship after the enactment of the peace treaty, so recognizing suffrage for those who would soon be noncitizens would cause confusion in the upcoming election.

Practices and debates among Japanese officials and police forces also signal that the Japanese authorities attempted to view Korean colonial migrants as Japanese citizens without equal sets of rights, including suffrage—arguably the most important civil right in citizenship. This may seem counterintuitive from today's standpoint: Why would the Japanese state try to continuously recognize colonial migrants as Japanese citizens when they simply wanted to exploit and exclude them? The same colonial logic that underpinned the Japanese Empire applied in this context to control these populations. The postwar Japanese state wanted to confine colonial migrants, especially Koreans, within the legal boundary of Japanese citizenship in order to coerce them into having a legal obligation to obey Japanese laws and authority rather than living as liberated people whose rights and treatments were under the protection of the Allied Powers. In other words, recognizing Koreans as Japanese citizens allowed the Japanese government to control the Korean population more effectively and legitimately via police forces. This double-bind status—de jure Japanese and de facto alien—was a familiar colonial tactic used during the imperial period. Although the circumstances shifted drastically from the imperial to the Cold War context, these two historical time periods were connected through the legacy of colonialism. The motive behind creating such a double-bind status remained consistent between the two periods: the government wanted to effectively control the Korean population within its territory while also distinguishing them as an exploitable, marginalized group. This fact severs the causal link between nationhood and citizenship or migration policies and shows the fluid and contingent nature of this nexus.

The response that the Japanese authorities gave on March 22, 1946, to the representatives of Korean residents' organizations also supports this point. In their response, the Japanese authorities clearly stated that Koreans in Japan would be treated exactly the same as Japanese civilians and that Koreans must obey Japanese laws; no exceptions would be made in applying Japanese laws to Koreans (Park 1989, 105). In September 1946, Prime Minister Yoshida Shigeru emphasized in a parliamentary discussion that Koreans and Taiwanese would be "Japanese citizens" and treated as such until the San Francisco Peace Treaty was signed. The Japanese Supreme Court also supported this position (Hida 1980).

American policy was also paradoxical. Occupation authorities defined Koreans and Taiwanese in Japan as "liberated people" who were guaranteed protection, while at the same time designating them as "enemy people," since their Japanese citizenship under the Imperial regime gave them the same negative status as Japanese citizens

(Gaimushō Seimukyoku Tokubetu Shiryōka 1950). Historian Kim Tae-Gi's in-depth analysis of American governmental archives about policies toward Koreans in Japan suggests that American intelligence and occupational forces shared the same concerns as the Japanese government (Kim 1997). That is, they were concerned about the Koreans' rising resistance as well as the Japanese discriminatory attacks against them. American authorities felt justified in this concern, citing a previous incident when Koreans were targeted by Japanese mobs in the aftermath of a major disaster (the massacre of Koreans by Japanese citizens following the Great Kantō Earthquake) (Kim 1997). American authorities, like their Japanese counterparts, assumed that such violent conflicts between the Japanese and the remaining Koreans were potentially the biggest obstacle to the postwar reconstruction of Japanese society (Kobayashi 1994). This was also a view held by American experts in Japanese affairs, including Edwin O. Reischauer. Thus, if the Koreans and the Taiwanese remaining in Japan did not cooperate, American authorities would view these Koreans as enemy combatants without the protection that would otherwise be offered to all foreigners in Japan (Kim 1997; Ōnuma 1978, 1993).

These paradoxical and malleable definitions of Taiwanese and Koreans' status in Japan in the aftermath of World War II underscores why these Koreans should be understood as "colonial migrants" who embody the continuing legacy of colonialism after the dissolution of empire. Taiwanese and Koreans' status cannot be fully captured in a binary fashion, nor did it transition from one category (imperial citizen) to another (liberated people). The contradicting and malleable definitions of their status emerged so that the state could maintain control over these populations even after losing its colonial territories.

As the following sections show, such a fluid definition and treatment of colonial migrants significantly affected the ways that Koreans viewed American and Japanese authorities. It made Koreans increasingly frustrated with Americans, as they had expected that American authorities would protect their interests and rights in the face of Japanese oppression. Their frustration manifested in numerous demonstrations and protests—an outcome that both American and Japanese authorities feared and wanted to avert. In turn, their growing dissent efforts invited the authorities' violent response, laying bare the hostility of Americans and Japanese toward Koreans. Eventually, these sentiments against Koreans became institutionalized in postwar Japanese immigration policies, which were developed under close supervision of the United States. Their laws were designed to be restrictive and exclusionary, based on the national security interests of that time. The main target of these laws was colonial migrants, particularly Koreans—the majority of the non-Japanese population on Japan's soil at that time. The subsequent sections in this chapter track the trajectory of this development and discuss how such restrictive legal measures resonated with the birth of the homogeneous ethnoracial self-image of Japan as a postwar democratic nation.

The Shift from Being "Deemed Japanese Citizens" to Being "Deemed Aliens"

A mass exodus of Koreans from Japan occurred immediately after World War II. As we saw earlier, the Japanese government encouraged the return of these Koreans. Figure 3.1 shows the sharp decline in the number of Koreans after the war.[10] Approximately 1.4 million Koreans left Japan, leaving about 600,000 Korean migrants (Morita 1996, 103; Tonomura 2004, 267). The remaining number might have been much lower had it not been for the restrictions placed on the amount of assets that these immigrants could take out of Japan and the uncertain economic and political conditions on the Korean peninsula at the time (Morita 1955; Nishinarita 1997). Most of the Koreans who remained

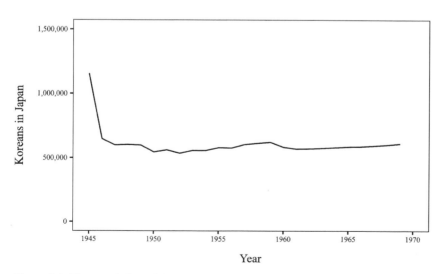

Figure 3.1. The population of Koreans in Japan, 1945–1969. From *Zainichi Chōsenjin Shakai no Rekishigaku-teki Kenkyū* (Tonomura 2004, 367).

had been settled in Japan for over a decade. Their families had been born and raised in Japan and only spoke the Japanese language. The lack of enough legitimate jobs drove many Koreans to engage in the black market, which led to a significant number of arrests.[11]

Rapidly changing political conditions and dire economic conditions in Korea convinced many returned Koreans to go back to Japan by whatever means possible, including unauthorized entry. Japan's leading newspaper, *Asahi,* published an article titled "Tightened Control toward the Third Country National," featuring the following statements by Minister of Foreign Affairs Ōmura Sei'ichi (1946):[12]

> Because the living conditions in Korea are not good, there is a strong trend of reentry to Japan among Koreans who once returned to their homeland[,] . . . I imagine about ten thousand illegal entries every month. . . . Among those Koreans and Taiwanese, there are quite a few who are willing to peacefully live here as good Japanese citizens, but there are also many malicious ones. Many Koreans today have a mistaken sense of superiority to Japanese as liberated people, and some even hold a grudge against the Japanese treatment of them during the colonial period.

It is revealing that Ōmura Sei'ichi called these undocumented Koreans' reentries "illegal," since Koreans and Taiwanese were deemed "Japanese citizens" at that time. Koreans were restricted in their right to free movement between the colonies and metropole, despite their status as Japanese citizens. The increasing reentry of undocumented Koreans, coupled with their growing support for communist ideology and the emerging Japanese labor movement, posed serious concerns to Japanese and American authorities. These circumstances also had important correlates in civil society within the Korean community in Japan.

Recognizing the uncertain future and poor living situations they faced in postwar Japan, many Korean intellectuals, activists, and workers mobilized to protect their rights. Because there was no homeland state that would represent and advocate for the rights of Koreans in Japan, numerous Korean advocacy and organizing efforts mushroomed during the postwar period. One of the most influential and largest organizations was Chōren (Zainihon Chōsenjin Renmei), which was operated mainly by Korean members of the Japanese Communist Party (Yang 1994b). Another notable organization, Kendō, was led by Park Yul, an influential and charismatic leader of the prewar Korean ethnic independence movement. He had been jailed in northern Japan for a few decades for treason against the Japanese emperor but was released after the war.[13] Although Chōren invited him to join the organization, Park Yul preferred not to associate his activism with communist ideologies. Instead, he started his own organization based on the goals of unifying their homeland and improving living conditions for all Koreans in Japan. Though this organization attracted many anticommunist youth activist groups (such as Kensei) as well as Koreans who had worked for the Japanese authorities during the colonial period and were thus excluded as "traitors" by Chōren members, Kendō did not grow as quickly as Chōren during its early years.

In the context of the rising communist influence, the founding father of North Korea, Kim Il-Sung, returned to the Korean peninsula from Manchuria with the Soviet forces in order to unite emancipated Korea. His policies and actions influenced many Koreans, including those in Japan, as evidenced by their increasing inclination toward communist ideology and the alliance they forged with the Japanese labor movement. This phenomenon created serious concerns for American authorities, who sought to minimize communist influence in East Asia and turn Japan into a military hub against the USSR. To control the remaining Korean residents, whom Japanese and American authorities perceived as an obstacle to Japan's postwar recovery, the Japanese government reversed their previous position that the remaining Koreans would be regarded as bearers of Japanese citizenship. On May 2, 1947, under the newly legislated Alien Registration Ordinance (Gaikokujin Tōroku Rei), released as the last Imperial Ordinance under Japan's Imperial Constitution, the Japanese government required all Koreans to register as legal aliens. Under this law, all Koreans were to be tentatively deemed alien until the Peace Treaty further specified their status in detail. In other words, Koreans were transformed from being "deemed Japanese citizens" to being "deemed aliens" under the Alien Registration Ordinance. This seemingly sudden 180-degree reversal as to the definition of Koreans' status shows how fluid the situation was for Koreans in Japan and also how malleable the boundaries of Japanese citizenship were in postwar Japan.

This Last Imperial Ordinance of Alien Registration was released just one day before the enactment of Japan's new democratic constitution, drafted under direct American supervision. The order of these significant events—the oppressive Alien Registration Ordinance as Japan's last imperial ordinance, immediately followed by the adoption of a brand-new liberal, democratic constitution—seems to suggest that both American and Japanese authorities were aware that the restrictive Alien Registration Ordinance squarely contradicted the principles of liberal democracy. Hence, authorities might have sensed that it should be out *before* the new democratic constitution. Whether or not this was indeed the motivation for this ordering of events, the suggested meaning of the sequence—that Koreans, as the legacy of Japan's colonial and imperial past, were to be excluded in postwar Japan—was transparent to Koreans in Japan. To them, this new alien status preserved the Japanese colonial legacy. Thus, many Koreans initially resisted the Alien Registration Ordinance and did not willingly register themselves as aliens out of fear of losing their residential rights in Japan (Park 1989). As the subsequent section explains, Koreans' concerns were confirmed by the introduction of a series of Japan's new immigration laws in 1952, which made Koreans' residential status in Japan precarious.

However, their voices demanding Japanese citizenship were hardly unified. Historical documents that capture discussions among Korean activists and their Japanese allies regarding their legal status and rights in the late 1940s reveal that they were keenly aware of the importance of defining Koreans' legal status and belonging in order to have their rights protected by both international and domestic laws (Mizuno 2005; Park 1989). The nation-state-based conceptualization of their citizenship rights reflected the dominant framework of the international community in the 1940s. In the post–World War II context, international treaties and laws regarding individuals' rights were based on the Westphalian model (McCorquodale 2003; Orakhelashvili 2001): that is, they assumed belonging to a particular nation-state as a prerequisite for the protection of basic human rights. Thus, stateless former colonial subjects by definition fell outside the protection of any laws, domestic or international, at that time. This explains the paradoxical fact that American authorities defined Koreans as "enemy people" on the grounds that they had Japanese citizenship prior to 1945; despite classifying Koreans as "liberated people," they did not provide Koreans with the same level of protection that other foreign nationals enjoyed in postwar Japan. Consequently, American authorities allowed the Japanese government to continue to control the Korean population as colonial migrants through its police force.

Not surprisingly, after decolonization many Koreans aligned their national belonging with Korea instead of Japan. Many Korean activist leaders argued that all Koreans in Japan should be recognized as a "liberated population" of Korea and, thus, as not Japanese. Through such self-identification, they sought to secure protection from the occupational forces for their rights and status in Japan. Invoking the nation-based framework used in international laws and occupational policies, Korean activists stressed the urgent need to clarify their national belonging—the critical basis for their rights at that time in world society.

Statements released on Korean suffrage in Japan by Korean activists reveal the nation-based conceptualization of rights shared among Koreans in this period. This conceptualization contrasts with their later framework, which emphasized universal personhood as the basis of their rights, a strategy that the next chapter addresses. When the Japanese government unilaterally revoked the suffrage of colonial immigrants from Korea and Taiwan in 1945, many Korean activists feverishly discussed whether or not they should seek suffrage in Japan. Initially, Chōren released a statement that all resident Koreans should pursue suffrage in Japan to secure their rights of political participation. However, this position was soon criticized by Korean activists who believed that requesting suffrage in Japan would contradict their national self-identification as Koreans.

Han Duk-Su, a prominent Korean activist who later became head of the pro–North Korea organization Chongryon, released a statement about the issue of Korean suffrage in Japan in May 1948. His statement makes it clear that the nation-based conceptualization of rights prompted Chōren to abandon its initial prosuffrage position:[14]

> By accepting the Cairo Declaration and the Potsdam Declaration, we have regained and restored our self-identification as Koreans, and recovered our rights as Koreans. We are fully non-Japanese, and thus insist that we should be treated as foreign nationals, rather than as an ethnic minority within Japanese society. . . . We understand that we cannot receive suffrage right away. But in a future progressive nation, we should make our lives in each region more comfortably, not as the subordinated, but as independent individuals.[15]

This reasoning, shared among activists in early postwar Japan, indicated that their conceptualization of rights was anchored in the nation-state framework. Many Korean activists believed, as did many policymakers and jurists in the 1940s, that citizenship rights, particularly suffrage, should be closely coupled with one's national belonging. Thus, the most plausible tactic for them was to employ a nation-state-based framing in order to legitimize their goals and maximize public attention and support for their movement.

However, there was a notable voice of dissent to this nation-based argument. Fuse Tatsuji, a prominent Japanese activist, Korean ally, and attorney, was well respected among Koreans and was often referred to as the "Japanese Schindler for Koreans" for his fierce advocacy for marginalized Koreans during and after the Japanese colonial rule. He was the first Japanese citizen to posthumously receive the Order of Merit for National Foundation by the South Korean government for his relentless support for the Korean Independence Movement during Japanese colonial rule. Fuse attended a meeting with Korean and Japanese activists, including Han Duk-Su, at the headquarters of Chōren on May 17, 1948, and talked with them about various challenges that Koreans faced in postwar Japan. At this meeting, he argued that Koreans' rights should be recognized and secured in Japan *regardless* of national belonging, stating that "the main problem [was] that citizenship status is a prerequisite for suffrage in the nation" and that this prerequisite "must be removed."[16]

Fuse separated citizenship rights from national belonging. His conceptualization of rights was close to the conceptualization of noncitizens' rights by contemporary advocates. Though his idea was deemed "progressive" by other participants at this meeting, it was not considered a viable option at that time. The fact that Fuse's advocacy for a framing of rights based on people rather than nation was dismissed among Korean activists in early postwar Japan has an important theoretical implication. The framing of rights as belonging to people and not nations became popular among later generations of Korean activists (as I explore in a later chapter), suggesting that a shift in the larger normative and ideational climate had a significant impact on actors' understanding of what would constitute a viable and effective strategy for their movement.

Chōren's rival organization, Mindan (Zainihon Chōsen Kyoryū Mindan), shared a similar conceptualization of rights and self-identification as anchored in a nationalized framework.[17] For example, in 1947, one year before the meeting involving Korean activists and Fuse Tatsuji, Mindan released the following statement against Chōren's initial prosuffrage position. "Throughout world history, there is not a single case where one can exercise suffrage in a country without its citizenship. . . . What we desire is not suffrage in Japan, but what we want is privileged treatment as foreigners and as liberated people" (Park 1989, 136).

With this nation-based understanding of their rights and self-identification, Korean activists eventually agreed to cooperate with Japanese authorities to register as "alien." They hoped that a clear definition of their national belonging would stabilize their status as "liberated people" in Japan and protect their rights once their homeland became a sovereign state after the San Francisco Peace Treaty. However, this optimism quickly abated. A series of new immigration-related policies and laws following the peace treaty produced the opposite outcome: the institutionalization of marginalized status for Koreans in Japan.

HANSHIN EDUCATION STRUGGLE

Koreans in postwar Japan were concerned not only about their political rights but also about their cultural rights. Shortly after the war, many Koreans founded their own schools, where they could freely teach their children the Korean language and culture, which had been prohibited under Japanese colonial rule. By 1947, about five hundred ethnic schools were established across Japan (Nakayama 1995). Initially the Japanese government tolerated the development of these Korean schools. The official notification concerning the schooling of Korean children by the Ministry of Education (Monbushō) to the directors of education, issued on April 12, 1947, argued that Korean children in Japan had the same obligation to attend compulsory school education as Japanese children and that there was no problem in them attending their own ethnic schools.

However, Japanese's supportive attitude toward these Korean schools was short-lived (Ghadimi 2018; Kim 1988). As Kim Il-Sung's Soviet-supported army exerted political influence over the Korean peninsula, American and Japanese authorities united to attack and minimize the communist influence in Japan. This situation prompted both American and Japanese authorities to be wary and more vigilant about any sign of homegrown communist influences. The rapid sprouting of these ad hoc Korean schools attracted negative attention, first from the Japanese government and then from SCAP, who began to consider these schools a means of spreading communist ideology.[18] The first directive against Korean schools was issued on January 24, 1948. Titled

Figure 3.2. Korean school established in Yachimata, Chiba Prefecture, in 1945. Photo from the History Museum of J-Koreans, Tokyo.

"On the Treatment of Korean Schools," it was sent by the Japanese Ministry of Education to all prefectural governors in Japan. In this directive, the Japanese Ministry of Education imposed an obligation on Korean families to send their children to Japanese schools in an attempt to end the ethnic schooling of Koreans in Japan.

Following this January 24, 1948, directive by the Ministry of Education, the municipal governments started ordering Koreans to shut down their privately run schools from March through April of the same year. This sudden reversal of the Japanese state's policy toward Korean schools was met with fierce resistance from furious Koreans. Many Korean protesters in Kobe and Osaka, where the largest number of Koreans lived, promptly organized on the street and vigorously expressed their dissent against this order. These multiple organized protests in the spring of 1948 are now known as the Hanshin Education Struggle. The execution of the school closure order that took place in Osaka City on April 20, 1948, triggered a protest in Osaka City three days later that drew 10,000 protesters. Within a few days, the number of protestors on the street had grown to 13,000 people, and it is estimated that more than 20,000 people eventually participated in the protest (Yang 1994a). As the City of Kobe similarly executed the order of Korean school closures on April 23, 1948, thousands of Koreans gathered around the mayoral building of Kobe City to protest the order. Given that the size of the George Floyd Black Lives Matter Protest on June 6, 2020, in Washington, DC, was estimated to have around 10,000 participants, one could imagine how intense these Korean protests were at that time.[19]

The Koreans' protests continued for days and remained relatively peaceful, but they were met with violent police suppression, resulting in hundreds of arrests and the unprovoked death of Kim Tae-il, a teenage Korean student. An account by a witness gives us a sense of the contentious atmosphere and the rage, desperation, and sorrow shared by participants in the protest:

> The boy [Kim Tae-il] was standing close to me—so close that he would have turned around if I were to reach his shoulder to get his attention. He was suddenly shot down. . . .
>
> I wondered how someone in a black school uniform ended up being involved in this chaotic scene [of the protests]. . . . His face was covered with blood, and his eyes remained open and pointing toward the police force who just shot him. . . . My hands were covered with his blood and I finally realized he was dead. I called for help. I could not leave the scene but all I could do was to glare at the police's loud water-cannon vehicle.[20]

SCAP—a supposed guardian of democracy—had little to no sympathy for Korean protestors. Struck by the intense display of Koreans' discontent with the Japanese authorities' unilateral school closure, SCAP quickly declared its very first (and the only) state of emergency in postwar Japan. With this declaration, they promptly mobilized forces to suppress the Korean protestors. The American and Japanese authorities did not hesitate to use physical force to achieve their goals, as Kim Tae-il's unprovoked death makes clear. The American authorities' strong reaction was a reflection of their own fear and quandary about Koreans. The Koreans' defiant assertion of their identity and rights on the streets of postwar Japan confirmed American authorities' paranoia about Koreans in Japan: these Koreans represented the threat and growing force of communist ideologies. The United States desperately wanted to wipe away such a threat in postwar Japan— the country they defeated with their powerful display of nuclear weapons and then attempted to turn into a stable ally. A statement by US Colonel George Jones, released after the Hanshin Education Struggle

100 *Chapter 3*

to the Japanese newspaper *Asahi Shinbun,* succinctly summarizes this sentiment. "I believe that this incident was influenced by the Communist Party, as in Korea. The Communist Party is using the Korean education problem as a political tool in order to incite riots."[21] The same article directly refers to Koreans in Japan as a "dangerous species" who were largely led by communists, nakedly exhibiting America's growing concern over the shadow of communist influence in Korean mobilization.

Park Jubeom—the Korean activist mentioned at the beginning of chapter 1—participated in this protest. He was arrested and accused of being a leading figure in this organizing effort against the closure of Korean schools. Park Jubeom came to Japan in 1927 as a colonial labor migrant and settled in Kobe City. He created a co-op in Korea Town and taught Korean children the Korean language at night. He was on the frontlines of the Hanshin Educational Struggle and attracted the attention of both Japanese and American authorities. He was sentenced to four years and nine months of forced labor. He was allegedly tortured during his imprisonment and was released temporarily after he fell ill. He died a few hours after his release, on November 25, 1949. More than 10,000 Koreans attended his funeral, and his name was engraved in the collective memories of Koreans in Japan (Chōsen Sinbō 2008).

Considering that this was the first and last state-of-emergency declaration issued by the SCAP during its occupational period, tensions between Koreans and both Japanese and American authorities was unmistakably high. After this struggle, American authorities closely collaborated with Japanese authorities and unequivocally suppressed any political activities among Koreans in Japan. Those who challenged them were arrested, and many were jailed. After the Hanshin Education Struggle in 1948, two of the largest and most influential Korean organizations, Chōren and Minsei, were forcefully disbanded by Japanese authorities. All of these facts demonstrate how Japanese and American Cold War political interests vigorously shaped perceptions about and the subsequent treatment of Koreans in Japan.

In April 1952, nine days before the San Francisco Peace Treaty was enforced, the Japanese government unilaterally revoked Japanese citizenship from resident Koreans. Following this treaty, the Alien Registration Law (Gaikokujin Tōroku Hō), which replaced the previously issued Alien Registration Ordinance, went into effect. With this law, the government formally cemented the alien status of Koreans in Japan. The peace treaty also marked the end of the American occupation in Japan, which meant that the Japanese government, without having to consult with American authorities, could legitimately control and deport Koreans because of their formally defined alien status.

Japan's postwar citizenship policy was specifically designed to define the boundary of postwar Japan and exclude the remaining colonial population from the shrunken territory of postwar Japan. This exclusionary policy was popularly and mistakenly viewed as having unbroken continuity with Japan's feudal national isolation policy. However, historical evidence suggests that the restrictive treatment of colonial migrants, especially Koreans in Japan, was instead a by-product of the emerging political and economic interests of a new regional geopolitical order after World War II, as well as the Japanese state's reaction to defiant Koreans in Japan. The new geopolitical dynamics merged the interests of Japanese and American authorities and fostered their unified perception of Koreans as unwanted outsiders and thus as the subject of exclusion.

THE COLONIAL LEGACY IN POSTWAR IMMIGRATION POLICIES AND LAWS IN JAPAN

Koreans' dissent efforts against the colonial legacy—evident in the Hanshin Education Struggle and in their demands to be recognized as "liberated people"—ironically validated American and Japanese authorities' negative conceptions about Koreans, prompting Edwin Reischauer to call them "annoying complications." Such negative conceptions were reflected in the new "immigration" policies in postwar Japan. Unlike the colonial period, the postwar Japanese government no longer needed to use obscure local laws, including *koseki,* to disguise its desire to control colonial migrants. Instead, it could openly create new immigration policies and laws and use them to control the remaining colonial migrants as "aliens/foreigners." The majority of such aliens were Koreans. The American occupational authority became "partners in crime" with the Japanese government as architects of these policies. Erstwhile enemies, the United States and Japan collaborated closely to effectively control the remaining colonial migrants in Japan, and this collaboration was based on their shared concerns about the Cold War. Through this process, the legacy of colonialism

102   *Chapter 3*

and Cold War interests deeply penetrated postwar Japanese migration policies and laws.

Under the new Alien Registration Law that the Japanese government introduced following the San Francisco Peace Treaty, Koreans became "aliens" who would be controlled as "immigrants." In 1950, a few years before the treaty, American authorities prompted the Japanese government to prepare and draft official postwar immigration policies and laws. A retired senior official of the US Immigration and Naturalization Service, Nicholas D. Collaer, was brought in to supervise the construction of Japan's migration law. In 1951, Japan's "Migration Control Ordinance," equivalent to today's Immigration Law, was enacted on October 4 and executed on November 1. Historian Tessa Morris-Suzuki's work (2006, 137) about undocumented migration in postwar Japan demonstrates that "the resulting Migration Control Ordinance of October 1951 reflected Collaer's intense concerns about the 'subversive' potential of immigrants at a time of rising Cold War tensions." The ordinance gave authorities the comprehensive ability to deport any foreign residents whom they deemed at odds with the interests of the state. Authorities could deport undocumented immigrants and people with criminal records, mental illness, and transmittable disease; those who had become a burden to the state or local authorities due to poverty, vagrancy, or disabilities; and anyone "determined by the Minister of Justice to be performing acts injurious to the interests and public order of the Japanese nation" (Morris-Suzuki 2006, 13).

GHQ gave great discretionary and administrative authority to Japanese bureaucrats and to the minister of the governmental branch in handling admission and deportation. This practice was the international norm at that time. In fact, GHQ ordered the Japanese government to ensure that their immigration policies and laws would adhere to the international standards of the time (Shinozaki 1955; Takaya 2014). For example, GHQ instructed the Japanese state that police should not handle immigrants like criminals as they had under imperial Japan during the prewar period. This might explain why the Japanese government initially placed the Office of Immigration (Nyūkoku Kanribu), which later became known as the Immigration Bureau (Nyūkoku Kanrikyoku),[22] under the Ministry of Foreign Affairs (Gaimushō). Suzuki Hajime's (1966, 31) recollection of his intentions and goals as the first director of this bureau reflects the logic behind this decision:[23]

My first order of action as a newly appointed Director of Immigration Bureau—the office dealing with foreigners—was to teach my officers of the bureau that "Koreans were foreigners. In our treatment, there should be no distinction between Caucasians and Asians. No abuse of power against them was tolerated. Officers of (Immigration) Bureau should be the frontline diplomats." I firmly believed that commitment to humanitarianism was the only way for Japan to overcome the stigma of war defeat and reenter international society.

However, placing the immigration office under the Ministry of Foreign Affairs was seen as deviating from international standards of the time. Thus, the Immigration Bureau was eventually transferred into the Ministry of Justice (Hōmushō) in August 1952 and remains under its jurisdiction.[24]

Although the United States and Japan held two contrasting positions—the United States as a victorious occupational force and Japan as a defeated nation in the subordinate position—political elites in both countries shared common concerns about reconstructing Japan, albeit with different motives and for different purposes. One such concern was national security in the context of the Cold War. Around the same time that Japan's Alien Registration and Immigration Laws were drafted and enacted, American lawmakers were working to pass a key postwar immigration reform bill in the United States: the Immigration and Nationality Act of 1952, known as the McCarran-Walter Bill (Marinari 2016). This bill's debate was filled with American lawmakers' Cold War–related anticommunist sentiments, such as the desire to avert communist espionage and expose sympathizers within the American government. Cold War paranoia and anticommunist sentiment gave incentives to lawmakers to pursue more restrictive immigration policies, linking the issue of immigration with national security.

In this context, Democratic senator Pat McCarran and Democratic congressman Francis Walter joined forces and combined their proposed bills into the McCarran-Walter Bill, which advocated for continued national origin quotas and discriminatory restrictions. Although the bill was opposed by the more liberal Democratic lawmakers and vetoed by President Harry Truman, Truman's veto was overridden by a two-thirds supermajority vote in Congress, and the bill became US law. The overwhelming majority support for this restrictive act reflects the wide penetration of anticommunist sentiment among lawmakers at that time. The restrictive immigration act was in place until the passage of immigration legislation in 1965 that overhauled the national origin quota altogether. Considering how Cold War paranoia permeated American immigration legal reform at that time, it was neither coincidental nor surprising to see parallel restrictive measures introduced into postwar Japanese immigration law, which was directly supervised by a former senior official of the US Immigration and Naturalization Service.

Suzuki Hajime's humanitarian ideals and commitments were not translated into actual practice among the municipal-level bureaucrats and officers who directly faced and dealt with Koreans in Japan.[25] At the municipal level, Japanese prejudice against Koreans continued among bureaucrats, public servants, and police officers (Shinozaki 1952, 1953, 1955). The fact that Japanese returnees from the former colonial Korea were assigned to the Immigration Bureau as well as to alien registration duties in municipal offices across the country allowed the direct transfer of the colonial mentality and prejudice against colonial subjects into postwar Japan. These public servants and bureaucrats' colonial mentality was reflected in the ways they applied the new immigration and alien registration laws to colonial migrants. Koreans in Japan have complained for decades about how they were treated by the bureaucrats at the Immigration Bureau and municipal offices, and historical evidence in the journal *Alien Registration (Gaijin Tōroku)* suggests that their perception of a colonial mentality among public servants was not entirely without basis.[26]

The journal was created by the National Councils of Alien Registration Offices (Gaikokujin Tōrokujimu Kyōgikai Zenkoku Rengōkai) in 1957, nearly a decade after the law was enacted, and was supported by the Immigration Bureau. Because it was published monthly and circulated among municipal servants, its content gives us a rare window through which to observe how public servants and bureaucrats felt about their day-to-day interaction with colonial migrants—the majority of the population they needed to register under this law. The transcript of the meeting held on May 29, 1964, gives us a glimpse of who these public servants and bureaucrats were and how they felt about their jobs and about Koreans (Shin 2010).

In 1964, seven years after the Alien Registration Law was enacted in 1957, six bureaucrats from the Immigration Bureau and the municipal offices gathered in Tokyo to collectively reflect on what it was like to implement the new immigration law in postwar Japan.[27] During this meeting, Hida Kōhei, a bureaucrat in the Immigration Bureau at the Ministry of Justice, casually mentioned that many bureaucrats engaged in the Alien Registration and Immigration Affairs Department had deep connections to colonial Korea. He referred to fellow attendees Hayashi Toshimasa (former chief of records in Kanagawa Prefecture Office) and Minematsu Tamesaku (chief of the Department of Public Liaison and Record at Nagasaki Prefecture) as "Koreans": "Yes, my father was transferred to the Colonial Government in Korea; thus, I was born over there. While I was 'made in Korea,' my citizenship is Japanese. . . . (*laughter*). Speaking of which, Mr. Hayashi and Mr. Minematsu here have been there [colonial Korea] for a very long time. So these are basically all *chōsenjin* [Koreans] (*laughter*)" (*Gaikokujin Tōroku Jimu-kyōkai Zenkoku Rengōkai* 1964a, 4). Hida's reference to himself as "Korean" shows these bureaucrats' deep ties to and experiences with colonialism in Korea. During this meeting, Minematsu mentioned that he was a police officer in colonial Korea and cited his experiences in Korea as a reason for him to engage with the alien registration duty at Nagasaki Prefectural Municipal Office. Their remarks underscored the chaotic situation involved in handling alien registration processes with non-Japanese residents—most of whom were Koreans—at the time of the law's enactment.

While some of these bureaucrats and public servants expressed sympathy toward some Koreans whom they had gotten to know better, they nevertheless candidly expressed contempt for many Koreans and for other non-Japanese people who resisted or reluctantly complied with this registration requirement. These bureaucrats and public servants sorted colonial migrants into two categories—those who obediently followed and respected Japanese laws, and those who acted entitled and disobedient. The former made their duty worthwhile, while the latter distressed them. This bifurcated view of colonial migrants mirrored the ways colonial subjects were viewed and treated during the colonial period. As chapter 2 revealed, the Japanese respected and supported Park Chungeum, the first Korean elected official of Imperial Japan, while they despised and mistreated dissenting Koreans. During this meeting, they also mentioned that their own opinions and efforts were later incorporated into revisions of immigration laws in postwar Japan.[28]

The Japanese bureaucrats' ethno-racialized sense of superiority against Koreans was not subtle to many Koreans living in Japan who interacted daily with municipal workers. From many Koreans'

106   *Chapter 3*

perspectives, the new immigration and registration laws were simply "old wine in a new bottle." The legacy of colonialism was on full display even after colonial rule ended. In the following section, I discuss how Cold War tensions impacted Korean social movements for social justice and rights and how the lack of international awareness and support negatively affected Koreans in Japan.

The 38th Parallel Divide in Japan

After World War II, the fate of the Korean peninsula was no longer in the hands of the Japanese, nor was it under the control of the Korean people. Instead, it was largely influenced by the power struggle between two major hegemonic powers, the USSR and the United States, which led the Korean peninsula to be divided into two occupational zones along the 38th parallel. This division became the foundation for the Korean civil war that followed between communist North Korea, led by Kim Il-Sung and backed by the USSR, and anticommunist South Korea, led by Rhee Syngman and backed by the United States. In 1953 a cease-fire was finally established through the United Nations, and the Korean peninsula was formally divided into two territories and separate sovereign states.

Colonial migrants from Korea and Taiwan became stateless after the Japanese government unilaterally stripped away their Japanese citizenship status. Two new Korean states, North and South Koreas, began competing over the representation of the remaining Korean colonial migrants in Japan. Their eagerness to represent the remaining colonial migrants in Japan merely reflected their political motives, however, rather than genuine concern for the welfare of their fellow Koreans. Both states understood that Japan's most pressing interest was the treatment of the remaining Koreans in Japan. Thus, both South and North Korean governments used Japan's concerns to leverage political and diplomatic gains, establishing a formal relationship and opening up dialogue about colonial reparations with the Japanese state.

The recording of nationality in the alien registration process for Koreans in Japan reflects these states' political interests.[29] As the South Korean government began to prepare its own national registration for its citizens, it requested that the GHQ instruct the Japanese government to list the nationality of remaining Koreans in Japan as Kankoku (South Korea) or Daikanminkoku (Republic of Korea) to legitimize their representation of the overseas Koreans. Having received GHQ's instruction, the Japanese government began to use the terms "Kankoku" (South Korea) and "Daikanminkoku" (Republic of Korea) for official documents. According to historian Kim Yong-Dal (1987, [1980] 1990), who analyzed the government's records on alien registration in this period, the Ministry of Justice cited variable preference among Koreans to explain why the terms "Chōsen" (Korea), "Kankoku" (South Korea), or "Daikanminkoku" (Republic of Korea) were used in their registration record. Koreans were also allowed to change their nationality record from Chōsen (Korea) to Kankoku (South Korea) or Daikanminkoku (Republic of Korea) at the municipal office. According to the Ministry of Justice, this kind of flexibility to change one's nationality record was thought to prompt Koreans to register and to make the registration transaction go smoothly (Kim 1987, 65–67).

The Japanese government insisted that these terms simply referred to one's *regional* origin rather than to one's national belonging or identity. Nevertheless, the creation of separate labels had significant implications for Koreans in Japan. Having experienced the negative impact of unilateral changes to their status, many Koreans were wary about the way they were classified by authorities on this official record. Furthermore, even if both labels meant the same set of rights for Koreans in Japan at that time, these separate labels led many Koreans to become more self-conscious of their national identification and political affiliation. Many Koreans in Japan began to associate the term "Chōsen" with North Korea, as North Korea is referred to as "Kita Chōsen," while South Korea is referred to as "Kankoku" or "Daikanminkoku" in the Japanese colloquial language. These terms, therefore, signaled their political affiliation and identities. This explains why some Koreans asked local governments in Japan to change their record from "Chōsen" (North Korea) to "Kankoku" (South Korea), or vice versa, after the Ministry of Justice began to allow such a change (Kim 1987).

In 1951, the Japanese government decided to separate these nationality labels more specifically and restrictively. They put a stop to Koreans being able to change the nationality information on their alien registration record through a simple request at a municipal office. The government sent internal notifications to municipal offices instructing them to require Koreans to present a South Korean National Registry certificate issued by the representative office of the South Korean government along with their request for a change of nationality information on their registry record in Japan. This change probably reflected the fact that the Japanese government was at the time prepared to recognize the South Korean government, but not communist North Korea, as an official sovereign state of the Korean peninsula (Kim 1987). Thus, the Japanese government limited any further changes from South Korea (Kankoku or Daikanminkoku) to North Korea (Chōsen) in Koreans' local registration records.

The provisional South Korean government, led by Rhee Syngman, demanded that the Japanese government grant them approximately 17 billion yen in reparations; they put this demand in a request to the American government, which was overseeing this process (Ōta 2003).[30] The United States initially planned to propose a robust reparation process for Japan, but this plan was revised extensively after Clifford Strike, a chair of the Special Committee on Japanese Reparations, argued that a large reparation requirement would put too much constraint on the Japanese economy and thus delay its recovery (Bennett 1948). As the delay would cause the United States both military and economic burdens, the United States reversed its initial position and rejected South Korea's request, describing it as unrealistic. Considering Japan's tenuous economic condition, the American government argued that all the monetary reparations that Korea received would ultimately come from American tax money (Ōta 2003).

In the eyes of American and Japanese authorities, Korea's reparation demand might have been unrealistic. However, in the eyes of Koreans, it was equally unrealistic to reconstruct their country without any reparation from its former colonizer, who severely exploited them for over thirty years. Nonetheless, the Far Eastern Commission concluded that Korea, which was not a part of the Allied Powers, had no legal right to claim reparations from Japan. This rejection was not unusual in the context of the mid-twentieth-century world society, where there was no normative or legal expectation for Western empires to offer reparations to their former colonial countries. From the perspective of Allied Powers, who possessed their own colonial territories, recognizing Korea's demand for reparations from Japan would open a floodgate for similar demands from their own colonies. This was a fault line the Allied Powers dared not to cross. As Cold War tensions mounted in East Asia, it was in America's interest to help Japan promptly reconstruct its nation and economy and to turn Japan into a stable regional ally and military base in Far East Asia.

Both the South and North Korean regimes grew frustrated as the United States tried to suppress their pursuit for reparation. They became even more eager to utilize their fellow Koreans in Japan as political capital to advance claims for reparations to the Japanese government. Both Korean regimes were aware that the Japanese state was eager to resolve any outstanding issues concerning both the remaining Koreans in Japan—including the determination of their legal status—and the remaining Japanese in both South and North Korea. The South Korean government took full advantage of Japan's predicament over the remaining colonial migrants and made a move to start its dialogue with Japan before the North Korean government approached Japan. While the United States served as an intermediating observer, the Japanese government and South Korea agreed to have a preliminary discussion with the goal of establishing a formal diplomatic relationship between the two countries in the not-too-distant future. At first the Japanese government was willing to discuss only the issue of the remaining Korean colonial migrants. However, South Korea, whose main concern was reparation, insisted that the agenda of their meetings must include the remaining colonial migrant issue *and* reparations (Ōta 2003). Japan reluctantly agreed, and their first preliminary negotiation meeting took place in 1952. However, during the preliminary meeting, the South Korean government did not prioritize the issue of the remaining Koreans in Japan; instead, it attempted to focus on colonial reparations, which frustrated both the Japanese government and Koreans in Japan.

The North Korean state did not miss the opportunity to negotiate with the Japanese state either. In 1955, the North Korean minister of foreign affairs called for a meeting with Japan in order to discuss the matter on Koreans in Japan and other pending issues, including colonial reparations (Takasaki and Park 2005). They too intended to establish a diplomatic relationship with Japan. However, sensing North Korea's political motives, the Japanese government rejected this request. Japan argued that Allied Powers did not recognize the legitimate sovereignty of the North Korean provisional government and that henceforth no official diplomatic relationship could be established between Japan and North Korea. To persuade Japan to establish political diplomacy, the North Korean government continuously attempted to utilize the repatriation of Koreans in Japan and Japanese in North Korea as a political capital to achieve this end.

110 *Chapter 3*

The Japanese government was particularly concerned about the situation at the Ōmura Detention Center near Nagasaki, where those who violated immigration laws were held (Takasaki and Park 2005).[31] The number of Korean detainees was steadily rising as unauthorized entries among Koreans increased after the enactment of new restrictive immigration laws. The Japanese government wished to deport these Korean detainees because it considered them a source of crime and disturbance in postwar Japan. Some of the Korean detainees were anti–South Korea political activists, and they wished to be deported to North Korea rather than South Korea, as they feared execution by the South Korean government. However, the Japanese government was reluctant to deport them to North Korea, a country with no formal diplomatic relationship with Japan. To prompt their release to North Korea, many Korean detainees began a hunger strike. This further motivated the Japanese government to deport these detained Koreans as quickly as possible (Kim and Takayanagi 1995).

While Japan and the two Koreas manipulated the issues of Koreans in Japan for their own political gains, Koreans in Japan—most of them living in poverty—concentrated on daily survival. These ordinary Koreans' primary concern was securing their rights and achieving better living conditions in Japan. Although some Korean activists attempted to promote the idea of the unification of Korea, the idea did not gain much traction from Koreans in Japan at first (Park 1989). However, the political division and tensions between the South and the North gradually penetrated the minds of Koreans and began to influence their self-identity and political beliefs. Eventually the political division between the South and the North further fragmented the interests of Koreans in Japan.

The penetration of the South/North division within the Korean community in Japan was demonstrated in the existence of two separate Korean organizations. A prominent Korean activist in Japan, Park Yul, led a new Korean organization, Mindan, whose proclaimed goal was initially to prioritize the improvement of their living conditions in Japan rather than to promote a specific political agenda or ideology of their homeland (Lee 1980). After the Japanese authorities broke up the more unified Korean organization, Chōren, a more politically defined and pro–North Korea organization, Chongryon, was formed under the leadership of Han Duk-Su in 1955 (Lee 1980; Yang 1994b).[32] Chongryon also began to collaborate with the Community Party and Socialist Party in Japan. However, as with Chongryon, which supported the North Korean regime, the top organizational leaders of Mindan began to exhibit explicit support for the South Korean government, especially after the Mindan leader, Park Yul, developed a close relationship with Rhee Syngman, the first president of South Korea (Yang 1994b).

When the US-sponsored South Korean government was established with Prime Minister Rhee Syngman, Mindan began to function as a South Korea–endorsed organization rather than as a civil organization for Koreans in Japan. Beginning in 1948, the South Korean government also appointed Mindan to perform some consular responsibilities, such as identifying and registering overseas Koreans (Lee 1980). This tactic was designed to solicit support for South Korea among Korean colonial migrants in Japan. Because most Koreans in Japan were originally from the southern geographical part of the Korean peninsula—within the territory of South Korea—they needed to register as South Koreans through their affiliation with Mindan to visit their relatives in South Korea. But their increasing political dependency on the South Korean government propagated dissatisfaction among some members, who believed that the South Korean government was not serving the best interests of Koreans in Japan. As a result, although it avoided the Japanese and American authorities' suppression, Mindan lost many members, significantly undermining its organizational solidarity.

Repatriation to North Korea suddenly became a viable and attractive option to many Koreans in Japan in the late 1950s. In 1959, Chongryon and the North Korean regime began to promote the idea of repatriation of Korean colonial migrants and their families to North Korea so they could join their comrades to rebuild their nation with a promise for better living conditions in the North (Chang 1991; Kim and Takayanagi 1995; Komatsuki 2004). Over 90,000 Koreans went back to North Korea with hope for a better life. However, previously sealed International Committee of the Red Cross documents written by Japanese officials before 1959 and declassified in 2004 reveal that before the North Korean effort to promote repatriation in 1959, both the Japanese government and the Japanese Red Cross Society closely cooperated in promoting the repatriation plan as a way to get rid of Koreans in Japan.

While the Japanese government and Japanese Red Cross Society contemplated the repatriation of Koreans back to North Korea, the Ministry of Health and Welfare (Kōseishō) was conducting a campaign

112   *Chapter 3*

to slash the limited welfare benefits available to Koreans in Japan, and many Koreans had their welfare payments reduced or canceled.[33] This government welfare cutback, along with the promotion of repatriation to North Korea, made moving to North Korea a more appealing option to many struggling Koreans in Japan and motivated them to consider the option.

Sending Koreans back to North Korea may have served as a solution to ease public sentiment against Koreans in Japan, but it also prompted another diplomatic challenge for Japan. Japan and South Korea were still in the middle of preliminary negotiations to establish an official diplomatic relationship. Given Cold War tensions in Korea, it was expected that the South Korean government would react antagonistically toward the Japanese government's plan to send Korean colonial migrants to its rival regime. To reconcile these two competing interests—getting rid of Koreans who were in its territory while deterring South Korea's antagonism toward this plan—the Japanese government concealed its true motives by pursuing its objectives through a nongovernmental agency, the Japanese Red Cross Society. The Japanese government emphasized that these were strictly "humanitarian efforts" by the Red Cross, independent of any state's political motives. The following statement by Inoue Masutarō, director of external affairs at the Japanese Red Cross Society, emphasized its humanitarian intentions:

> The problem is the fact that Koreans suffer most severely from the high unemployment rate. Most will face unemployment no matter how much better our economy in Japan becomes and even worse if our economy declines. . . . There is no solution for them but repatriation back to Korea. Even if there is another solution, it will not come in time. Their problem needs immediate action, and if we don't do anything now, there will be many illnesses and deaths among them. This is a very serious humanitarian issue.[34]

However, as the declassified documents revealed, the statement was nothing but a performative political maneuver based on coordinated efforts between the Japanese government and the Japanese Red Cross Society. As historian Tessa Morris-Suzuki's (2005) analysis of these declassified documents revealed, Director Inoue explained to a visiting official of the International Committee of the Red Cross that the Japanese government wanted to get rid of impoverished and communism-inclined Koreans and that doing so would resolve the security and budgetary concerns for Japan, as supporting these Koreans was costly. These declassified documents also revealed Director Inoue's strong anti-Korean sentiment.

The International Committee of the Red Cross (ICRC) in Geneva sensed Japan's naked political motives and was also concerned about the reality of living conditions in North Korea. Thus, they demanded that the Japanese authorities publicly and fully inform Koreans in Japan of their genuine choices to remain in Japan or leave for North Korea. In doing so, the ICRC attempted to ensure that the Japanese government was committed to the Koreans' right to remain in Japan. The Japanese Red Cross Society reassured the ICRC on behalf of the Japanese government. They alleged that there was generous welfare support by the Japanese government for Koreans, making it appear as if Koreans had viable choices—staying in Japan or leaving for North Korea. Scholars specializing in the issues of the Koreans' exodus to North Korea agreed that the Japanese Red Cross Society intentionally misled the ICRC in order to get rid of Koreans on Japan's soil (Morris-Suzuki 2005; Takasaki and Park 2005). The ICRC did not press the Japanese Red Cross Society to provide further evidence to verify their reassurances; instead, the ICRC finally agreed to lend its name to the Korean repatriation project. This collaboration between the Japanese government and the Japanese Red Cross Society vividly shows how the concept of universal human rights was weakly enforced and practiced at the local level in this specific Cold War context in the 1950s. Consequently, the ICRC failed to protect the human rights of an oppressed subaltern group.

The Japanese Socialist and Communist Parties also supported North Korea; this Korean repatriation project was mainly based on their concern about the Koreans' poor living conditions and severe social discrimination against Koreans in Japan. In 1958, Japanese intellectuals and politicians established a group in support of the Korean repatriation project (Zainichi Chōsenjin Kikoku Kyōryokukai). This group consisted of numerous politicians and intellectuals, such as Iwamoto Nobuyuki as chair (a representative of the Lower House), Arita Hachirō (former minister of foreign affairs), Hatoyama Ichirō (former prime minister), Asamura Inajirō (secretary of Japan's Socialist Party), and Miyamoto Keiji (secretary of Japan's Communist Party). However, it was mainly run by the members of Japan's Socialist and Communist Parties, who supported communist ideology and regarded the project as a humanitarian effort to help poor Koreans go back to

114   *Chapter 3*

their communist homeland. These parties also believed that helping poor Koreans return to a communist country would promote public understanding of their socialist and communist ideals in Japanese society (Wada and Takasaki 2005, 107).

By 1971, approximately 90,000 Koreans had gone back to North Korea. This number reflects the level of their yearning for emancipation from racism and poverty in Japan, especially given that Korean repatriates knew that they might never have the chance to come back to Japan or South Korea once they repatriated to North Korea. Nonetheless, their hopes were quickly dashed once they arrived. Oral accounts of North Korean political refugees later explained that many repatriates died upon their return due to lack of food and the horrible living situation in North Korea (Chang 1991; Wada and Takasaki 2005).

The eventual fate of these Korean repatriates was of no concern to the Japanese Red Cross Society, as a callous comment by former director Takagi Takezaburō makes clear: "If there were some people who went back to North Korea believing that it was their paradise and who were disappointed with the living conditions in North Korea after their arrival, then those must be real suckers."[35] His coldhearted account illustrates how hollow and performative the concept of human rights and norms of humanitarianism were in postwar Japan in the context of the Cold War. This case also demonstrates that the absence of effective normative pressure to ensure the protection of human rights in a meaningful manner is detrimental to vulnerable subaltern groups. Conversely, the presence of strong globalized norms of human rights could serve the interests of subaltern groups, as I show in the next chapter.

Korean repatriation to North Korea eventually declined, in part corresponding to the rapidly changing geopolitical climate in East Asia. In South Korea, after Rhee Syngman's regime fell in 1960, Chang Myon's new government was overthrown by General Park Chunghee through the May 16 coup d'état in 1961. As Cold War tensions in Asia became aggravated, the United States began to assert more interest in foreign affairs in Asia. In this political context, the Japanese government started prioritizing a formal diplomatic relationship with South Korea and focused less on North Korea. The South Korean government—led by Park Chunghee, the former general and new president, who was keenly interested in South Korea's economic recovery—wasted no time in proceeding with the normalization of diplomatic relations with Japan in order to allow Japanese reparations and for capital to flow into South Korea. In 1965, when the Japan-

Korea Normalization Treaty was finally signed, the possibility of any diplomatic relationship between Japan and North Korea virtually vanished.

As the diplomatic relationship between Japan and South Korea improved, the pro–South Korea organization Mindan regained many members from the Korean community in Japan. Koreans in Japan found the affiliation with South Korea beneficial because it allowed them to freely travel back and forth to South Korea, where they originally came from and where their relatives lived. Membership in Mindan soared, especially after the 1965 normalization treaty between South Korea and Japan improved the legal status and expanded the rights of self-identified South Korean nationals. After the normalization treaty was signed, the Japanese government granted the status of permanent residency, with the right to enter the National Health Insurance Plan, to those who registered as South Korean nationals on the alien registration. This legal status and these social rights were not extended to those who identified as North Korean in Japan. These changes prompted many previously stateless Koreans to acquire South Korean citizenship in order to secure their legal status in Japan (Kim 1992b).

This situation caused a further divergence between Koreans in Japan. Koreans with South Korean passports had more secured legal status and rights than self-identified North Koreans. While both faced similar discrimination in Japan, North Koreans faced more disadvantages. Because the Japanese government had not established a diplomatic relationship with North Korea, the latter had no embassy in Japan that could issue North Korean passports to Koreans there. Consequently, self-identified North Koreans continued to remain "stateless" and outside the protection of both domestic and international laws. This divergent treatment between South and North Koreans as a result of heightened Cold War politics fragmented solidarity among Koreans and undermined their social movements.

The bifurcating force of Cold War politics impacted not only Koreans in Japan but also postwar Japanese intellectuals. However, it yielded a different outcome for Japanese intellectuals than for Koreans in Japan: rather than dividing them, it facilitated a unified self-identification among intellectuals from opposite ends of the political spectrum. The next section shows how Cold War politics and postwar conditions shaped the psyche of postwar Japanese intellectuals and led them, despite the incompatible differences in their intellectual positions and scholarly disciplines, to embrace the same type of national

116   *Chapter 3*

self-image—as an ethno-racially homogeneous nation. The next section shows how the discourse on mono-ethnic Japan constructed by these intellectuals played a key role in facilitating public support for postwar Japan's exclusive citizenship and migration policies.

POSTWAR INTELLECTUALS AND THE RETURN OF ETHNIC NATIONALISM

The dismantling of Imperial Japan by the United States was humiliating to many intellectuals in Japan. During the US occupation, Japan did not have full sovereignty. Japan's southern islands of Okinawa became a territory of the United States, and the American military built bases there to guard against growing communist vigor in East Asia. Meanwhile, the Japanese military was dismantled and Japan's economy deteriorated. Emperor Hirohito, once considered the inheritor of absolute divine power, was reduced to a secular national symbol in the postwar Japanese constitution.[36] After the exhaustion of warfare, many Japanese people were living in poverty, many children became orphans, and some women turned to sex work for American soldiers to make ends meet (Dower 1999). American occupational forces brought back some of the political elites who were willing to collaborate with them to run the postwar Japanese government. In the eyes of many Japanese people, their government seemed to be nothing but a puppet of the United States. Their nation was undeniably in extreme fatigue, physically and psychologically.

Facing this corrosion of their nation, many intellectuals in postwar Japan held "a shared sense of the need to articulate the meaning of the wartime experience" (Koschmann 1993, 396). Most of them were also highly critical of militarism in prewar Japan and discredited their own government, but they were also contrite about their collaboration with fascism and failure to resist the war. Many antiwar and antifascist radical intellectuals released from prison after the war were welcomed back as heroes. Leftist and radical ideologies were quickly embraced and became popular in postwar Japan. It was in this context that discourse about the mono-ethnic nation (*tan'itsu minzoku kokka*) emerged among radical leftists in the disciplines of history and social sciences as part of an effort to seek new foundations for national unity and pride. It may seem counterintuitive that such an exclusive conception of nationhood became celebrated among the most radical and liberal group of intellectuals in postwar Japan. However, as I show

Homogeneous Nation-State 117

below, radical leftists in postwar Japan found the theory of mono-ethnicity to be an invigorating and effective symbolic tool through which to achieve their end.[37]

The fact that the mono-ethnicity theory emerged from remorseful progressives challenges the conventional argument that it was Japan's exclusive sense of mono-ethnic nationhood that caused postwar Japanese policymakers to exclude colonial migrants from Japanese citizenship. As earlier sections of this chapter revealed, it was a combination of colonial legacy and Cold War political calculations that motivated the Japanese state to adopt exclusive citizenship and immigration policies against the remaining colonial migrants in postwar Japan. Reviewing the genesis of postwar Japanese ethnic nationalism shows that similar geopolitical contexts inspired the theories of mono-ethnic Japan, revealing a far more complicated relationship between nationhood, citizenship, and migration policies in postwar Japan.

Even after the American occupation officially ended in 1952, American influence lingered in Japan. Although the prewar intention of the United States was to transform the ultranationalist Imperial Japan into a more progressive, civic, and democratic nation, the United States quickly reversed course and molded Japan into its subordinate Cold War partner as its political interests in East Asia grew (Doak 1997; Takemae 2002). This allowed the return of conservative political elites to the postwar Cabinet and led the Japanese bourgeois to embrace capitalism. Over time this situation intensified the economic disparity between the well-to-do and the poor. Facing this contradictory reality, some intellectuals in postwar Japan attempted to genuinely embrace democracy and peace in postwar Japan. Toward this end, Japanese intellectuals reflected on the nation's trajectories since the Meiji Restoration and on how Japan—a nation that became an imperial power in a quest to emulate Western nations—fell into the hands of the United States. Most intellectuals, regardless of their political inclinations (whether they were radical leftists or conservatives), were almost uniformly critical of the prewar authoritarian regime. They were also aware of their failure to effectively argue against prewar ideologies that emphasized pan-Asianism, which they condemned for leading prewar Japan to senselessly invade neighboring nations.

Rejecting a pan-Asian ideology anchored in militarism and imperial expansionism was an important logical step that many intellectuals felt was necessary in order to emancipate Japan from the cultural colonialism of US imperialism. To criticize American militarism and

118   *Chapter 3*

dominance, however, intellectuals needed to negate Japan's own militaristic past. At the same time, they felt a need to revitalize the Japanese populace by providing them with a new symbol of national unity. Postwar intellectuals therefore found ethnic nationalism "an effective tool for criticizing, simultaneously, the capitalist postwar Japanese state and the cultural colonialism of US imperialism" (Doak 1997, 303).

One of the most influential radical postwar historians, Ishimoda Shō, published *The Discovery of the Ethnic Nation* (*Rekishi to minzoku no hakken: rekishigaku no kadai to hōhō*) in 1952. In this book Ishimoda underscored the importance of ethnic nationalism as a foundation for unity among the popular masses in postwar Japan. Another influential Marxist historian, Tōma Seita (1951, 292–293), argued that to emancipate Japan from US global imperialism, historians should provide "a tool to unify varying ethnic strata into one ethnicity," adding, "We need to promote a psychological commonality among nationals and to let them have self-confidence" in their traditions and culture and a sense of ethnic pride. These historians carefully distinguished their concept of ethnic nationalism from that of prewar ultranationalism. They claimed that unlike prewar nationalism, which was based on a pan-Asian concept of nationhood that led Japan to expansive imperialism, the postwar ethnic nationalism, which was based on a mono-ethnic concept of nationhood, prevented Japan from being imperialistic. At the same time, the concept also allowed them to return to their ancient ethnic roots of a pacifistic nation based on a unique culture (Oguma 1995).

Conservative historians also took part in this intellectual endeavor of trying to find a new source of Japanese nationhood. Preeminent historians such as Tsuda Sōkichi ([1946] 1968) and Watsuji Tetsurō (1948) asserted that the symbolic emperor system could serve to create unity. It was a well-known fact that American authorities forced the postwar Japanese government to transform the Japanese emperor's role from symbolic sovereign to a symbol of a nation that had a new democratic constitution. Tsuda and Watsuji had always questioned, even during wartime, the erstwhile dominant theory of a Japanese multiethnic origin as the source of their dominance in Asia and the world and had advocated for the possibility of a mono-ethnic origin of Japan. In fact, Tsuda was arrested by imperial police for challenging the multiethnic origin theory. Yet both historians' scholarship became popular after the end of the war.

Ethnic nationalism was empowered by various cross-disciplinary theories of Japanese mono-ethnic nationhood. The racial origin theory provided, albeit unintentionally, "a bridge between the otherwise irreconcilable camps of conservatives and Marxists" (Doak 1997, 301–302). For conservatives and rightists, ethnic nationalism could serve as an effective tool to restore the emperor system as the foundation for postwar Japanese unity and solidarity. For radical leftists, ethnic nationalism was a legitimate tool to emancipate Japan from the shadow of US imperialism and prevent postwar Japan from returning to a militaristic empire. With a growing voice to support independence among the colonies in Indo-China and Africa in the 1950s and '60s and to echo Stalin's criticism of Western imperialism, ethnic nationalism gained further legitimacy. It was celebrated among those postwar Japanese intellectuals who wished for Japan to be liberated from Western—or, more accurately, American—imperialism.

This explains why for postwar Japanese intellectuals, sending the remaining colonial migrants back home appeared to be a reasonable solution that they did not contest. For conservatives, the solution allowed Japan to sweep away any foreign elements from postwar Japan, which further reified their ideal notion of ethnic homogeneity, while for leftists it resonated with their spirit of ethnic independence, supported by Stalinist and Marxist dogma. In fact, Japanese communist Terao Gorō (1959) published a book about North Korea in which he passionately portrayed North Korea as a country of promise. His book was allegedly among one of the most important push factors that convinced many Koreans to go back to their homeland (Takasaki and Park 2005).

The discourse of Japanese homogeneous ethnic and racial origins continued growing throughout the 1960s and 1970s. A new generation of social scientists, literature scholars, and anthropologists continued to elaborate theories of Japanese uniqueness and homogeneity. These efforts to define and reify the unique and homogeneous origin of the Japanese nation, ethnicity, and race eventually formed their own theoretical field, known as Nihonjinron, which literally means "theory of Japaneseness" (Befu 2001). These intellectual theories about Japanese homogeneity were widely used among both conservative and radical activists and policymakers to achieve very diverse objectives.

The notion of a mono-ethnic and homogeneous Japan was also widely incorporated into policies across various spheres, including political, economic, and educational spheres. In fact, the theory of a

120   *Chapter 3*

mono-ethnic national character was used not only to justify Japan's treatment of immigrants and foreigners but also to justify economic and political positions and policies about trade and international relations (Befu 2001). This is evident in the repeated references to Japan's homogeneous ethnicity in parliamentary debates on various issues. As the following two quotes from the parliamentary debate on April 40, 1965, illustrate, two policymakers, despite their different political positions, took ethnic homogeneity for granted and used it as a point of comparison to European nations when discussing their economic policy and labor disputes in Japan. Ueda Shinkichi, a member of Japan's Socialist Party, stated, "Our country consists of one ethnic group known as Yamato. . . . We should learn a great deal from Western developed nations' unified efforts to increase productivity through the human harmony, and their governments' supportive policies toward this objective. Since Japan is a mono-ethnic Yamato nation . . . , our labor and management should cooperate and unite together."[38] Minister of Internal Affairs Takahashi Mamoru of Japan's Democratic Liberal Party replied, "Now, with regard to the previous statement about the American and European situation and in comparison to them, there is a strong conflict between labor and management in Japan, which is very difficult to reconcile; in spite of the fact that we are a mono-ethnic nation, I cannot agree with you more."[39] This exchange is one of many references that exemplify how the concept of Japanese mono-ethnic nation penetrated and became embedded in the minds of Japanese political and intellectual elite groups by the mid-1960s.

It is important to remember that postwar Japan's decision to strip citizenship rights and status from its colonial migrants on its soil predates the penetration of this intellectual and political discourse of mono-ethnic nationhood. As we saw earlier in this chapter, state policymakers, by and large, did not act with a coherent nationalist ideology; rather, they acted on their lingering colonial mentality and Cold War political interests and concerns. Thus, we should consider that the discourse about mono-ethnic and racial nationhood in Japan *justified* rather than *caused* the development of exclusive citizenship and immigration policies in postwar Japan. As an earlier section discussed, the Cold War's bifurcating force severely weakened Koreans' organizing ability to challenge this continuing oppression, which in turn allowed the further institutionalization of ethno-racial inequality and structural and symbolic oppression against Koreans in postwar Japan. The popularized myth of ethno-racial homogeneity of Japan endorsed and perpetuated institutionalized racism against Koreans and other minority groups, while masking the connections between the legacies of colonial oppression and structural inequality.

A review of postwar Japanese intellectuals' efforts to revive ethnic nationalism as well as the Japanese government's treatment of Koreans also reveals some similarities and contrasts in the process of remaking nationhood between the imperial and Cold War contexts in Japan. As in the imperial period, defining a new boundary of national self-image in postwar Japan also required othering. This composition of the other in the Cold War context did not differ much from its composition in the imperial period. Postwar Japan found two subjects of otherness in this process. The first was the United States, which defeated and occupied Japan; the second was Koreans in Japan, who embodied Japan's lost empire. Although other minority groups—such as Ainu, Okinawans, Taiwanese, and Burakumin—were also important in defining the Japanese national self-image, Koreans continued to remain the focus of othering, especially through the process of citizenship and immigration policymaking in postwar Japan. As we saw in the previous chapter, Imperial Japan defined its national self-image in relation to Western imperialists who were about to colonize them. These Western imperialists were replaced with one particular Western nation, the United States, after World War II. Imperial Japan utilized the colonial population to postulate its pan-Asian hybrid nationhood. In contrast, while postwar Japan exploited the labor of colonial migrants, it did not absorb them into its nationhood. Instead, postwar Japan chose to exclude them from it by stripping away their Japanese citizenship status—their legitimate right to reside in Japan. Shedding the idea of hybrid ethno-racial nationhood, postwar Japanese intellectuals developed a new self-image as a homogeneous nation based on the mono-ethnicity theory, and policymakers eventually embraced this myth and used it to justify their exclusionary policies against immigrants and minority groups. In both cases, colonial migrants and Western nations served as a marker for the Japanese to specify the boundaries of their own national self-image, and the self-image from the two periods had contrasting ramifications.

DISCUSSION

In the two decades following the end of World War II, the status of Koreans and the boundaries of Japanese citizenship were redefined based on the complicated and entangled interests of various state and nonstate actors. In postwar Japan as in the imperial era, an exogenous impact sharply influenced the interests and choices that the state made regarding the boundaries of citizenship and the conception of immigration. But this time the exogenous factor was the Cold War bifurcating the world into Eastern and Western blocs, led respectively by the USSR and the United States. As a war-defeated nation, postwar Japan did not have much autonomy to determine its own boundaries of nation via citizenship and immigration policies.

This should have given Koreans in Japan ample opportunity to exert their interests and demand their rights through collective action. That is exactly what they did in the postwar period. But their influence over the citizenship and immigration policies in postwar Japan was limited, as their internal solidarity was fragmented by the same bifurcating force, the Cold War. The political position each nation-state occupied in the larger world society, along with their political stance in relation to Cold War ideologies, put constraints on the level of influence that Koreans in Japan could exert in the process of citizenship and immigration policymaking in postwar Japan.

In a mid-twentieth-century world largely dominated by Western countries, both North and South Korea were denied the ability to claim war and colonial reparations from Japan by the Allied Powers. This denial subsequently led these two states to consider the issue of repatriating the remaining Korean colonial migrants in Japan, acknowledging them as part of their own political capital as they sought colonial reparations from Japan. In the aftermath of Japanese colonial exploitation and a bitter, divisive civil war, both South and North Korea were suffering and lacked the means to reconstruct their nations' economies and militaries. Thus, they prioritized their own interests in reparations from Japan over the well-being of the disfranchised overseas Koreans in Japan. Initially, North Korea succeeded in attracting Korean colonial migrants in Japan with its communist ideology, embellished with hollow promises of egalitarianism and fairness. However, as North Korea was unable to establish a formal diplomatic relationship with Japan, many Koreans in Japan eventually chose South Korean citizenship, which allowed them a more secure legal status in Japan and freedom to travel to their homeland.

An earlier section of this chapter discussed the phenomenon of Japanese who served as public servants and bureaucrats in colonial Korea, then returned to Japan and took positions in municipal offices or new democratic government branches or were assigned to the duties of the Alien Registration Office and Immigration Bureau in Ministry of Justice. The exact number of bureaucrats with direct colonial connections is unknown, but historical evidence suggests that some of the bureaucrats in prominent positions in these offices had direct life and work experience in colonial Korea. These bureaucrats perceived their former colonial subjects in Japan through the same colonial gaze, and treated them in similar ways, but at a new site—municipal offices in Japan. These bureaucrats played crucial roles in institutionalizing the colonial legacy in postwar Japan's citizenship and immigration laws and reminding Korean migrants of the persistent colonial legacy that continued into the postwar period.

Furthermore, as the case of the Red Cross and the North Korean repatriation project of the 1950s and '60s illustrated, the lack of normative support for former colonial nations and the limited penetration of robust human rights norms made displaced colonial migrants vulnerable to the manipulations by powerful actors. Because of the Cold War fracture as well as the absence of larger normative supports for their claim, Korean colonial migrants could not exert enough normative pressure to constrain the Japanese government's treatment of colonial migrants in the postwar context. As the case of the International Committee of the Red Cross and the Japanese Red Cross Society illustrated, supranational institutions in the mid-twentieth century did not yet have strong influence over the internal affairs in each nation-state. This point becomes more noticeable when we compare the postwar period to the global period in the next chapter, when the presence of globalized normative support for the subaltern claims reinvigorated the minority's social movement, exerted significant pressure on the public and policy debate, and thereby affected its outcome.

This chapter also highlighted the United States' decisive role in keeping the colonial legacy alive and well in postwar Japan. The mounting Cold War tensions in Asia prompted the United States to reverse its course: instead of being a guardian for civic and democratic values and peace, they rearmed Japan and allowed the return of conservative politicians to the Cabinet. In combination, these circumstances allowed postwar Japan to adopt exclusive immigration policies under the direct supervision of the United States and to further marginalize Koreans in their society without facing any international scrutiny. These empirical facts show that citizenship and immigration policies are *not* simply the result of one particular state's interests or a production of elite engineering within a single country. Rather, such policies are the result of a clash of conflicting interests between involved states, nonstate actors, and subaltern populations who were also keenly influenced by the larger political context at a given historical juncture.

The postwar Korean community's experience didn't follow the pattern predicted by the existing theory, which suggests that the institutionalization of racial and ethnic categories by the state could facilitate solidarity among the marginalized (Espiritu 1992; Marx 1997). Although Koreans strongly protested the ban on ethnic education in Japan just after World War II, the threat of deportation had a chilling effect on that mobilization effort. The division of the Korean peninsula after the outbreak of the Korean War also divided the Korean community in Japan and severely weakened its solidarity. Hence, the 1952 act's definitive stripping of Koreans' Japanese citizenship did not reinvigorate the unified social movement, as previous scholarly work had predicted.

Postwar Japan's exclusion of Koreans occurred during the process of liberalization and democratization of the Japanese state by the American-led SCAP. This directly echoes earlier work by scholars that also reveals the democratic origin of racist immigration policies in other countries (FitzGerald and Cook-Martín 2014; Ngai 2004; Paul 1997). The very different dynamics underlying the development of the new exclusionary citizenship in Japan after World War II involved the same set of forces as the dynamics that produced the inclusive policies of the Japanese Empire. During the colonial and imperial period, the impulse for inclusion was animated by the need to absorb different groups into its empire during colonial expansion. After World War II, the impulse for exclusion originated in the need to reabsorb large numbers of Japanese returnees (i.e., troops and administrators) from the shrunken empire. In both cases, protests by domestic minorities—particularly Koreans—frustrated initial policies and led to evolving and sometimes contradictory administrative policies as the government both offered concessions to the resistance and developed new devices for more effective social control. And in both cases, the jagged policy path was decisively affected by the exogenous dynamics of Japan's status in world society, especially in relation to the Western powers. During the imperial era, both the experience of European powers and their competition for dominance in East Asia shaped Japanese policy. During the postwar period, the confrontation with the communist world impacted initial postures and then became an ongoing factor as

Koreans in Japan made their own connections to communism, both in guiding their internal political philosophy and in relating to the divided Korea peninsula.

Thus, the same nexus of forces—the larger policy currents of the state and the elites, the subaltern actors' organizing efforts, and the placement of the nation-states within world society—operated in very different combinations during the postwar period, as compared to the imperial period. The path that postwar Japan took contrasts with those of other empires, such as Britain or France. Like Japan, those European empires also racialized and excluded their colonial subjects in practice, while they continued to recognize them as British or French citizens. Yet as a war-defeated nation whose economy was at rock bottom, Japan could not afford to retain its colonies; it also could not continue to recognize them as its citizens. On the other hand, unlike Germany, which also lost the war, Japan was protected by the United States from demands for war reparations by its former colonies and from international criticism against its discriminatory treatment of colonial migrants because of America's own political interests in Far East Asia. This allowed the postwar Japanese government to introduce exclusive citizenship and immigration policies.

Japan's exclusive citizenship and immigration policies were eventually buttressed by a new national self-image as a homogeneous nation, elaborated and analyzed in postwar Japanese intellectual and political discourses. As in the imperial period, intellectuals in postwar Japan sought compelling narratives for the history of Japan so that they could find an appropriate role and create goals for postwar Japan to pursue. They also carried this endeavor sensitively, corresponding to the external geopolitical context in which they found themselves. However, in the new geopolitical circumstances in which Cold War bifurcation expanded, the influence of the United States hovered over the nation, and voices demanding colonial independence echoed throughout the world, the concept of multiculturalism or pan-Asianism hardly carried positive connotations for many postwar intellectuals in Japan. In the shadow of bitter defeat, the idea of a hybrid and multiethnic nation was nothing but a dark legacy of a militarist past for many Japanese intellectuals. A return to ethnic nationalism and an embrace of mono-ethnic nationhood fit with Japan's pressing need to rebuild its nation.

In the 1960s, numerous scholarly works argued that the unique Japanese culture made it impossible for any non-Japanese person to

126   *Chapter 3*

be assimilated, even those who, like the Korean colonial migrants, were raised in Japan and educated in its language (Befu 2001; Yoshino 1999). This socially constructed national self-image gradually penetrated into the furthest corners of economic, political, cultural, and educational institutions in Japanese society, reinforcing the exclusive mode of citizenship and immigration policies in Japan and reproducing systematic marginalization against Koreans and other noncitizens. This myth then allowed Japan to mask the legacy of colonial oppression against Koreans in Japan, embedded in its laws and societal structure, while also rationalizing these dynamics as a reflection of a culture derived from Japan's ethno-racial homogeneity. The next chapter will discuss how the legacy of colonialism was brought to bear in the global arena by a new generation of dissenting Korean activists in Japan.

Chapter Four

THE FIGHT FOR SOCIAL JUSTICE AND HUMAN RIGHTS

Given Japan's relatively small foreign population for a few decades following World War II, it might seem on the face of it that postwar Japan succeeded in transforming from a pan-Asian hybrid empire into a homogeneous nation-state. Lawmakers assumed that these Koreans would either return to their homelands or become naturalized Japanese when the state introduced a series of new immigration and citizenship laws in postwar Japan (Suzuki 1966).[1] In fact, many Koreans were already assimilated into Japanese culture by the time the war was over, due to the state's colonial policies, which sought to suppress Korean culture. Many Koreans were sent to Japanese schools to learn the Japanese language after the forced closure of their ethnic schools. Racism discouraged them from embracing their Korean identity publicly, as doing so would lead to constant discrimination, bullying, and harassment by neighbors, coworkers, teachers, and peers. Koreans were supposed to remain "invisible" and "silent" inside the homogeneous nation.[2] Yet many Koreans neither returned to their divided homeland nor became invisible and remained silent. Instead, they not only survived structural racism but also fought back. This chapter traces the trajectory of their fights for justice from the 1970s on. It shows how their voices of dissent have reached global audiences since the 1980s, and how advocacy on their behalf by their ancestral homeland state, South Korea, and supranational institutions such as the UN forced the Japanese state to recognize the legitimacy of their claim-making.

Today many Koreans in Japan have the most stable legal status among noncitizens in Japan, and they enjoy a series of citizenship rights that were previously denied. This liberalized extension of citizenship rights to noncitizens has been cited as a sign of emerging postnational conceptions of citizenship (Jacobson 1996; Sassen 2002; Soysal 1994). In Europe, the driving forces behind extending citizenship rights to noncitizens, or the "decoupling" of citizenship and nationhood, have usually been based on strong public support for diversity initiatives and a large presence of foreign populations in a society. However, neither of these factors is present in contemporary Japanese society. The total population of registered noncitizens in Japan gradually increased in the 1980s and grew to over 1 million by 1990. By 2005, it had risen to over 2 million people. The number of registered noncitizens temporarily decreased during the 2008 Great Recession and again in 2021 due to pandemic-related border restrictions.[3] However, it continued to increase again to over 2.9 million registered noncitizens, or about 2.4 percent of the total population, in 2022.[4] Chinese individuals make up the largest group of registered noncitizens in Japan in 2022, followed by Vietnamese, Koreans (North and South Korea), Filipinos, and Brazilians. It is important to note that Chinese individuals in

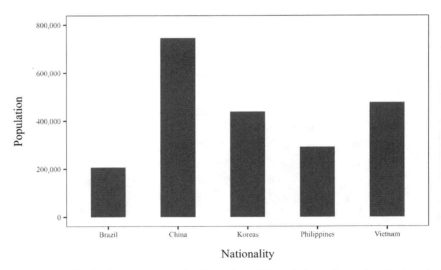

Figure 4.1. The five largest groups of registered noncitizens in Japan by nationality, based on the statistics on foreign residents in Japan (or *zairyū gaikokujin tōkei*) collected in June 2022 and published in December 2022 by the Ministry of Justice, Immigration Service Agency in Japan or Hōmushō Shutsunyūkoku Zairyū Kanrichō (2022a).

figure 4.1 are people from the People's Republic of China (PRC); the figure does not include individuals from Taiwan. Furthermore, figure 4.1 includes both North and South Koreans, but only 6 percent of the Koreans are North Korean. Approximately 62 percent of all Koreans in this data are Special Permanent Residents.

While the steady increase of immigrants in Japan is notable, in comparison with other industrialized countries—especially other G7 countries—this figure is strikingly low (see figure 4.2). Even with a sharp increase in the immigrant population and an economic dependency on immigrant labor, the Japanese government and its people do not view themselves as a country of immigrants.

The state continues to restrict the flow of newly arrived immigrants, especially unskilled workers, and the duration of their residency in ways that are similar to how it handled colonial migrants from Korea and Taiwan many decades ago. Japan's relatively small immigrant population is repeatedly cited by the popular media and lawmakers to reify the image of Japan as an "ethno-racially homogeneous nation" that is based on one ethnic and racial population and culture. This statistic is also often used to justify restrictive treatment toward immigrants and noncitizen residents in Japanese society. As I noted at

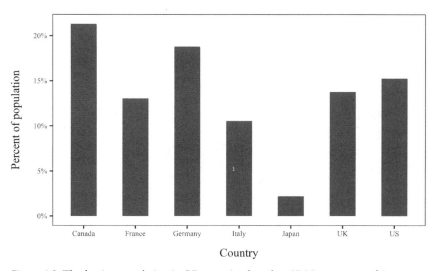

Figure 4.2. The foreign population in G7 countries, based on UN Department of Economic and Social Affairs, Population Division 2020. The UN's data set presents an estimate of international migrants (the definition of which varies from one country to another) based on official statistics published by each nation-state.

130 *Chapter 4*

the beginning of this book, few problematize the fact that the Japanese government's census does not collect data about one's ethnic or racial background or identity.

In Japan, despite continued restrictive immigration policies and an image of being a homogeneous nation, there has also been a notable extension of citizenship rights to non-Japanese populations, especially Koreans. While recent legal reforms give the impression that Japan is following the global trend of extending citizenship rights to noncitizens, a closer examination of the practices of citizenship and immigration laws reveals that the liberal extension of citizenship rights is not evenly applied to all noncitizens. The extension is, instead, limited to Special Permanent Residents (Tokubetsu Eijyūsha), who are Korean and Taiwanese colonial migrants and their descendants. Thus, what is transpiring in contemporary Japanese society seems perplexing and poses an important question to ponder: How did Koreans end up enjoying a set of numerous citizenship rights without becoming naturalized Japanese citizens in today's Japan?

This chapter explains how the interplay of the same three sets of forces—the larger policy currents of the state and the elites vis-à-vis state's policymaking process, subaltern mobilization against the state's policies, and the placement of countries within world society— triggered a series of citizenship and immigration policy changes, especially for colonial migrants and their descendants in the new context of globalization. As I explained in chapter 1, this book calls the decades from the 1970s on the "global context" and applies a sociological concept of world society and world culture (Meyer 2010; Meyer, Boli et al. 1997) to understand the impact of globalized norms of human rights on Koreans' fight for social justice. This context warrants separate analytical attention, as distinctive new features began to emerge and influence the interactive dynamics between the three key forces under discussion. Since the 1970s, Japan's economic, security and political interests in world society began to gradually shift as its economy became increasingly more competitive in the global market. We also observe an increasing demand for restorative justice for the colonial past and its legacy from Japan's former colonies as well as from colonial migrants and their descendants, especially in the 1990s.

This chapter analyzes how these forces interact with one another in the new context of globalization, comparing and contrasting these interactions with those of past historical contexts. Specifically, it examines the impact of supranational institutions, primarily the United

Nations, as well as globalized norms of colonial reparations and human rights on the interactions among these three forces. This chapter examines these dynamics alongside the ones examined in the previous two contexts, and discusses the theoretical implications of the parallels and differences in the process of transforming citizenship and immigration policies within these three distinctive historical and geopolitical contexts. By comparing these three contexts, chapter 4 sheds new light on globalization's impact on the process of remaking nationhood, citizenship, and migration policies in societies.

The next section explains the complexities of the legal status of Koreans in Japan and how their self-identification has shifted gradually as their legal status has changed. This frequently overlooked detail is actually a key element in understanding the shift in their framing and their strategies of collective resistance. The rest of the chapter also pays attention to changes within Japanese society—namely, how people in Japan began to understand the issues of Koreans' struggles and marginalization. These two changes manifested in the strong alliance formed between Korean and Japanese activists in the time period covered in this chapter. The chapter closes by examining the impact of shifting power dynamics in East Asia and world society on Japanese state's attitude and policies concerning citizenship, migration, and Koreans' demands.

From Deportable Aliens to "Privileged" Special Permanent Resident Aliens

As discussed in an earlier chapter, the Japanese citizenship status of colonial migrants from Korea and Taiwan was unilaterally revoked by the Japanese government at the time of the San Francisco Peace Treaty. After this unilateral revocation, these colonial migrants were made to be noncitizens or aliens (*gaikokujin*) who were subject to postwar Japan's immigration laws. However, the process of transforming them from citizens into alien residents was anything but simple. Immigration law normally requires immigrants to hold a passport issued by their homeland's sovereign state and a visa issued by a consulate abroad. However, colonial migrants had neither, because they entered Japan as imperial citizens and had already been living in Japan. Their homeland lost its sovereignty due to Japan's colonization; thus, there was no international border for them to cross with a visa. Therefore, the Japanese government needed to create a separate law to specify

132   *Chapter 4*

the conditions under which it could recognize Koreans and Taiwanese' residency status in Japan. That law was the "Act on Measures concerning Orders Related to the Ministry of Foreign Affairs Pursuant to the Imperial Ordinance on Orders Issued Incidental to Acceptance of the Potsdam Declaration No. 126-2-6," known simply as Act No. 126 (Hōritsu 126 Gō). This law was enforced on April 28, 1952, the same day the San Francisco Peace Treaty was signed.

Koreans were given "temporal residency status without any fixed term" by Act No. 126 until their citizenship status could be clearly specified.[5] In other words, the law stipulated that those who had lost their Japanese citizenship due to the 1952 peace treaty and who had been living in Japan prior to September 2, 1945, including children born between September 3, 1945, and the enforcement of the law on April 28, 1952, could stay in Japan until their residency status was adjudicated. This would consequently determine how long they were allowed to stay in Japan (Park 1995, 2006). This temporary status is sometimes referred to with the acronym "Act No. 126 status." Act No. 126 status did not require an annual renewal, nor did it specify the duration of residency. However, there were a significant number of Koreans who did not qualify for this temporary residency—including those who had been living in Japan before September 2, 1945, but who left Japan temporarily and reentered Japan after that date. Because no noncitizen was technically allowed to enter Japan after September 2, 1945, all reentries of Koreans who had been living in Japan prior to the end of the war but who just happened to have temporarily left mainland of Japan were considered "illegal or unauthorized." Koreans who had made "illegal or unauthorized entries" were excluded from the provisions of Act No. 126 and became subject to detention and deportation when discovered. As a result of Act No. 126, the number of detainees in the Ōmura Detention Center near Nagasaki increased steadfastly.

Act No. 126 created a haphazard legal limbo for many colonial migrants. Colonial migrants who were deemed to have entered Japan "illegally" were given a different status, called Tokubetsu Zairyū, or Special Residency Status. Unlike Act No. 126 status, Special Residency Status had a fixed term and required a renewal every few years. Also, those children and grandchildren of colonial migrants who were born after the enforcement of Act No. 126 (on April 28, 1952) were also excluded from this provision and were given other separate residency statuses in Japan: Tokutei Zairyū, or Specific Status, was issued for children of Act No. 126 residents, and Tokubetsu Zairyū, or Special Status, was issued for grandchildren of Act No. 126 residents. In short, those who fell outside the purview of Act No. 126 ended up having a more precarious residency status in Japan. Considering that significant numbers of Koreans went back and forth between the metropole and their colonial homeland due to familial ties, such precarious statuses diminished the quality of lives for many Korean colonial migrants in Japan. As a result of the different residency statuses assigned to Koreans, it was fairly common to have two or three different types of residency status—some permanent and some fixed-term residencies—within the same Korean family at that time.[6] Consequently, many Koreans and their families had to live with the constant fear of detention and deportation, which essentially meant family separation.

The 1965 treaty between the Japanese and South Korean governments was supposed to resolve this issue of overly complicated residency statuses among Koreans in Japan. Per the agreement of the 1965 bilateral treaty, the Japanese government agreed to extend Kyōtei Eijyūken (Treaty-Based Permanent Residency)—the more secure legal status with reduced risk of deportation—to those Koreans who identified themselves as South Koreans and who applied for this permanent residency status.[7] The status could be passed to children of treaty-based permanent residents, and it was to be determined twenty-five years from 1965 whether this status would continue and be passed on to the Korean colonial migrants' grandchildren.

As mentioned in the previous chapter, this treaty triggered a schism between those who self-identified as South Korean and as North Korean in Japan; those who identified with and supported the North Korean regime did not benefit from the treaty-based residency status. This resulted in different experiences of legal marginality and precarity among Koreans in Japan. In 1981, the Japanese government reformed its immigration laws and introduced different types of permanent residency statuses. First they introduced Tokurei Eijyūken (Special Case Permanent Residency) and Ippan Eijyūken (Regular Permanent Residency). With this reform, all colonial migrants and their descendants (the subjects of Act No. 126), regardless of nationality, could obtain Special Case Permanent Residency in Japan if they applied for that status between January 1, 1982, and December 31, 1986. Those Koreans who did not apply for Treaty-Based Special Residency, as well as Chinese immigrants who came to Japan during the colonial period, were extended Regular Permanent Residency status. However,

134 *Chapter 4*

Table 1. Koreans' Legal Statuses in Japan since 1952

Year	Status types of Koreans in postwar Japan	Who qualified	Duration
1952–1991	Act No. 126	Colonial migrants from Korea and Taiwan who were already living and born in Japan before or on Sept. 2, 1952	Unspecified
	Specific Residency (Tokutei Zairyū)	Children of colonial migrants with Act No. 126 status who were born on or after Apr. 29, 1952	3 years
	Special Residency (Tokubetsu Zairyū)	Grandchildren of colonial migrants with Act No. 126 status and/or a child of Tokutei Zairyū; those who lost Act No. 126 status and/or made irregular entries to Japan	Up to 3 years
1951–1991	Regular Permanent Residency (Ippan Eijyū)	Colonial migrants and their descendants who did not qualify for other statuses	Unspecified
1965–1991	Treaty-Based Permanent Residency (Kyōtei Eijyū)	South Korean colonial migrants and their children with Act No. 126 status	Unspecified
1981	Special Case Permanent Residency (Tokurei Eijyū)	All colonial migrants and their children who applied for this status, regardless of nationality	Unspecified
1991	Special Permanent Residency (Tokubetsu Eijyū)	All colonial migrants and their descendants who lost Japanese citizenship due to the San Francisco Peace Treaty	Unspecified

Note: A majority of colonial migrants and their descendants had statuses described in this table, while a very small number held different statuses not listed in this table. See Osaka Zainichi Chōsenjin no Jinken o Mamorukai 1978; Yamada and Park 1991.

compared to the Treaty-Based Special Permanent Residency that only South Koreans were qualified to obtain, Regular Permanent Residency, or Ippan Eijyūken, was less secure in terms of deportation risk.

This heterogeneity in legal status among colonial migrants and their descendants was resolved in 1991, when the Japanese and South Korean states made another agreement to further secure the legal status of Koreans in Japan.[8] This prompted the introduction of a new permanent residency status, Tokubetsu Eijyūken (Special Permanent

Residency), which was more secure than previous categories of permanent residency in Japan's postwar immigration legal history had been. This Special Permanent Residency was extended to all Korean and Taiwanese colonial migrants and their descendants—regardless of current or previous legal status in Japan or citizenship status or the lack thereof—who had lost their Japanese imperial citizenship status at the time of the San Francisco Peace Treaty. With this reform in 1991, all colonial migrants from Korea and Taiwan and their descendants in Japan—regardless of citizenship status—became "Special Permanent Residents of Japan" who would enjoy the most secure legal status among noncitizens in Japan. (For an overview of the types of legal status for Koreans in Japan since 1952, see table 1.)

While a more secure legal status was a welcome outcome for Koreans in Japan, this wasn't necessarily a sign of the declining significance of ethno-racism against Koreans or other non-Japanese residents in Japan. The improvement of Koreans' rights and status was met with heightened attacks from right-wing racist Japanese groups and individuals. Hate speech on the street and online remains prevalent, and racially motivated violent attacks against Koreans continues in Japanese society. The following section discusses how overt and covert racism have impacted Koreans' self-identification in Japan as well as how they perceive Japanese society. Understanding their self-identification is an important step to understanding how their collective activism changed since the 1970s and managed to effect a series of changes in Japan's citizenship and immigration policies in the late twentieth century.

Ethno-Racial Formation in Japan and Citizenship as an Identity Signifier

As with their legal status, Koreans' sense of self is hardly monolithic or homogeneous. In the 1990s, Japanese sociologist Fukuoka Yasunori (1993) interviewed Korean youths and classified their self-identification into several neatly delineated types and displayed those types in a diagram (see Fukuoka and Kim 1997). His finding—that young Koreans develop diverse self-understandings depending on social relations and upbringing—was neither distinct nor novel as a sociological finding, but it did receive public attention. And the very fact that a Japanese sociologist finally created a basic study of Koreans' self-identification in the late twentieth century, several decades

136 *Chapter 4*

after Koreans came to Japan, demonstrates in and of itself the general lack of scholarly and public interest and understanding of Koreans in Japan, despite their persistent presence in society.[9]

Despite such confirmed diversity, Koreans are often referred to by a few uniform labels in today's public and intellectual discourses, such as "Zainichi," "Zainichi Kankokujin/Chōsenjin" (South and North Koreans), or "Zainichi Korian" (Korean). The term "Zainichi" literally means "Resident Koreans in Japan" or "Koreans Living in Japan," and today it is usually used to refer to colonial migrants and their descendants in Japan. As I explained in the first chapter, this book intentionally avoided this now-popular label because it could obscure the complex sociohistorical processes in which their diverse self-identification and legal statuses developed in Japanese society, the very processes that this book is capturing. Whether intentional or not, such obscuring could then run the risk of essentializing this diverse group of people—the antithesis of my goal. Instead of using a pervasive term to uniformly address a diverse group for the sake of pragmatism or convenience, I pay close attention to the very sociohistorical process in which a diverse sense of self had developed among Koreans in Japan, and how this diverse sense of self was intimately connected to the ways in which Korean activists and their allies challenged Japan's nationhood and its citizenship and immigration policies since the 1970s.[10]

Today most Koreans with Tokubetsu Eijyūken (Special Permanent Residency Status) are descendants of colonial migrants from Korea who were born and raised in Japan. Many do not speak the Korean language well or at all and have never been to or lived in either of the two Koreas, and quite a few use only Japanese names in their daily lives. Thus, unless they "come out of the closet" about their Korean identity, they could easily pass as Japanese. To avoid overt racism, some Koreans do pass as Japanese in their everyday life. However, this does not mean that their ethnic and racial background is "optional" for Koreans in Japan. Similar to how race and ethnicity are mandatory for minority groups while they are optional for the White majority in the United States, as articulated by sociologist Mary Waters (1990), they are also "mandatory" for Koreans in Japan. Many Koreans have long argued that even if they became assimilated or naturalized, they would still be considered "perpetual foreigners" whose presence in Japanese society is constantly questioned and contested. The perpetual foreigner syndrome is not unique to Koreans in Japan, as it has been documented for minorities in other countries, most notably Asian Americans (Zhou and Ocampo 2016). The number of Koreans who have become naturalized Japanese citizens is ongoing, a trend often mistakenly understood as showing the "declining significance" of ethno-raciality for Koreans in Japan. Yet a significant number of Koreans still continue to maintain permanent residency status and thus do not have Japanese citizenship. This often leads to one of the most commonly asked questions about Koreans in Japan: "Why don't Koreans become naturalized Japanese citizens?"

For those who grew up in societies that adopt the jus soli principle, in which citizenship is treated as a birthright, naturalization seems like a logical and rational practice for immigrants and refugees who settle in the country of their residence without any intention of returning to their ancestral homelands. Thus, retaining their ancestral homeland's citizenship over multiple generations in lieu of citizenship from the country of their permanent residence often appears an odd and irrational practice, especially if this means that they cannot enjoy equal rights, including suffrage. For many Koreans in Japan, however, choosing to retain the citizenship of their ancestral homelands is just as logical as choosing to become naturalized Japanese.

Unfortunately, however, Koreans' retention of their Korean citizenship in Japan is often portrayed in a binary fashion in public discourse, as either a reflection of their irrational, emotional sense of nationalism or as a reactionary sense of victimhood against the dominant myth of Japanese homogeneity. Such a binary categorization lacks the sociological imagination evident in more recent sociological work, which reveals that the nature of identity is far more strategic and complex (Lee 2021; Sasaki 2001, 2006; Tai 2002). To adequately understand this aspect, we should rely on sociological perspectives that are neither Anglo- nor Euro-centric. In other words, we should avoid applying perspectives based on experiences in Western countries alone, where birthright citizenship and dual citizenship are commonly accepted norms. Otherwise, we implicitly treat experiences in those regions as a standard and the rest as anomalies or deviations. Instead, we must first pay attention to the particular sociopolitical and legal circumstances in which Koreans in Japan have developed a conceptual understanding of their self, rights, and duties.

To this end, the relational approach in sociological theories on race, ethnicity, and citizenship is useful. European anthropologists Fredrik Barth ([1969] 1998) and Richard Jenkins (1994) explained decades ago that group boundaries are constructed through social encounters and interactions between groups who decide to perceive each other distinctively.[11] Their approach was later coined the "relational approach" among social scientists. Sociologist Charles Tilly (1998) applied the relational approach to explain how socially constructed categories emerge from our social relations, become institutionalized, and are then used to justify unequal and unjust allocations of scarce resources between groups in societies, resulting in what he called "durable inequality." Citizenship is a key institution for what sociologists call "social closure"—the practice of drawing boundaries based on imagined differences in order to monopolize material or nonmaterial resources for one's own group while excluding others from accessing them. Political scientist Anthony Marx (1997, 5) notes that citizenship "selectively allocates distinct civil, political, and economic rights, reinforcing a sense of commonality and loyalty among those included." Marx (1997, 5) adds that "by specifying to whom citizenship applies, states also define those outside the community of citizens, who then live within the state as objects of domination."

As we saw in previous chapters, citizenship serves as a key institution for social closure in Japan. Citizenship and nationhood were decoupled and recoupled throughout the course of the twentieth century in Japanese society. In the colonial period, the imperial state of Japan decoupled citizenship from nationality, which they defined ethno-racially, and established an empire that was externally expansive and inclusive while also being internally exploitative and exclusive. In the postwar period, lawmakers and their allies closely coupled citizenship and nationhood to establish an externally and internally exclusive democratic nation-state. In both historical junctures, citizenship and other institutions, such as the family registry or *koseki,* were used to demarcate subtle but discernible boundaries between Koreans and the Japanese.

Over time, people in society internalized and normalized such boundaries and applied them in order to make sense of the characters, skills, and practices of those they considered outsiders or others. Scholarly literature inside and outside Japan that essentialized an ethos of Japanese national character supplied a plentiful lexicon to verbalize and express such boundaries, as other scholars have noted (Befu 2001; Selinger 2019). In this process, minority groups such as Koreans in Japan were "ethno-racialized": in other words, they are now seen as groups that are culturally and physically distinct from the majority. Commonly used expressions like "contaminating blood" (*chi ga kegareru*) and "mixing blood" (*konketsu*) to describe marriage between Japanese and non-Japanese people and the children born from such a union clearly indicate that invisible phenotype-linked factors such as "blood" have played an important role in facilitating the imagined boundaries between Japanese and Koreans or other marginalized populations in Japanese society (Yoshino 1999). This point was explicitly displayed in hate mail targeting Korean fingerprint objectors. Here is an example of the vitriol that Koreans faced: "Follow Japanese law and surrender your fingerprint. If you want to refuse it, then go back to Korea, you idiot. You Koreans, stop acting so entitled in our country. You contaminate our Japanese blood."[12]

Because there are no visible cultural and phenotypical differences between Japanese and Koreans in Japan, it became important for both Japanese and Koreans to rely on something more tangible and visible, such as citizenship and the family registry, to reify the imagined differences between them. The fact that the Japanese state continues to maintain a strict jus sanguinis principle in citizenship and immigration statutes (where legal statutes are passed through blood lineage) further facilitates the conceptual overlap between ethno-racialized self-identification and citizenship statutes in Japanese society.

What transpired in twentieth-century Japan is similar to what Omi and Winant ([1986] 2014) describe in their work on racial formation. But in the case of Japanese society, the formation was not just racial but ethno-racial: both race and ethnicity simultaneously became an autonomous field of social conflict, political organization, and cultural/ideological meaning that was at play. As Omi and Winant ([1986] 2014) explain in their theory of racial formation, race—a socially constructed category—operates at both micro and macro levels. At the micro level, it influences individual identity formation, while at the macro level, it contributes to collective social structures. When these two levels interact or when individuals mobilize and respond to structural injustice, Omi and Winant ([1986] 2014) argue that a social movement is formed in a society. This dynamic was also noted in Marx's (1997, 5) aforementioned comparative work on race and nation:

> Such imposed exclusion inadvertently may serve as a unifying issue, mobilizing the excluded group to seek inclusion in the polity as a central popular aspiration. Gradual expansion of citizenship is then gained

140 Chapter 4

through protracted contestation. The goal of gaining citizenship rights, which were not originally universal, thus has often served as a frame for mobilization. Extending a provocative analogy, groups use their voice to overcome their enduring and forced exit from the polity.

The same dynamic can be observed among Koreans in Japan in the 1970s and 1980s (Katō 2008, 28). Though many Japan-born Koreans identify more closely with Japanese society than their homelands, many second- and third-generation Koreans became keenly aware of the structural barriers to opportunities in Japanese society, as discussed later in this chapter. They also felt stigmatized and struggled with a sense of self-hatred as they faced both subtle and overt racism from peers and teachers. This point was illustrated in the following recollections of Kim Kyung-Duk (1995, 56), a renowned Korean attorney and activist in Japan. He was born in Japan as a second-generation Korean in 1949 in Wakayama Prefecture. He fought to obtain eligibility for a legal license and became the first noncitizen licensed attorney in Japan. He wrote this about his childhood experience of ethno-racism from his teacher and peers:

> When I was little, I could not understand either the context behind Koreans' poverty and their restless lifestyles or the injustice of Japanese discrimination. All I wanted to do was to escape from everything associated with Koreans, whom the Japanese despise so deeply. This feeling intensified after I entered elementary school. Simply because I am Korean, an older student physically assaulted me whenever he was with me at school. I don't know why but he just kept scratching my face with so much hatred and contempt. . . .
>
> There was a schoolteacher who . . . criticize[d] Koreans throughout class and told all the students in our classroom that before the end of the war, Japanese treated Koreans equally, but after the war, Koreans forgot what they owed the Japanese and acted as if they had defeated Japan, even though they weren't at war with Japanese.

For much of the latter half of the twentieth century, it was not uncommon for Koreans such as Kim Kyung-Duk to hold such sentiments about their positionality in Japanese society (Sasaki and Wagatsuma 1981). A sense of shame, stigma, self-hatred, and confusion was pervasive among Koreans in Japan. These sentiments continue to exist today, though perhaps to a different degree than for generations past, because the public has begun to understand more about the issues surrounding this injustice and some Korean celebrities have begun to publicly embrace their identity.

The majority of Koreans today attended Japanese schools instead of ethnic schools. Thus, they barely had a chance to learn their own history of colonialism and colonial displacement, as this history was rarely discussed or taught in the Japanese schools that many of them attended. Deep down, many recognized a sense of injustice for what they faced in their day-to-day lives in Japanese society. As they grew older and learned for themselves about colonial history, they became aware that they were shunned from various job opportunities not simply because of their noncitizen status but also because of the colonial legacy that led to institutionalized forms of exclusion and discrimination against them. Unlike racialized minorities in the United States and elsewhere, Koreans in Japan could not rely on visible phenotypical identity signifiers such as skin color, hair texture, facial features, or stature to delineate their status and to embrace their identity as a minority. Nor could they rely on cultural identity signifiers such as languages and names. Under circumstances where visible identity signifiers are not readily available, citizenship or color of passport became a discernible identity signifier to express their distinct sense of self. And gaining citizenship rights became a frame for mobilization for many Koreans in Japan—an important tool for collective action (Benford and Snow 2000; Snow et al. 1986).

Their non-Japanese citizenship epitomized the complex history of unjust colonial exploitation and its legacy. It also served as the common ground where the Korean minority in Japan could meet, regardless of differing political affiliations—with North or South Korea—or demographic differences such as gender, class, cities of residence, and religion. Thus, citizenship functioned not just as a legal status or a bundle of rights and duties but also as a significant source of identity and group solidarity—just as skin color or religious symbols did for oppressed groups elsewhere. The different color of their passports symbolized the imagined difference in their blood, which was cited and used to separate them from Japanese people. This point was succinctly summarized in an opinion expressed by renowned Korean historian Kang Jae-eun: "The majority of our fellow Japan-born Koreans rely on [Korean] citizenship as a basis for ethnic identity because they have lost other ethnic traits such as cultural lifestyle. In other words, citizenship is the last fort standing to protect their ethnic identity against forces of

142   *Chapter 4*

assimilation and absorption into mono-ethnic Japan. It is also the precious legacy that the first-generation [Koreans] have protected."[13]

The next section discusses how Koreans framed citizenship-based exclusion as ethno-racial oppression against them and started a social movement to fight back. Then they began to shift their frame from an identity-based claim to one of universal human rights. This allowed further mobilization and became fuel to expand citizenship rights in Japan for Koreans and other noncitizens through the 1990s.

FROM PARTICULAR NATIONHOOD TO UNIVERSAL PERSONHOOD

In the 1970s, a new generation of Koreans in Japan—in collaboration with sympathetic Japanese citizen activists—began to mobilize and protest against the discrimination they faced in Japanese society, and they won critical legal battles (Shin and Tsutsui 2007). Their strategies, framing, participants, and claims differed from those of previous social movements among Koreans; more importantly, their activism was getting more respect and attention from both within and outside Japanese society. The most notable contrast from previous periods was that, for the first time, their movements led to a series of significant changes in Japan's immigration and citizenship laws. Minority organizational newsletters and petitions demonstrate that the globalized concept of human rights contributed significantly to the emergence of renewed social movements among Koreans and the Japanese. Supranational institutions such as the UN also critically influenced their claim-making and the movements' subsequent outcomes.

In contrast with earlier social movements, Korean social movements since the 1970s have put less emphasis on the relationship with their homeland states and more on unity between Koreans and non-Koreans (both Japanese citizens—including minority groups such as Burakumin, Okinawans, and Ainu—and other foreign nationals in Japan). This was evident in a job discrimination lawsuit brought against the Hitachi Corporation in 1970 by a young Korean male—the third Park mentioned at the beginning of this book—which marked the beginning of a new wave of social movements by Koreans.[14]

Although he did not know it at the time, Park Jongseok made history when he applied for a job in August 1970 in the software systems department at Hitachi Corporation in Japan. The eighteen-year-old Japan-born Korean male applied for the job using his Japanese name, the only name he had used up until that point in his life. (Using a Japanese name was a common practice among Koreans in Japan.) Instead of listing his ancestral origin for his family registry or *koseki* on his résumé, he wrote the name of the Japanese city where he was born. He took a screening test with Hitachi and passed it. The following month, he received an offer letter in which Hitachi asked him to bring a copy of his family registry record, certificate of diploma, and other items. Park contacted Hitachi and explained that he could not submit his family registry record because he was a Korean citizen and thus did not have a family registry record in Japan. He offered to bring his alien registration, which contained the equivalent information for non-Japanese citizens residing in Japan.

Matters quickly turned sour between Park and Hitachi. When Hitachi learned of his Korean origin, they rescinded their job offer, claiming that they would not hire any foreigners. They also accused Park Jongseok of lying about his citizenship on his résumé. Park Jongseok contested Hitachi's decision to rescind his job offer. In response to his questioning, Hitachi allegedly provoked Park to sue the company if he wanted to hold them accountable for alleged discrimination. Park filed a lawsuit against Hitachi Corporation, and this unknown young man's bold actions caught the public's attention (Nakahara 1993).

Park Jongseok's path and legal fight against Hitachi is a perfect window through which to observe how organically the alliance of different nonstate actors emerged. In October 1970, just two months before he filed a lawsuit against the Hitachi Corporation, Park reached out to several student activists from Keio University with whom he had had a chance encounter near Yokohama Station. These activists were leafletting to spread their views in opposition to the Vietnam War and government control of Koreans in Japan. Soon after this encounter, the student activists began to help in Park's fight for justice. With their help, Park filed a lawsuit against Hitachi in December of that same year. One of the lawyers who joined Park's legal team was twenty-five-year-old Sengoku Yoshito, who later became a key member of the Democratic Party and served as a Chief Cabinet Secretary under Prime Minister Kan Naoto in 2010. This was his first case as an attorney, and Sengoku and Park have remained friends. Choi Seungkoo, a Korean youth activist at Kawasaki Christian Church, learned about Park Jongseok's legal fight in a newspaper article and decided to join the cause. Choi prompted the pastor, Lee Inha, to form a "group for Mr. Park," or Paku kun o Kakomukai. This group of young student activists and attorneys organized to strategically plan for Park Jongseok's lawsuit against one of Japan's corporate giants. The group met many professional activists during this time period, including self-identified Buraku minority schoolteacher and activist Nishino Hideaki, who preached to them about the importance of fighting against discrimination (Fukuchi and Nishino 1970; Tsukajima 2016). Inspired and encouraged by this diverse group of activists, including other minorities such as the Burakumin, Park realized that he was not alone in this fight.

Park Jongseok's fight for justice was not smooth sailing, however. He met with criticism from other Korean groups. Neither Chongryon nor Mindan—two major Korean organizations in Japan at the time—initially supported his lawsuit, because both organizations regarded the case as promoting the cultural assimilation of Koreans in Japan. Supporting a second-generation Korean who wished to work for a Japanese company using a Japanese name instead of his "true" Korean name was not a cause that either of these organizations was eager to support (Kim 1978). These pro–North Korea and pro–South Korea organizations defined their identities in relation to their ancestral homelands, while Park and his supporters were trying to define his identity in relation to Japanese society. This criticism from fellow Koreans was disappointing to Park Jongseok. However, he remained committed and continued to receive support from many progressive and sympathetic Japanese activists, lawyers, teachers, and religious leaders (Choi 2006).

Prior to his trial, he and his supporters protested in front of Hitachi headquarters. One of his supporters, Choi Seungkoo (2006, 34–73), recalls that over two hundred people participated in this protest. It is apparent that Park's sense of justice matured through collective activism, as evident from his lengthy autobiographical statement of intent, presented to a judge, where he explains that he gave up applying for a competitive job because of his teacher's disparaging words:

> In my senior year of high school, I saw so many job ads on the school bulletin board. . . . Thinking that no Japanese company would hire Koreans like me, I looked for a job ad that did not require the *koseki* information. I found one foreign company, called "IBM computer," and asked my teacher if I could apply for a job there. Then my teacher coldly said, "It is not the kind of place where you could get in." (Paku kun o Kakomukai 1974, 248–249)

Social Justice and Human Rights

Then he explained why he used his Japanese name instead of his Korean name when he applied for a job at Hitachi, clearly defining his belonging in relation to Japanese society rather than in relation to a country he has not been to or lived in:

> Since I was born, I received a Japanese education. I continued to believe I was a member of Japanese society and that I could continue to live as one, . . . [and that] so long as I worked hard and earned good grades, I would be respected by Japanese [and have] some degree of experience that would give me confidence. . . .
>
> I was determined to apply for a job and started writing a résumé. Then I paused and realized that I had swiftly written down Arai Shōji—the real name I had used thus far. . . . Because I had never used any other name besides Arai Shōji, Park Jongseok was a very unfamiliar name to me.
>
> Then, in the "Legal Domicile" [honseki] section on my résumé, I did not know what to write. . . . I had repeatedly heard from my brothers and older classmates how large Japanese companies would not hire Koreans at all. . . . What if I couldn't even take a screening test just because I wrote "Korea" down there? I could not bear that thought. So to be safe, I wrote down my parents' address, the place of my birth, for "Legal Domicile." (Paku kun o Kakomukai 1974, 252–253)

Park Jongseok concluded his statement with a strong conviction and a sense of justice:

> I feel ashamed of my own ignorance, lack of self-awareness, and immaturity. However, as I have become aware of my own identity as a Korean, I find a confident conviction that it is the right decision to call out Hitachi Corporation's act of injustice. . . .
>
> I used to believe my parents were small. In fact, I hated them. But right now, I now realized how they endured discrimination and tried to raise all nine of us with as much love as possible. When I think of that, I cannot hold back my tears. For the sake of my aging parents, I must swear to become a human being who can fight against injustice relentlessly. (Paku kun o Kakomukai 1974, 260)

Park's defiant fight against Japanese corporations for justice and fairness promoted public awareness of the issue. Japanese media covered his story extensively. One of Park Jongseok's supporters, Pastor

146   *Chapter 4*

Lee Inha, was a vice chair of the Program to Combat Racism at the World Christian Conference, and he publicized the Hitachi Discrimination Case internationally (Paku kun o Kakomukai 1974, 33). Choi Seungkoo also shared the story of Park Jongseok with student activists in South Korea while he was studying at Seoul University.[15] South Korea's media also picked up the story of Park Jongseok's case, igniting a boycott against Hitachi products in South Korea. As public attention loomed large, this case was also discussed in the Japanese Parliament. In 1974, Park won the lawsuit, and his victory inspired many other Koreans who quietly suffered the same racism and discrimination. Following Park's case, similar lawsuits against Japanese companies surfaced, and mass protests against the local government for housing discrimination occurred sporadically across the nation (Park 1999).

As exemplified in Park's job discrimination case, throughout the 1970s, small pockets of local grassroots activism sprouted spontaneously among previously disconnected individuals from diverse backgrounds. Unlike the Korean organizations of the postwar period, these new activist organizations in the 1970s consisted of ordinary citizens—store owners, schoolteachers, doctors, housewives, senior citizens, and so on—most of whom were not full-time activists. Although many local Korean organizations emerged across the nation in early postwar Japan, the interests and political ideologies of the earlier organizations were far more fragmented than those in the 1970s and 1980s. Furthermore, while the early postwar Korean organizations comprised a relatively homogeneous group of individuals in terms of gender, age, class, education, religious background, and political orientation, the grassroots activist groups of the 1970s and 1980s were far more heterogeneous in terms of their demographic backgrounds. Despite this diversity, they were inspired by common ideals—to fight for ethno-racial injustice and promote the protection of human rights for noncitizen residents. They voluntarily and spontaneously came together without any central guiding force or figure to organize themselves and to fight for shared causes. This diverse grassroots effort would become even more salient in another notable collective action, this one against the fingerprint requirement of the Alien Registration Law.

Pastor Lee Inha, one of Park Jongseok's most emphatic supporters, led another grassroots organization called Mintōren. This group was also made up of diverse citizen activists with a shared sense of ethno-racial justice. Reviewing Mintōren organizational newsletters from this time signals a distinctive shift in their framing that helped

Social Justice and Human Rights   147

to unify these heterogeneous actors. Unlike activists in the imperial or postwar period, who used a nationalized framing, activists in this period began to use a broader framing to address problems of discrimination, hoping to appeal to both Korean and Japanese peoples. In other words, their social movement was no longer anchored in the language of national rights and tied to a specific nation; rather, it was tethered to conceptions of universal human rights that recentered the individual as deserving of equal treatment regardless of nationality status (Shin and Tsutsui 2007). This is evident in their first organizational newsletter, published in July 1975, in which they reflected on the victorious outcome of their movement against the Hitachi Corporation job discrimination case. "We learned [from the Hitachi discrimination case] that fighting against ethnic discrimination is always a collaborative effort between Japanese and Koreans in Japan. . . . Because the Hitachi Discrimination Struggle had a universal meaning for both Koreans and Japanese, we were able to appeal our cause to both Japanese and Koreans who wished to fight against ethnic discrimination."[16]

As in any social movement, it is not possible to isolate the exact moment or the first individual who started using a new framework, because collective ideas, norms, and beliefs often permeate society gradually. To be clear, the language of human rights (*jinken*)—rights that belong to universal personhood rather than particular nationhood—was used among a group of lawyers who worked on behalf of Koreans before the 1970s. However, the concept was much more pervasive in the global context than in the previous colonial context, as subaltern actors came to use it frequently. The language of human rights became a shared and common vocabulary among Korean activists and their allies during the global context.

Furthermore, activists who propelled the social movements that emerged during this period made claims that appealed to a sense of belonging in relation to Japanese society rather than their ancestral homeland (Katō 2008). This was another critical departure from the collective struggles of previous generations of Koreans. Mintōren was among the organizations that used universal human rights frames explicitly from the beginning, as we can see in one of the protest letters that it submitted to local governments refusing to provide welfare benefits to Koreans on the basis of their alien status: "The municipal government should take a humanitarian approach and eliminate all forms of institutional discrimination in order to allow Korean residents in Japan to live their life as human beings" (Minzoku Sabetsu to Tatakau Renraku Kyōgikai 1975, 12). Such grassroots activism led to some limited success at the local level, but it was not until the 1980s that the human rights frame became more pervasive and facilitated a national social movement with a large number of Korean and Japanese participants.

If Park Jongseok's fight was the advent of Koreans' self-awareness against systematic racism and of a universal human rights framework for Koreans, then Han Jongsok's fight against the fingerprinting requirement for alien registration in 1980 signaled the maturity of Korean social movements. In September 1980, Han Jongsok refused to comply with the fingerprinting requirement at a municipal office in Tokyo. Soon after Han Jongsok's refusal, the twenty-one-year-old Korean woman Choi Sun-ae Lois and her father, Korean Christian pastor Choi Changhwa, also refused fingerprinting (Choi 2000; figure 4.3). Like Han Jongsok, they publicly expressed their dissenting voice against this requirement. These individuals' fierce defiance reinvigorated other Koreans as well as other foreign residents in Japan and ignited a nationwide fingerprinting refusal movement in the 1980s, which led to numerous street demonstrations and protests.

Figure 4.3. Fingerprint objectors Pastor Choi Changhwa and his daughter Choi Sun-ae Lois speak to the press. Photo from the Korean Christian Church in Japan.

Social Justice and Human Rights 149

The fingerprinting practice was often understood by Koreans as one of the most salient symbols of the colonial legacy, because it invoked the negative Japanese treatment of Koreans as "criminals" or "outlaws" during the colonial and postwar periods. The fact that it used the same "rotating" method used for criminal suspects by police was humiliating for many Koreans. Any violations of this law and a refusal to submit one's fingerprint were subject to punishments such as less than one year of imprisonment and a fine of less than 30,000 yen (Ōnuma 1993, 480). Koreans' negative sentiments against this requirement were not entirely unfounded. As chapter 3 explained, this requirement was implemented in the Alien Registration Law in 1952, when the state viewed Koreans as a source of societal ill and disturbance. Given this history and the ways the law was being implemented, this fingerprint requirement carried more significance than just bureaucratic identification; it represented the unbroken continuity of Japanese colonial oppression against Koreans in Japan and Koreans' generational trauma.

As I discussed in the previous chapter, many Koreans fiercely opposed the Alien Registration Law since its enactment, out of fear that the law would further marginalize them. Nonetheless, their earlier mobilization against such policies did not receive strong support or attention from the general Japanese public or the international community. Their earlier activism was not able to abolish the fingerprinting practice; it could only prevent its practice from getting more restrictive. For example, prior protests managed to delay the actual implementation of the fingerprinting practice by three years (Kang 1994). In the 1960s, they also successfully prevented virtually all proposed revisions of the law that sought to tighten control over their lives through increased penalties and more burdensome registration procedures (Zainihon Daikanminkoku Mindan Chuō Honbu 1997).[17] But while many Koreans found this fingerprinting requirement humiliating, they reluctantly complied to avoid severe punishment.

The 1980s movement, on the other hand, was determined to get rid of this requirement entirely. After a few brave Koreans publicly defied the requirement in the 1980s despite the punishment and penalties, many Koreans in Japan fiercely mobilized against the fingerprinting requirement. This movement was supported by second- and third-generation Koreans in Japan who viewed themselves as a part of Japanese society rather than identifying with their ancestral homelands. These Korean activists and their allies advocated for all Koreans

150 *Chapter 4*

in Japan with the same conviction that they shared common interests regardless of political affiliation or legal status (Eun 1983). They began to reconceptualize the basis of their rights from particular nation-hood to universal personhood. Their concept of human rights, or *jinken ishiki,* allowed them to transform their activism from a movement about specific ethnic nationalism to a human rights movement. Their rallying cry was no longer "ethnic awareness" (*minzoku ishiki*) or "ethnic independence" (*minzoku dokuritsu*); now it was "human rights" (*jinken*). This helped to make their causes and claims relatable—for themselves, the Japanese, and the rest of the world.

Various testimonies by Korean fingerprinting objectors reveal the strong impact of the human rights discourse on the Koreans' finger-printing refusal movement. One notable objector was Han Jongsok, director of a Korean students' scholarship organization in Japan, who refused to surrender his fingerprints at the time of his registration re-newal in 1980 and was later sued by the Tokyo District Public Pros-ecutors Office for this violation of the Alien Registration Law. During his trial, Han succinctly and passionately explained to a judge why he refused to comply with the fingerprinting requirement:

> I have lived in Japan prior to the birth of Japanese postwar constitu-tion, and I live under Japan's constitution, just as Japanese people do. So long as the Japanese constitution recognizes equality and dignity under the law, and the persons elected as its representative under this constitution have signed the International Covenants of Human Rights, it is my conviction that my action would be proven legitimate by the constitution and the [International] Covenants of Human Rights. There-fore, mine is an act of self-defense; I simply defended my own human dignity and self-respect for my own ethnicity based on the constitution and the International Covenants of Human Rights. (Hitosashiyubi no Jiyū Henshū I'inkai 1984, 123–124)

Japanese jurist Iwasawa Yuji (1998) noted that Han Jongsok was not the only one maintaining that this fingerprint requirement violated Koreans' human rights; many Korean objectors charged with refus-ing to be fingerprinted argued before courts that this degrading and discriminatory fingerprinting practice violated Article 7 of the Inter-national Covenant on Civil and Political Rights (ICCPR), Article 14 of the Japanese constitution, and Articles 2 (1) and 26 of the ICCPR (Iwasawa 1998, 102). Other activists also referred to the idea of uni-

Social Justice and Human Rights 151

versal human rights to advocate for the abolishment of fingerprinting requirements. Christian activists also found that the universal human rights concept deeply resonated with their Christian values and thus actively participated in the movement (Terashima 1995). One of the most notable Christian activists was the Rev. John McIntosh from the Presbyterian Church of Canada, who came to serve Koreans in Japan in the 1960s. In solidarity with Koreans and in a spirit of social justice, Reverend McIntosh also refused the fingerprinting requirement and consequently faced a deportation order. Archival records on his fight for justice show the intense harassment and scrutiny he faced from the xenophobic racist public and authorities. It also shows a strong solidarity between Christian activists and Korean activists. Reverend McIntosh filed a lawsuit against the government for his deportation order and later won (McIntosh bokushi no zairyūken soshō o shien surukai 1987).

Through fierce and persistent advocacy, the Korean social movement was able to change public conception about the fingerprinting practice from a bureaucratical necessity to an unwarranted violation of universal human rights inflicted on all noncitizens.[18] This shift also broadened the basis of solidarity among subaltern activists, as evident in the following note made by a group supporting Han Jongsok:

> The unique aspect of collective activism on fingerprint refusal is the fact that it has transcended the various conflicts and schisms of previous movements. . . . This activism is deeply entwined with basic rights as humans. A sense of unity [has] bridged the gap between the Zainichi first generation and second and third generations as well as across the 38th parallel line (Chongryon and Mindan together organized the meeting in Kawasaki), the discrepancy between Asian and European Resident Aliens, and the differences between permanent residents and temporary residents. Furthermore, this type of activism usually develops as a "men's fight," but what's striking is that women are also actively involved and mobilizing their own collection action. (Han-san no Shimon Ōnatsukyohi o Sasaerukai 1990, 66)

What changed was not only the public perception of the issue but also the ways that other Koreans perceived their own rights—what they were entitled to refuse and request as their rights. As more Koreans began to see refusal as an act of social justice for their own human dignity and rights, the number of objectors to fingerprinting gradually

152 *Chapter 4*

increased. In 1982, the number of objectors was only twenty-one, but it increased to over eighty in 1984 (Park 1999, 54). This may seem small, but this number is significant, considering that objectors would face serious consequences, including but not limited to large fines and the inability to travel into and out of Japan.

In 1982, the government introduced a revision that raised the minimum age for the fingerprint practice from fourteen to sixteen and that extended the interval of Alien Registration Renewal from three to five years, while at the same time raising the fine for refusal from 30,000 yen to 200,000. Han Jongsok and his allies believed that this reform was the Japanese government's attempt to slow the movement's growing momentum. They pointed out that the "two-year" extension interval period would effectively create a two-year dormant period for Alien Registration and renewal cases. Thus, if there were few individuals eligible for registration or renewal during those two years, few could refuse fingerprinting. Activists argued that by creating this period of dormancy, the government was trying to tame and weaken their movement.

After this reform was passed, the government also began to punish objectors by limiting their freedom of movement. Under Japanese immigration laws at that time, all noncitizens were required to request a reentry permit before leaving Japan, and they could not return, regardless of their legal status, because the Japanese Immigration Bureau denied the objectors' request for reentry permits. The inability to travel abroad could hinder some objectors' ability to make a living because many of them, including Han Jongsok, needed to travel for work but couldn't under these new restrictions. Han also needed to raise money for his own trial to defend his objections against fingerprinting, while his livelihood was in serious jeopardy.

Despite the hardships, Koreans' movement against fingerprinting did not fade out but remained strong during those two years. Han Jongsok's trial played an important role in keeping momentum alive, as it began to expose many unjust aspects of fingerprinting requirements. During Han's trial, it came to light that Japanese police authorities unlawfully targeted Koreans by using registration fingerprints in their criminal investigations. It also became clear that the municipal office's public servants lacked proper training and the skill to accurately verify individuals' identities through their fingerprints. These revelations challenged the validity of the government's claim that fingerprints were necessary for the purpose of identification rather

Figure 4.4. Young Korean activists protest against the fingerprinting requirement and the Alien Registration Law in August 1982. Photo from the History Museum of J-Koreans, Tokyo.

than for the purpose of policing. These exposed contradictions further galvanized Koreans in Japan.

By 1985, it was expected that a significant number of Koreans would have to renew their registration as a result of the 1982 reforms. Activists patiently waited for this moment to reignite their movement and organize collective actions of fingerprinting refusal. Indeed, the number of objectors rose to more than 10,000 (Iwasawa 1998, 150)—a huge leap from eighty cases in 1984. Civilian associations such as the National Committee of Lawsuits against Fingerprinting (established in 1983) also played an important role in orchestrating the collective refusal across the country. The Japan Federation of Bar Associations (Nichibenren) and the Japan Civil Liberties Union publicly condemned the fingerprinting practice (Han-san no Shimon Ōnatsukyohi o Sasaerukai 1990; Jiyū Jinken Kyōkai 1984). In 1985, the government revised the fingerprinting provisions again; they alleged that they would further "reduce the psychological pressure felt by foreigners at the time of fingerprinting" (Administrative Order No. 125 of May 1985) by replacing the "rotating" method of using thick black ink with a "flat" fingerprinting process that used a colorless ink. In 1987, they made additional revisions, requiring fingerprinting only at the initial registration. Nevertheless, the government was showing no sign that it would abolish the requirement completely.[19]

154   *Chapter 4*

Meanwhile, Han Jongsok's legal battle against the government ended in his defeat at both the lower and high courts. Defiant, Han appealed to the Supreme Court. While he was awaiting trial, however, he and thirty-four other prosecuted objectors were granted an amnesty pardon as a result of the death of the Shōwa emperor Hirohito in 1989. Unlike pardons in the United States, one cannot refuse the amnesty pardon in Japan. In fact, one of the community activists and objectors, a second-generation Chinese colonial migrant, Jo Sui Chin, attempted to refuse this amnesty pardon by filing a civil lawsuit in 1989 in Osaka.[20] She fought all the way to the Supreme Court but lost in 2002 (Jo 2020). Many objectors, including Jo Sui Chin, were dismayed and humiliated by this abrupt end to their legal fights. The fact that this pardon derived from the death of Shōwa emperor Hirohito—the supreme symbol of colonialism and generational trauma—made them feel even worse. Their bitter sentiments were well summarized in the following dissent statement, issued by objectors in response to the pardon: "We have been trying to prove our innocence and [to prove that] the Alien Registration laws—including its requirement for fingerprinting and carrying the registration card at all times—are against the Constitution and ICCPR. This pardon violates our right to make a legal argument and a call for justice. It does nothing but fabricate a false history" (Han-san no Shimon Ōnatsukyohi o Sasaerukai 1990, 93).

Koreans' domestic legal fight was abruptly ended by a unilateral pardon that they didn't ask for and could not reject, but their fight was far from over. In parallel to their ongoing domestic battle in Japan, Korean activists also mobilized transnationally. They heavily lobbied allies abroad, including civil rights activists in the United States and the UN. In 1980, Choi Changhwa, the Korean pastor and activist from southern Japan who refused fingerprinting along with his daughter, Choi Sun-ae Lois, utilized the 1503 procedure—the oldest human rights complaint mechanism, which allows any individual or group claiming to be the victim of human rights violation to submit a complaint and have it reviewed. In 1984, Kim Dong-hoon, a Korean legal scholar and activist, also made a similar complaint to the UN (Kim 1984; Tsutsui and Shin 2008).[21] While the Japanese government defiantly defended its practice, it was nevertheless humiliating for Japan to be internationally scrutinized by the commission (Gurowitz 1999).

Throughout the 1980s and 1990s, Korean activists and various pro-minority NGOs submitted reports to the UN Human Rights Committee, where they continuously advocated for the abolition of discriminatory and degrading fingerprinting requirements in Japan's immigration law (Kim D. 2003; Mushanokōji 1994). The committee that monitors the ICCPR also required the participant country's state to submit its reports and examined it with great care. In 1988, upon reviewing the reports from NGOs and the participatory government, the committee questioned the Japanese government about the legitimacy of the fingerprinting practice. Despite the Japanese government's defensive argument for its bureaucratic necessity, the committee nevertheless prompted the government to cease this requirement. In 1992, a few years after this deliberation at the UN committee, Prime Minister Kaifu Toshiki visited South Korea and promised that Japan would no longer require Koreans to be fingerprinted within two years of a signed bilateral memorandum. Following this announcement, the government announced that it would terminate the practice for Permanent Residents, including Special Permanent Residents—most of whom were Korean. This was a major, hard-won immigration reform for Koreans in Japan.

The government continued to retain the fingerprinting requirement for other foreign residents. This was problematized again at the UN Human Rights Committee in 1998 (Nichibenren 1999). The Japanese government again defended its practice, underscoring its ongoing efforts to minimize the psychological trauma for noncitizens, but they couldn't deter a strong objection against this continuing practice from the committee (Okamoto 1999). Shortly after this UN debate, in 1999, the Japanese government announced the abolition of the fingerprinting practice; that law was enacted in 2000.

The trajectory of Koreans' relentless fight for justice through the antifingerprinting movement suggests that the concept of global human rights played a significant role in these policy changes. However, it was not just a normative shift in world society that spontaneously or organically generated the external pressure that forced the Japanese government to change its policies. This norm was incorporated and mediated by the subaltern group's strong domestic and international mobilization efforts. By using this universally unifying framework, Korean activists in this time period successfully overcame the North/South political schism and promoted the participation of Japanese allies to support their cause. Such horizontal solidarity in both global and domestic arenas brought enough pressure for the state to consider drastic immigration policy changes. Koreans gradually formed a unified front and, referring to the International Covenant on Civil and Political Rights, were able to change the public perception of social

156 *Chapter 4*

justice issues in Japan. Korean activists and their allies successfully galvanized their base and forced the Japanese government to confront issues of injustice in both domestic and global arenas.

One could argue that the shift in framing by Korean activists since the 1970s may simply reflect a generational effect. As the literature on immigration argues, there is a generational difference in the level of interest and political participation in the host society between the first and second, or later, generations of immigrants (Ramakrishnan and Espenshade 2001). This generational shift was certainly an important factor for North and South Korean activists to overcome their previous political cleavage. However, the generational effect alone does not fully explain why since the 1970s these activists have specifically chosen a global framework, rather than a national framework, as a means of uniting their organizational body and legitimizing their claims to the public.

Analyzing the trajectories of these grassroots movements through historical documents and records, it is clear that many activists purposefully sought out a universalistic framework to unite these diverse actors. In contrast to the nationalized conceptualization of their rights, new activists for resident Koreans conceptualized universal human rights that they were entitled to regardless of their citizenship. This was exhibited most vividly in the demand for suffrage. As I discussed in chapter 3, Koreans and their Japanese allies, including attorney Fuse Tatsuji, explored ways to maintain Koreans' suffrage in postwar Japan. Fuse firmly argued that Koreans should be able to have their rights recognized and secured in Japan regardless of national belonging. However, Fuse's advocacy did not earn support at that time, and even Korean activists such as Han Duk-Su did not seem to believe that this idea would be feasible. However, a similar idea—of suffrage regardless of national belonging—once again emerged among Koreans in Japan, but in a renewed context. Invigorated by a series of changes in domestic laws, a group of Koreans started an alien or noncitizen suffrage movement in the 1990s. The court statement of Korean activist Lee Yonghwa, from his lawsuit against the Japanese government to recognize noncitizen's suffrage, sharply contrasts with earlier activists' conceptualization of rights:

> We do not request suffrage because we want to acquire material wealth or political power. We only wish to have equal rights. . . . We are aware of the history of African Americans' and black South Africans' enormous

struggles and sacrifice for their suffrage. However, history is not a [matter of] simple repetition, and we move forward with our history. Like blacks in the United States and South Africa, let us rejoice in becoming true members of society, even if we may still tread a thorny path. For those of us who do not have suffrage, legal action is the last stronghold of human rights. Please give us hope for suffrage, a dream of equality and justice. We sincerely desire that this lawsuit will mark the advent of the Japanese civil rights movement. (Lee 1993, 92–93)

When we compare this statement with the one by postwar Korean activist Han Duk-Su mentioned in chapter 3 (in which he accepted that Koreans lacked suffrage in Japan because they were foreign nationals), it becomes clear that the basis of Koreans' conceptualization of citizenship was shifting from one of particular nationhood toward one of universal personhood.

Lee refers to the civil rights movements in the United States and South Africa to bolster his argument, but the Korean social movement for suffrage is different from the American and South African examples. The baseline of such civil rights movements was that all "citizens" should have the same set of rights, whereas the Korean social movement called for recognizing the civil rights of noncitizens. In other words, they appealed for a shift—from particular nationhood to universal personhood—in the very basis for rights. Regardless of their non-Japanese citizenship status, Koreans in Japan demanded an equal set of rights, such as suffrage, under the umbrella of "universal, natural, and human rights" to which every human being was entitled. They were not arguing for "civil rights" limited to individuals with formal citizenship status.

Lee's claim was denied in court, and the proposed law for alien suffrage at the local level did not pass. However, in the series of petitions that these Korean activists wrote, we can observe a clear shift from self-identification as foreign noncitizens to self-identification as minority residents of Japan. We can also see that they came to see universal personhood, rather than particular nationhood, as the basis for their rights. This universalistic frame was also adopted by politicians in Japan who supported alien suffrage, indicating the extent to which the movements shaped policy discourse, although actual policy change had yet to take place.

This shift in self-identification—from alien to minority resident of Japan—is in line with Yasemin Soysal's (1997) work on postnational membership in Europe. Like Muslims in Europe, Koreans defined themselves as a "minority" and legitimized their claim by taking advantage of a growing globalized discourse regarding particular ethnic and racial identity as natural rights. All these shifts in this period reflect a larger normative change in world society and its gradual entry into Japanese public debates. As global human rights became a legitimate and even dominant framework for claim-making around the world, local activists recast their movements using human rights frames to reinvigorate their social movement. In the case of resident Koreans' social movements, this new framing was particularly effective, as it allowed Koreans to bridge the North/South split that had plagued their activism for decades. Universal human rights language facilitated this collaboration greatly, providing the basis of solidarity for a new social movement. The expansion of global human rights also provided a new venue for resident Koreans; activists pressured the Japanese government by appealing to international political forums such as the UN Human Rights Committee, often with help from other international activists, and gained some key successes in their activism. The following section addresses another exogenous factor contributing to this change—namely, the impact of transnational social movements for war reparations—along with the international relationship between Japan and other countries, including Japan's former colonies: China, South Korea, and Taiwan.

Japan's Place in World Society

In 1968, only twenty-three years after the end of World War II, Japan's GNP had become the second largest in the world. With its booming economy, Japan had become a rising sun once again in world society. A critical difference between Japan's progression in the early twentieth and the late twentieth century was that Japan asserted its presence in the world through economic ambition and technological advancement rather than through raw military or spiritual vigor and aggressive expansionism. Japan's rapid economic growth after its devastating war defeat in 1945 is often termed a "miracle" in popular discourse. It is celebrated by people in emerging economies in the non-Western world. However, what naive admirers of Japan's postwar economic success fail to notice is that Japan's quick recovery and advancement rested on the exploitation of colonies and colonial migrants' labor, similar to the relationships of Western empires to their colonies and colonial laborers. Unlike the United States or Europe, who had experienced an influx of labor immigrants, maintaining exploitative labor from the former colonized population was critical for Japan because the postwar Japanese government did not allow for a new stock of cheap labor immigrants from other countries to enter its country until the 1990s.

As Japan reclaimed its role as a significant global player in the economic sphere within world society, it also sought a more prominent role and position in the political sphere. To this end, the Japanese government attempted to obtain permanent representation on the Security Council at the UN. At the Twenty-Third and Twenty-Fourth General Assemblies, the Japanese foreign minister addressed Japan's aspiration to become a permanent member of the Security Council, and at the Twenty-Eighth General Assembly in 1973, US secretary of state Henry Kissinger expressed the United States' support for Japan's permanent membership on the Security Council. The United States' support for Japan's membership in the Security Council was confirmed by American president Richard Nixon in the Tanaka-Nixon Communique in 1973, where he stated that "a way should be found to assure permanent representation in that council for Japan, whose resources and influence are of major importance in world affairs" (Ogata 1983, 31).

Japan's economic resources began to have a strong impact on the UN. In 1983, Japan's assessed contribution to the organization was 10.32 percent, which came close to that of the second largest contributor of its time, the Soviet Union (10.54 percent).[22] By 1986, Japan's contribution surpassed that of the Soviet Union, and Japan became the second-largest contributor to the UN, after the United States (Ogata 1987). Despite its remarkable economic contribution, Japan struggled to gain due respect in the international community. Its aspiration to become a permanent member of the Security Council at the UN received little support from the other industrialized countries, such as the United Kingdom, France, and the Soviet Union, in part because these nations feared that Japan's membership may undermine their established power distribution. Also, the negative international image of Japan did not help the matter. Japan was often perceived as a passive international player in the political sphere, a country that rarely took a proactive leadership role in the international arena (Calder 1988). Particularly in the area of human rights, the Japanese government's attitude remained indifferent at best (Fujioka 2003; Peek 1992).

160   *Chapter 4*

For example, when the international discussion to empower the United Nations High Commissioner for Refugees (UNHCR) with the ability to impose sanctions on countries that severely violated civilians' human rights in the 1960s and '70s, the Japanese government did not support such a proposal, nor did they join the UNHCR.

Japan's unsympathetic attitude toward the issues of human rights reflects the complex intersection of political and economic interests in Japan's domestic sphere. In the first few decades after World War II, the Japanese government's foreign policy was by and large US-centric, in that it relied on close cooperation with the United States to protect its security and its economic interests (Irie 1966, 1991). However, US involvement in the Vietnam War led public opinion in Japan to question Japan's US-centric foreign policy. Furthermore, President Nixon's sudden effort to reconcile with China in 1972 shocked and humiliated the uninformed Japanese government (Farnsworth 1972). This sudden US policy change toward China is known as the "Nixon Shock" among Japanese analysts (Barnds 1976). After this instance of being sidelined in diplomacy, the voices demanding a more autonomous foreign policy became more salient, not only among the public but also among political elites within Japan.

Nonetheless, the Japanese government was still reluctant to pursue an active and independent role in humanitarian issues abroad, particularly in the area of admitting asylum seekers and political refugees onto its own soil. However, in the late 1970s, Japan became the target of severe global criticism over its reluctance to support political refugees from Southeast Asia when its closed immigration policies were exposed to the international media (Stokes 1979). As the Vietnam War ended and the communist regime triumphed in the mid- to late 1970s, many displaced anticommunist people from Laos, Cambodia, and Vietnam fled their homelands to survive by any means possible. Many used small fishing boats with the hope of being rescued by commercial ships from Western countries, seeking to make it to neighboring countries that would accept them as asylum seekers. These so-called boat people also docked in small Japanese ports in 1977, pleading with the Japanese government to let them land as political refugees.

The Japanese government refused to accept these refugees, however, and let them float in the open sea for over a month, stating that Japan did not have any governmental policy or law to accept political refugees. As a first-class economic power in world society, their apathetic treatment of these displaced vulnerable refugees begging for their lives on small ships in the open water attracted global media coverage. Many European and American media ran stories highlighting Japan's exclusionary immigration policies and juxtaposing the economic wealth of Japan and its lack of care for those refugees in open water. This was well summarized by an article in the *New York Times* on August 26, 1977: "Because of the disproportion between Japan's wealth and the small number of refugees that reach Japan's waters, their icy reception here is a token of the full measure of the distress of approximately 100,000 Indochinese refugees in Asia" (Kam 1977).

Facing fierce global criticism of its callous attitude toward refugees, the Japanese government attempted to recover its global reputation by accepting three thousand refugees (Malcom 1978). Although this was a much lower number of refugees than other industrialized nations accepted, it was indeed a significant step for the Japanese government, which had maintained restrictive immigration policies for over a few decades. The Japanese government also quickly and drastically raised its economic contribution to UNHCR, WFP, and UNICEF, which were all engaged in humanitarian relief for the Indochinese refugees. Shortly after this incident, a US-educated Japanese specialist of refugee issues, Ogata Sadako, was appointed director of UNHCR. In this context, the Japanese government also ratified two UN treaties, including the International Covenant on Civil and Political Rights and the International Covenant on Economic, Social, and Cultural Rights.

These ratifications resulted in opening eligibility for the national pension plan, which had previously excluded all non-Japanese resident aliens, to noncitizens, including Koreans in Japan (Kang 1994, 234; Shin 1995, 302–303). Despite the long-standing plea from Korean residents for the government to include Koreans in this plan, the government and the courts had been reluctant to comply with their demands.[23] One notable case was that of Kim Hyeon Gyun. In October 1960, a worker from the National Pension Office invited Kim to participate in the national pension program, which was solely for Japanese citizenship holders.[24] Kim at first declined because of his Korean citizenship. However, he was allegedly told by the worker from the pension office that if he wished to live in Japan permanently, he had to be enrolled in the pension program and that it was also a benefit for him.

162 *Chapter 4*

Thus, he continued to contribute to the pension program for twelve years, and when he turned sixty-five years old—the eligible age to draw from his national pension—he was notified that he was ineligible to receive his pension due to his Korean citizenship status. In 1979, he sued the director of Social Insurance in Japan and appealed its decision to refuse his request to receive his pension. On September 22, 1982, the lower court of Tokyo rejected his claim, stating that the law clearly referred to Japanese citizens and that it was obvious that those without Japanese citizenship would be excluded. Furthermore, the court argued that social rights—the rights to receive social services and welfare—belonged to citizens and not foreigners, and thus that the law does not contradict the Japanese constitution. Finally, the court argued that whether or not citizenship should be an eligibility requirement was at the discretion of the state (Tanaka 2013).

However, the lower court's decision was overturned in a matter of one year by the higher court of Tokyo. On October 29, 1983, the higher court sided with Kim, citing two international treaties that the Japanese government had ratified. The first was the International Covenant on Economic, Social and Cultural Rights (ICESCR), which holds ratifying countries responsible for promoting policies protecting the social rights of noncitizens, and the second was the convention relating to the status of refugees. Because international treaties are accorded higher authority than domestic law by Japan's constitution, the government also had to amend its laws and make noncitizens, including Koreans, eligible for the national pension plan to comply with the spirit of ICESCR. As a result of the ratification, the citizenship requirement was removed from social benefits, including the national pension, childcare subsidies, the Special Child Care subsidy, and the Disabled Child subsidy.

The direct effect of UN treaties was undeniable, as clearly noted by Hida Yuichi, a lifelong civil and human rights activist for Koreans and other noncitizens. In calling for the ratification of the UN treaty, Hida said, "Black ships [*Kurofune*] have arrived!"[25]

> Exclusion from the national pension plan didn't end even if those excluded Koreans such as Kim [Hyeon Gyun] sued the government agency. But it ended so quickly as a result of the ratification of the Convention Relating to the Status of Refugees. As one who participated in this movement, I felt somewhat powerless, seeing that the law that our activism could not change was so easily modified by external pressure. . . . Thanks

Social Justice and Human Rights 163

to these newly arrived Vietnamese refugees, Koreans also became eligible for the national pension. What an ironic story it is. (Hida 2004, 2)

After a few decades of maintaining restrictive immigration laws, the Japanese government began to relax them, albeit slowly and reluctantly. The order of these events made it seem as though the Japanese government yielded to external pressure, or *gaiatsu* (Miyashita 1999). This is a popular interpretation of Japan's sudden immigration policy changes. However, we miss an important point if we reduce Japan's reluctant modification of its immigration laws solely to a response to external pressure from the UN. Some of the changes made in the immigration laws were not necessarily just a passive reaction to external pressure; rather, they were a response to a combination of internal and external pressure.

Prior to this external pressure, there had been a wave of subaltern mobilization among minority groups in Japan demanding changes in Japan's restrictive citizenship and immigration laws, arguing that they violated their human rights. Admitting three thousand Indochinese refugees was not a major concern for the Japanese government. What worried the government was that admitting non-Japanese populations onto its soil, albeit an extremely small number in comparison to the numbers admitted by other industrialized countries, might create the need to modify its policies for all the other non-Japanese populations residing in Japan, including Koreans. This point is succinctly summarized in a remark made by a Foreign Ministry official in response to the foreign press's inquiry about whether the number of admittances was too small when considering the wealth of the Japanese nation: "This is not a quantitative but a qualitative question" (Kam 1977).

The few thousand refugees did serve as "black ships" in that they opened the floodgates for the already rising demands of Koreans in Japan. Thus, the interaction of new external and internal pressures influenced the Japanese government.[26] Japan's new interests in world society produced a series of policy changes in immigration law and challenged the national self-image. These dynamics were in direct contrast to those of previous periods. In the next section, we see how Japan's renewed relations with other nation-states in East Asia, including Japan's former colonies, exerted influence on this process, adding more pressure on the Japanese state to respond to the demands of activists to extend more citizenship rights to Koreans in Japan.

Rising New Global Powers and the Unresolved Colonial Past

By the 1980s, Japan's position as a global economic superpower was firmly secured. In fact, its economy became so strong that it triggered strong American criticism against the growing trade imbalance between the two countries, as well as anti-Japan sentiment in American media and the larger global public in the 1980s. When the iron curtain was removed in 1989, signaling the end of the Cold War, Japan once again had to define its position and role in world society. As discussed earlier, it had become clear to many Japanese policymakers as well as the public that having a bilateral relationship with the United States alone was no longer adequate for Japan to stay relevant in a globalizing world. Japan needed to redefine its relationships with and policies toward rapidly emerging new economic and political powers in Asia and the rest of the world (Auslin 2005). Although its relationship with the United States continued to be significant to Japan for both economic and security reasons, cultivating good relationships with its Asian neighbors was also becoming vital to Japan's future economic, political, and security well-being.

By 1989, China became Japan's second largest trading partner in Asia. The economic relationship between Japan and China was more intimate than ever. In 1990, Japan gave China $617.8 million in official development assistance funds, becoming one of its most important investors. By 1992, China had become Japan's top choice for investment in the automotive, transportation, and banking industries, as Beijing liberalized its economic policies (Matray 2001). A similar economic intimacy was growing between Japan and South Korea as well. South Korea became one of Japan's three largest trade partners, while Japan became South Korea's second largest. As South Korea was also transitioning to a stable democracy, South Korea and Japan became the most stabilized democratic allies to the United States. The two countries increasingly began to assert their significance as the new Asian core. Furthermore, as the military threat from the increasingly isolated North Korea became prominent, they also began to share a common security concern, thus further collaboration was desired.

Parallel to the development of a close economic relationship between Japan and the countries that were its former colonies, a demand for historical reparations among citizens and intellectuals in China, South Korea, and Taiwan was also rapidly growing. One of the most prominent examples of this trend was the rise of transnational political movements for wartime sex slaves or so-called comfort women in the late 1980s (Moon 1999). The issue of military comfort women was not discussed between the South Korean and the Japanese governments when these two governments negotiated war reparations during the postwar period. The South Korean government did not spontaneously prioritize the issue of these sexually exploited women by imperial Japan partly because of its desire for the flow of Japanese capital into its country as a means to economically rebuild. To South Korean political elites, the victims of colonial exploitation and violence—whether comfort women or remaining colonial migrants—were nothing but diplomatic capital at best.

The silence of these victims was broken when feminist political activism led by Korean female intellectuals internationally publicized the issue of the military comfort women and demanded reparations by the Japanese government. Quite a few Japanese and Korean scholars and activists in Japan, including but not limited to Yamashita Yon'e and Kim Puja, also engaged in the restorative justice movement for these victims (Kim 2008; Suzuki 1992; Yamashita 2008). South Korean activists also appealed to their own government in South Korea to reopen reparation discussions with the Japanese government in order to make Japan readdress the issue of sexual exploitation during the colonial period. While appealing to both South Korean and Japanese governments, these women's rights activists fostered transnational coalitions with women's activists in Japan as well. Together, they initiated an international campaign to promote public awareness about comfort women's issues both domestically and internationally. In 1992, they conducted international rallies in major American cities, and they appealed to the UN Commission on Human Rights. The movement's successful results are well documented in recent scholarly works (Tsutsui 2006).

This movement was followed by a series of lawsuits among Koreans, Chinese, and Taiwanese victims of various war crimes during the imperial period, both in and outside Japan. For example, Liu Lianren, a Chinese forced laborer who hid in the Japanese mountains after escaping the inhumane labor environment of a northern Japanese mine, was among the plaintiffs suing the Japanese government. These transnational reparations movements, led by activists in Japan's former colonies, also inspired Korean activists in Japan, who were already reinvigorated by the same global norm of human rights and traditional justice. Some of the reparations lawsuits were also filed by Korean individuals in Japan who served the Japanese imperial military or who were victims of the atomic bombs in Hiroshima or Nagasaki. They were not eligible for a military pension or victim aid from the Japanese government because they were not Japanese citizens. Japanese courts ruled against these plaintiffs, citing time limitations and state immunity that the Japanese government and corporations had used in their defense.[27] However, efforts to continue lawsuits against both the Japanese government and corporations did not fade out in Asia.

The public attention that these historical redress movements received forced previously apathetic political elites in South Korea to seriously engage with the economically disadvantaged victims of the colonial past, including the Korean minority in Japan. Responding to the persistent pleas from Koreans in Japan, to growing transnational voices calling for redress of the colonial past, and to demands from activists in South Korea, the Japanese and South Korean governments started negotiating the legal status of third-generation Koreans residing in Japan since 1988. In 1990, the South Korean government urged the Japanese government to abandon fingerprinting for all Koreans. Unlike in the 1960s, when neither Japan nor South Korea listened to the demands of Koreans in Japan, the discussion between these two countries in the late 1980s and the early 1990s was far more attentive and sensitive to the voices of Koreans in Japan. To support this fact, the Japan–South Korean Memorandum signed in 1991 by both governments' foreign ministers indicated that the practice of fingerprinting of Koreans would be halted by the end of 1992, directly reflecting the acute demands of Koreans in Japan (Iwasawa 1998, 155–156). In parliamentary debates between 1989 and 1993, Japanese policymakers cited a memorandum cosigned by the South Korean government, as well as demands from Koreans in Japan, as the most important factors in mediating these laws.

These contentious dynamics in East Asia since the late 1980s suggest that the new position of Japan's former colonies in world society as rising economic and security rivals and/or partners with Japan, combined with increasing international collaboration among activists within and beyond Asia, put significant pressure on the Japanese government. This pressure prompted the Japanese government to revisit its colonial past and to pay more attention to the demands of Koreans in Japan, who were living proof of Japan's colonial legacy. The amount of pressure that these movements created in order to alter the

Japanese government's attitudes and policies toward both the colonial past and colonial migrants was unprecedented. However, the transnational collaboration among subaltern activists was not an entirely new phenomenon limited to the global context. As I discussed in chapter 2, the March First Movement in 1919 also involved a vast international collaboration among political refugees abroad.

However, the fundamental difference between the transnational movements in the imperial and global contexts was the amount of global attention and support gained by the movements in the global context. This signals the emergence of "world culture"—the global diffusion of normative ideas impacting local actors, which sociologist John Meyer conceptualized (Meyer, Boli et al. 1997; Meyer 2010). In spite of successful collaboration among Korean activists across national borders during the imperial period, their movement did not attract much attention from the international community, where there were few normative incentives to promote the rights of colonial populations among Western imperial powers. Rising voices from Korea colonized country in the Far East, were largely ignored, even though activists' petitions were sent directly to Western countries at the Paris Peace Conference in Versailles in 1919 or the Washington Naval Conference (regarding naval disarmament) in 1920. As chapter 2 discussed, the lack of international support eventually resulted in Imperial Japan's forceful suppression of the movement.

On the other hand, Korean-led transnational movements in the latter part of the twentieth century took place against the background of a growing global trend to redress past and present human rights violations (Barahona de Brito, González Enríquez, and Aguilar 2001; Gibney and Roxstrom 2001; Ludi 2006). The emergence of global norms about condemning past human rights violations committed during the colonial period in world society and the relative openness of the global political system allowed these social movements to publicize and receive public support for their claims internationally (Tsutsui 2006). The renewed power balance between Japan and its former colonial countries in world society that centered global norms of human rights and social justice served as a key to uncovering the colonial past that Japan had buried decades before.

All the unfinished business between Japan and its former colonies became the agenda to discuss whenever the Japanese government attempted to proceed with discussions and negotiations about economic and security concerns with China, South Korea, and other

168   *Chapter 4*

Asian countries. One example was the territorial dispute around Dokdo/Takeshima, uninhabited small islets around the Exclusive Economic Zone in the Sea of Japan / East Sea. Neither Japan nor South Korea could agree on territorial borders. The dispute dates back to the end of World War II, when US peace settlement drafters failed to specify which country, South Korea or Japan, had sovereignty over the islets. The territorial dispute persisted but remained relatively dormant (Weinstein 2006). But after the Cold War ended, their common strategic interests began to shift attention and course. An economically confident South Korea provocatively voiced its interests in the islets, and discomfort over Japan's claim to them, in 2005, which quickly turned into a heated nationalistic debate between the two countries. The United States, which had spurred this dispute but had quickly forgotten it, took a rather ambivalent diplomatic pose toward the dispute between the two countries. Its ambivalence demonstrated that US interests in Asia no longer skewed toward Japan. This was evident in a vague and ambivalent response that Secretary of State Condoleezza Rice gave to a South Korean journalist who asked whether the United States endorsed Japan's move toward global expansion at the height of political tensions over the Dokdo/Takeshima Islands dispute:

> It is obviously our view that when Japan and the United States and South Korea are working together, we have demonstrated how much good we can do in a region like this, where the United States maintains an alliance with Japan, an alliance with South Korea, that has promoted peace and stability, not just on the Korean Peninsula but in the entire region. . . . I really believe that these great democracies can deal with issues as they emerge.[28]

Secretary Rice's vague response indicates that Japan was no longer America's only or most important partner in East Asia. South Korea was also quickly becoming an important security and economic partner to the United States. Hence, the United States was no longer granting Japan special protection as it did during the early phase of the Cold War. This shift in American attitudes and in the power dynamics between Japan and its former colonies in world society meant that Japan would now face this issue on its own and deal directly with its increasingly important economic and security partner South Korea, the rapidly growing global power China, and a defiantly independent-minded Taiwan. Japan could no longer dominate the center stage of Asia at the turn of the twenty-first century.

As the position of the former colonial countries became elevated in world society, activists were able to turn the tables and prompt their homeland states to work on their behalf. This point is drastically different from what we observed in the Cold War context, when their homeland states—North and South Koreas—utilized subaltern claims among Koreans in Japan as political capital on which to prioritize their political and economic interests, instead of protecting the subaltern concerns. Furthermore, as the shifting political climate (the end of the Cold War and the hegemonic interests of the United States) became distributed more discursively, this allowed former colonial states to prompt the Japanese government to redress past colonial problems, including the rights of colonial migrants and their descendants in Japan. In sum, the changes in Japanese immigration and citizenship laws leading up to the 1990s should be understood as a result of the renewed interplay of three familiar forces—the state's policymaking process, subaltern mobilization against state policies, and the placement of nation-states within world society. As these empirical facts illustrate, the strength of each force shifted, reflecting drastic changes in the geopolitical and economic climates in world society.

Searching for a New Self-Image for the Future

Intellectual discourse on Japanese nationhood or national self-image has also been transforming, sensitively corresponding to the rapid changes in geopolitics and in the power dynamics between Japan and its former colonies. Since the 1980s, a series of scholarly works that criticize and challenge *nihonjinron* (theories/discourse on Japaneseness) and the myth of Japanese homogeneity have been published. Some of them come from a new generation of intellectuals in Japan (Oguma 1995; Ōnuma 1993; Sugimoto and Mouer 1990; Yoshino 1999; Yun 1997), while others come from Japanologists in North America and Europe (Befu 2001; Dale 1986; Lie 2001; Mouer 1982; Weiner 1997). Historians have tirelessly uncovered a series of documents that portray the multiethnic past of Japan, while social scientists have documented the growing number of non-Japanese immigrants increasingly entering Japan (Brody 2002; Tsuda 2003). The myth of Japanese homogeneity

170   *Chapter 4*

has been vigorously challenged, questioned, and analyzed, both internally and externally (Befu 2001).

Reflecting this change, prominent scholars and policymakers who had previously advocated that Japan had a homogeneous self-image and ethno-racialized origin have modified their position. This trend is illustrated in a remark made by a leading anthropologist in Japan, Umehara Takeshi, who was appointed as director of the International Japanese Cultural Research Center, a research center established by Nakasone Yasuhiro—one of the most prominent nationalistic and conservative prime ministers in postwar Japan—to construct the Japanese national self-image. Umehara commented: "These days, I have stopped thinking of the Japanese as mono-ethnic. The Japanese was a hybrid ethnicity . . . that emerged as a result of the Yayoi ethnic group's domination of the native population in Japan" (Oguma 1995, 397).

This shift in the perception of Japanese nationhood was not limited to intellectuals. Key politicians began to modify their previous positions. For instance, Ishihara Shintarō, the governor of Tokyo and an influential writer in postwar Japan, wrote that Japan is not a homogeneous ethnic nation but, rather, comprises various different Asian ethnicities (Ishihara and Mohamad 1994). This contrasted with his previous writing in 1969: "There is no other example in the world [besides Japan] in which mono-ethnic nationals continue to maintain their own unique culture by speaking one language that has no commonality with that of other nations" (Ishihara 1969, 365).

As these changes suggest, Japan began to reimagine itself, once again, after the demise of Cold War logic. However, the Japanese government and the larger public did not abolish the rhetoric of Japanese homogeneity entirely; nor did they embrace the diversity of their nationhood or call for more inclusive citizenship and immigration policies. As external and internal challenges against Japan's self-image as a homogeneous nation increased, counterarguments also surfaced among right-wing critics in Japan (Buruma 1994). Beginning in the 1990s, heated debates over Japan's imperial past and growing ethno-racially diverse reality due to the increasing number of non-Japanese immigrants on its soil became frequent topics in newspapers and magazine articles in Japan and other Asian countries. Newly arrived immigrants from South America, South Asia, and Southeast Asia were quickly marginalized and became new, unassimilable others in Japanese society (Brody 2002; Goodman et al. 2003; Tsuda 2003).

Social Justice and Human Rights   171

One of the most prominent arenas where this reimagining of Japan took place at the turn of the twentieth century was in history textbooks. With the backdrop of transnational movements challenging Japan's war past, the textbook became a site for different social actors to debate and compete over the depiction of Japan's imperial past (i.e., what Japan used to be) and its future (i.e., what Japan would or ought to become). As part of the effort to substantiate their claim for war reparations, many activists and intellectuals who took part in this movement uncovered and presented a series of documents that recorded war atrocities. Historians, journalists, and civilian activist groups also attempted to record oral histories of living victims of sexual exploitation, forced labor, military drafts, massacres, and atomic bombs. Books focusing on the Nanjing Massacre became landmarks of these efforts (Chang 1997; Honda 1987). Japanese textbooks began to incorporate this newly publicized evidence as historical fact.

At the same time, voices critical of such assertions that admitted Japan's wrongdoings during the colonial period also became louder inside Japan. A professor of education at Tokyo University, Fujioka Nobukatsu, and his colleagues established the Liberal View of History Study Group (Jiyūshugi Shikan Kenkyūkai) in 1996 in order to counter international criticism toward the Japanese colonial past. Fujioka and other intellectuals, such as Nishio Kanji, a German specialist, and Hata Ikuo, a military historian, also created a group called the Japanese Institute for Orthodox History Education (Atarashi'i Rekishi Kyōkasho o Tsukurukai) to write history textbooks that did not include negative assertions about Japan's war and colonialism. These scholars also directly challenged the authenticity and historical accuracy of various war crimes that activists and victims claimed took place (Hata 1999, 2006). Nishio criticized the popular juxtaposition between Japan's war conduct and German Nazism. He argued that Japan should not provide war compensation or reparations to the victims simply because Germany did so. He writes in his book *Is Japan as Guilty as Nazi(s)? (Nihon wa Nachisu to Dōzai ka?)* that "there is no evidence showing that Japan's Asia-Pacific War involved such large-scale and extensive crimes against humanity" (Nishio 2005, 123).

Governmental records of these events were not fully available. Furthermore, voices and images of vulnerable victims were rarely recorded and stored when actual events took place. In addition, many victims were elderly, and some had already passed away. The fragility

172 *Chapter 4*

and unavailability of archival documents and oral histories allowed these countervailing arguments to prevail and to further discredit the claims of sexual and forced labor victims. Their discrediting efforts provided a symbolic and moral backbone for some conservative politicians, including former prime ministers Koizumi Junichirō and Abe Shinzō, to assert their political stance in dealing with Japan's war history and Asian neighbors. This is most vividly displayed in their repeated visits to Yasukuni Shrine, a location that venerates war criminals: these visits fueled nationalistic sentiment among both the Japanese and the former colonial countries. These conservative politicians attempt to promote the idea of new "patriotism" (*aikokushin*) and to educate the Japanese to have a sense of pride as Japanese.

Japan's new national self-image in the twenty-first century is still under construction. However, this brief review of the late twentieth-century to early twenty-first-century debates over the colonial past and discourse on Japan's future national self-image shows that, as in two previous periods, three familiar forces—the state's policymaking process, subaltern resistance, and the position of the nation-states within world society—closely and contentiously interact to shape such an image. However, unlike in the two previous contexts, nonstate actors' voices were no longer negligible. In fact, their voices became and remained so loud that Japan could no longer imagine itself as a nation free from the history and reality of their colonial past and immigration politics. As we will see in the final chapter, the more legitimized and amplified the subaltern voices became, the more radicalized and violent racially motivated hatred grew.

DISCUSSION

People take for granted the privilege of citizenship rights, especially when they are born with it. Those who have been able to enjoy citizenship rights since birth would find it peculiar that many Koreans in Japan would mobilize and fight for their rights as noncitizens rather than as naturalized minority citizens. But if you weren't born with that privilege, then you are likely to normalize the deprivation of such privilege in order to cope with the disadvantages and obstacles associated with it. This phenomenon is labeled "internalized oppression" by psychologists and social scientists who study the behavioral patterns and psychologies of minorities (David 2014). These oppressed groups, including Koreans in Japan, have to learn, usually through education, why they do not have access to but deserve such privileges; after acquiring this knowledge, they understand their self-worth and contemplate how to achieve equity. And even when they figure out a way, it is an uphill battle. This chapter chronicled Koreans' trajectory from divorcing themselves from internalized oppression to recognizing their self-worth and then translating that knowledge into collective, organized action, all while living under circumstances that existed because of ties to a colonial past.

This pattern was evident in two landmark legal fights by members of the Korean minority in the 1970s and '80s—Park Jongseok's fight with Hitachi and Han Jongsok's fingerprinting refusal. These two men did not know each other, lived in different cities, and were decades apart in age, but both of them made historic decisions to challenge ethno-racial oppression. They began their fights alone as individuals but later collectively organized with other activists and allies. In casting spotlights on these individuals, I do not intend to imply that all Koreans followed similar paths. Many people couldn't embrace their Korean identities publicly because they could not afford to absorb the socioeconomic costs associated with coming out of the closet in a brazenly racist society. But a significant number of Koreans, despite this risk, did stand up and take action. By tracing claims from the 1970s to 1990s that were newly anchored in universal personhood rather than in particular nationhood, we gain insight into the significance of this overarching framing for activists' ability to successfully organize and achieve their desired outcomes.

This chapter has demonstrated how citizenship, immigration, and national self-image in Japan once again have undergone a drastic shift since the 1980s. These shifts reflect a larger normative change in world society and its gradual entry into the Japanese public debate, affirming sociologist John Meyer's theories on world society, polity, and culture. As global human rights became a dominant and legitimate framework for claim-making in the contemporary world, local activists recast their movements using the human rights framework to reinvigorate a fragmented social movement. In the case of Koreans' social movements in Japan, this new framing was particularly effective. First, it allowed Koreans in Japan to unite their divided social movements and overcome the North/South split that had haunted their activism for decades. Second, the language of universal human rights has facilitated the wide-ranging alliance domestically within Japanese society and transnationally with activists abroad. The expansion of global human rights also provided a new venue for Korean activists in Japan and other activists in Japan's former colonies, some of which are also Japan's current economic partners. These activists pressured the Japanese government by appealing to international political forums such as the UN Human Rights Committee and to states that were Japan's former colonies, often with help from other forms of international activism, such as transnational war reparation movements. Such actions helped activists achieve the key successes described in this chapter.

After more than four decades, citizenship and immigration laws in Japan slowly began to change. Although these recent reforms have not yet met all the demands of minority groups in Japan, they nevertheless illustrate the important role played by new global dynamics that empowered the subaltern movement in Japan—the emergence of new global norms such as the concept of human rights, a globally sanctioned normative repertoire of demands for reparations from the colonial era, and the increase of globalized economic transactions across national borders. These combined forces generated substantial policy changes in Japanese citizenship and immigration.

Nevertheless, though this shift from exclusion toward inclusion was animated by new dynamics, the forces at work were also familiar. They were, in fact, new versions of the same forces that shaped policy during the two earlier periods. Japan's economic engine was still operating, leading to the necessity of negotiating external relations with rapidly industrializing South Korea. Global relationships were key constraints not only because of the leverage exercised by South Korea but also because of the broader pressure brought to bear by emerging human rights norms that were enforced by the UN. In this instance, unlike in the earlier iterations, the protests of targeted minorities, notably Korean activists and their supporters, were able to exert a far more powerful driving force for change. These activists became stewards of human rights for noncitizens. The empirical analysis presented here shows that the same equation of forces, with a different balance and in contrasting combinations, was operating in all these instances and working together to shape Japan's new national self-image.

What transpired in the later decades of the twentieth century did not, however, result in more inclusive and humane immigration laws for all immigrant populations in twenty-first-century Japan. Instead, as the next chapter will discuss, the Japanese government shifted its target population from colonial migrants and their descendants to the newly arrived immigrant population. This fact contrasts with FitzGerald and Cook-Martín's assertion on the US case: that immigration policy in the United States has become far less racialized and that the connection between liberalism and racist immigration laws was fundamentally severed with the demographic change resulting from the passing of the Hart-Celler Immigration Act in 1965. In the case of Japan, even if legal treatment of colonial migrants and their descendants has become more liberalized and inclusive, citizenship and immigration laws toward other immigrant groups in Japan remain overtly exclusionary and restrictive. The final chapter of this book will analyze this phenomenon of uneven treatment among noncitizens in Japanese society and reckon with what we can learn from Koreans' experiences in relation to the current struggles of new immigrants in Japan.

Chapter Five

CONCLUSION
Toward Diverse and Inclusive Japan

On December 4, 2009, about eleven Japanese men showed up in front of a Korean elementary school in Kyoto with bullhorns and screamed ugly racial slurs and false accusations against Koreans for over forty minutes: "Korean school isn't school." "Cockroaches, maggots, go back to Korea." "North Korean spy factory. Get Korean schools out of Japan!" "Euthanize Koreans at the health center!"[1] According to the accounts of parents and teachers, frightened students burst into tears, while teachers tried to control the scene outside. According to the court document, the Japanese police were called, but they simply instructed the men to refrain from making noise and did not take any further action. The Korean elementary school in Kyoto sued these individuals in both civil and criminal courts, but the lawsuits did not deter them. They came back repeatedly and continued their hate speech and harassment in front of the school, intimidating the students and teachers inside. In April 2011, the lower court of Kyoto found the group's leading figure, Nishimura Hitoshi, guilty of "forcible obstruction of business" for interrupting the educational operation of the Korean school. He was also later found guilty of hate speech in a subsequent civil lawsuit.

These Japanese men are a part of a growing ultraconservative nationalist and racist group called Zaitokukai, an acronym for Zainichi Tokken o Yurusanai Shimin no Kai (Citizens Group against the Special Privileges of Resident Koreans in Japan). Members have been organizing anti-Korean demonstrations across Japan, inciting violent hate speech and protests against Koreans and other foreign residents in Japan. They frequently organize street demonstrations and protests and are said to have over 10,000 members (Higaki and Nasu 2021; Yasuda 2015). Zaitokukai has been placed on a watch list for its extreme right-wing, xenophobic, and nationalist ideology. International media, foreign governments, and a UN committee on the elimination of racial discrimination have condemned these extremist groups and the hate speech targeting Koreans and other foreign residents in Japan. They are urging the Japanese government to address domestic extremist groups that incite hate speech and xenophobic, ethno-racial violence against minority groups.

The incident at the Korean elementary school in Kyoto in 2009 invokes the bitter memory of the postwar state's suppression of Korean ethnic schools, which triggered the Hanshin Educational Struggle of 1945, resulting in the unprovoked death of teenage Korean student Kim Tae-il. Thus, it is tempting to link the rise of ultranationalist, anti-Korean, racist groups like Zaitokukai to the legacy of colonialism and to assume an unbroken lineage of Japanese exclusion and sentiment against Koreans and other minorities in Japan (Robillard-Martel and Laurent 2019). The idea that a persistent legacy of colonialism and imperialism continues in the form of inequality, oppression, civil wars, and political corruption has been eloquently presented by humanistic scholars, including Edward Said (1978). But such arguments must be made with substantive and systematic empirical evidence, since oversimplified linear arguments made without concrete evidence can invite unconstructive hearsay and unwarranted attacks against minority groups. A case in point was the controversy surrounding a paper by Harvard law scholar J. Mark Ramseyer (2019, 2021b). His paper's allegation that comfort women weren't victims but willing participants, made without any credible historical evidence by a scholar lacking academic qualifications as a historian, irked many activists and specialists in Japanese and Korean history.[2] As Ramseyer's case exemplifies, oppressors and provocateurs often weaponize an oversimplified linear logic to argue that Koreans have always been a source of social disturbance and criminal activity and thus do not deserve to live in Japanese society (Higuchi 2019; Higuchi and Oguma 2020).

Furthermore, such linear arguments from both sides of the political spectrum ignore the historical disjunctures presented in this book. Imperial Japan did extend some citizenship rights to Koreans despite their colonial oppression. From the late twentieth century through the early twenty-first, during the period of rising anti-Korean and anti-immigrant sentiment, Koreans gained access to many citizenship rights in Japan, while this liberalized access was largely denied to other immigrants. A simple linear argument of the colonial legacy fails to explain these disjunctures or the heterogeneous situations surrounding citizenship rights.

This final chapter discusses the complex interplay between the legacy of colonialism and the forces of globalization from the end of the twentieth century into the twenty-first. It addresses how this interplay led to what appears to be a revival of colonial racism against Koreans and other immigrant groups in contemporary Japanese society. In other words, history indeed repeats itself—but not in a linear and continuous manner. Instead, it moves in a dialectical, oscillating pattern, where a few familiar endogenous and exogenous forces interact.

Despite repeated reforms and revisions, citizenship and immigration policies and laws in Japan produce and reproduce durable ethnoracial inequality and injustice. However, the current targets, forms, and outcomes of these policies and laws are different from those in previous periods. This chapter also reckons with the future of Japan's nationhood, citizenship, and immigration policies based on what we have learned from the trajectories of Koreans' social movements in Japan and the making of Japan's nationhood, citizenship, and immigration in the twentieth century.

From Universal Human Rights to Particular Historical Rights for Reparations

From the 1970s to the 1990s, Koreans' social movements utilized a universal human rights framework to find common ground across different categories of immigrant groups—regardless of immigrants' heterogeneous backgrounds with respect to age, generation, ethno-racial origins, national origins, class, gender, religion, legal status, and so on. However, as transnational power dynamics shifted globally, especially in East Asia, the framing of the debate over Koreans' rights in Japan gradually shifted toward particular historical rights, especially with regard to historical reparations. References to the Japanese government's responsibility for the colonial migrants and their descendants have appeared more frequently and dominantly in the policy debate since the 1990s. In parallel to this shift, access to citizenship rights among different types of noncitizens has become unevenly distributed in Japanese society.

Conclusion 179

Korean activists have always used diverse types of framing, including that of the historical redress of colonial legacies, but this was never the primary framing. Beginning in the mid-1990s, references to the colonial past and its historical redress became a more dominant framing by both proponents and opponents. This tendency was particularly noticeable and salient in the alien or noncitizen suffrage debate. In the mid-1980s, the major Korean organizations started to consider demands for suffrage as part of their official agenda. In 1985, Mintōren, which led the fingerprint movement, considered suffrage the most significant part of its agenda (Higuchi 2011). In 1986, Mindan recognized acquiring suffrage in Japan as one of its official policy platforms.[3] The suffrage movement gained momentum in the early 1990s when a group of Koreans and other resident aliens began to file a series of lawsuits against local governments on the grounds that not recognizing their suffrage was unconstitutional. Their lawsuits eventually reached the Supreme Court. While the Supreme Court ruled against their claims in 1995, the judges did include a rare special addendum. In their addendum, the court asserted that even though the Japanese constitution does not guarantee alien suffrage, it does not strictly prohibit the state from making it possible by introducing a new law (Saikō Saibansho Dai 3 Shō Hōtei 1995). Issuing such an addendum at the time of the ruling was extremely rare for the Japanese Supreme Court and thus carried significant weight. It energized activists and the proponents for alien suffrage and sparked policy debates among intellectuals and lawmakers.

Many advocates for alien suffrage, including Korean activists, called for the extension of suffrage rights for *all* noncitizen residents in the name of universal human rights. However, a close review of the public debates reveals that this discourse was largely concentrated on the issue of historical redress between Japanese and Koreans.[4] As discussed in chapter 4, emerging transnational politics about historical redress exerted significant influence over domestic debates related to Korean minorities in Japan, and Korean activists in Japan started to mobilize transnationally as South Korean organizations, scholars, and celebrities started to pay attention to issues concerning the Koreans in Japan (Higuchi 2011; Tsutsui 2018).

In parallel to Koreans' transnational lobbying efforts with supranational organizations and their homeland state, both proponents and opponents of alien suffrage increasingly and explicitly referred to the Japanese government's historical responsibility for colonial migrants and their descendants in Japan. Proponents of alien suffrage often argued that the extending suffrage based on the recognition of Japan's colonial past was morally just given Japan's particular historical relations to the colonial migrants and their descendants. This perception was widely shared among proponents across different political parties. Nonaka Hiromu, an influential politician from Jiyūminshutō or the Liberal Democratic Party (LDP), frequently criticized Japan's inadequate efforts of historical redress. He explicitly supported local suffrage for Koreans (Nonaka and Shin 2009). Fuyushiba Tetsuzō from the Kōmeitō, a conservative political party supported by the influential Buddhist organization Soka Gakkai, also publicly expressed his support for this idea (Fuyushiba 1998; Higuchi 2017).

In 1998, when President Kim Dae-Jung of South Korea visited Japan, the debate over alien suffrage took an even more distinctive tone toward historical redress for colonialism. Mindan was heavily lobbying with sympathetic Japanese politicians about the issue of alien suffrage around the time of President Kim's visit (*Mindan Shinbun* 1998). When Kim Dae-Jung visited Japan, he requested that Prime Minister Obuchi Keizō consider alien suffrage for Koreans in Japan. President Kim also promised to pass a special law that would recognize alien suffrage so that Japanese residents living in South Korea would have the same rights. President Kim underscored the importance of resolving these existing tensions in order to heal past wounds and build future relationships between the two countries. The South Korean government eventually passed a law to recognize alien suffrage under Kim Dae-Jung's successor, Roh Moo-hyun. However, when minority parties submitted a similar proposal in Japan, it was quickly shot down by the majority in the lower house, which was controlled by the ruling party, the LDP. Nevertheless, this sparked a larger debate about alien suffrage among lawmakers.

Opponents who disagreed with Nonaka and Fuyushiba's arguments also began to use colonial history to frame their counterargument against alien suffrage, albeit with different interpretations of the same historical facts. An opinion expressed by journalist Sakurai Yoshiko, a leading conservative opinionator, demonstrates this point. She is known for her vocal opposition to alien suffrage and for her hawkish policy preference toward China and the two Koreas. She cited historical issues regarding the colonial Korean migrants in a discussion over alien suffrage in *Seiron,* a conservative opinion magazine, to justify her opposition to Koreans' demands for alien suffrage:

Conclusion 181

> Reviving a sense of nation is an urgent task and it also requires us to reflect on our history. Just recently, we had a seminar on this issue [of local alien suffrage] at the lower house of the Diet, where one Korean person in their seventies angrily argued that Koreans were unilaterally made Japanese nationals by the Japanese government and were then stripped of their Japanese nationality after the war. . . . While I can understand his sentiment, he misunderstands the historical facts. . . . Koreans were the ones who abandoned their Japanese citizenship. (Sakurai 2000, 65)

A series of conservative idealogues released similar sentiments in the early 2000s (Takaichi and Momochi 2000; Takubo 2001). This marked another crucial moment for the alien suffrage debate after its previous momentum in 1995 (Higuchi 2011). As the debate over alien suffrage heated up, both proponents and opponents of alien suffrage started developing their own proposals. One notable effort was made by a project team of lawmakers who focused on citizenship issues. This team was comprised of lawmakers from three conservative parties, including the LDP, Kōmeitō, and Hoshutō, a conservative party established by Ozawa Ichirō in 2000 that dissolved after subsequent election losses. This team drafted a tentative proposal titled "Proposal to Grant Special Permanent Residents Japanese Citizenship by Exception." This proposal suggested drastically swift and easy naturalization of anyone with Special Permanent Resident status (i.e., colonial migrants and their descendants) without any lengthy bureaucratic process.

Historically, Japan's naturalization procedure was criticized for its opaque processes, which forced applicants to hire expensive professional legal experts to assist them. Furthermore, some naturalization requirements invoked colonial assimilationist policies. For example, the Japanese word for naturalization, *kika*, originally meant "submission to the Imperial Sovereign's moral authority," and during colonial times, the term *kikajin* (naturalized people) was used in a derogatory way. The Japanese naturalization process also used to require applicants to adopt Japanese-sounding names that must be written with officially recognized Japanese letters and characters for names (*jinmeiyō kanji*). This Japanese name requirement largely excluded characters commonly used for Korean and Chinese family and personal names; thus, the process had been deemed an institutionalized form of Japan's persisting colonial mentality and of forced ethno-racial assimilationist policies for Koreans in Japan. Although the state

182   *Chapter 5*

began allowing an applicant's original name to be used, it continued to require the usage of officially recognized Japanese letters and characters, which basically meant that an applicant was forced to "Japanize" their name's characters. And the naturalization process also involved a series of financial and criminal background checks that many Japan-born Koreans found humiliating and derogatory. This proposal would reduce nearly all such cumbersome paperwork and get rid of the restrictions for allowable characters and letters for names for any naturalization applicants.[5] Rather than relying on the subjective discretion of the Minister of Justice, the proposed procedural reform would make the process transparent by specifying clear criteria. The Policy Affairs Research Council in the LDP considered this naturalization proposal to be a part of postwar atonement, as reported in an April 27, 2001, article in *Tōyō Keizai Nippō*: "There is no clear standard or criteria in the process of naturalization and there has been much criticism against the final decision resting in the discretion of Ministry of Justice. In particular, there are many opinions that question applying the regular naturalization process to Special Permanent Residents. Thus, we proposed a swift, simplified process. We consider this a part of our postwar atonement."[6]

The proposal nevertheless was met with harsh criticism from Korean activists. The same article from *Tōyō Keizai Nippō* reported that Mindan criticized the proposal for possibly attempting to avoid recognizing noncitizen alien suffrage. Chongryun also criticized the proposal, arguing that it was an assimilationist policy in disguise, and called for prioritizing the protection of human rights for Koreans in Japan. In the end, the proposal was never submitted for debate in Parliament. Meanwhile, tensions between North Korea and Japan escalated after the issue of returning Japanese abductees from North Korea gained momentum when Koizumi visited North Korea and returned with some of the abductees, and after a series of provocative missile tests by North Korea. An analysis of the ongoing debate about alien suffrage in the 2000s reveals a notable shift in framing: people increasingly centered their argument on competing historical issues (e.g., colonial reparation, historical reconciliation) rather than treating the matter as a universal human rights issue.

The alien suffrage debate became reinvigorated for the third time around 2010 (Higuchi 2011).[7] When South Korean political leaders proposed that Japan pass alien suffrage, they also addressed the importance of establishing a Northeast Asian Union where South Korea

Conclusion   183

and Japan would play a leading role. This plan was not supported by a majority of the LDP, but it certainly had an impact on opposition party members, particularly on Ozawa Ichirō. Ozawa saw alien suffrage for Koreans as an opportunity to establish a stronger alliance between Japan and South Korea. As one of the most influential politicians in Japan at that time, Ozawa played a significant role in the parliamentary power shift from LDP to the Democratic Party of Japan, or Minshutō (DPJ) in 2009. Ozawa submitted the proposal for alien suffrage shortly after his own party, DPJ, seized a historical victory in the 2009 general election, ending sixty years of LDP domination. This was no surprise to those who followed Ozawa's remarks on alien suffrage in the parliamentary debates. For example, in 2003, Ozawa repeatedly addressed his shared vision for Northeast Asian unity with the Korean president and pressed then–prime minister Koizumi Junichirō to support suffrage for Koreans in Japan.[8] Ozawa recognized the issue of Koreans in Japan as a key part of a solution for Japan overcoming the unresolved colonial legacy that continued to present an obstacle to potential alliances with its Asian neighbors. When he did not get support from Prime Minister Koizumi, Ozawa harshly criticized the lack of any concrete provisions on this specific issue in the Koizumi cabinet. After DPJ became the ruling party in 2009, Ozawa sprang into action and the debate over suffrage gained further momentum.

By then, however, the target population for suffrage extension had shifted from long-term resident aliens or noncitizens to aliens who are Special Permanent Residents (colonial migrants and their descendants). Similar to Ozawa, supportive policymakers largely framed this issue as a symbolic way to reconcile the historical sentiment with their current and future economic and political partner, South Korea. Opponents also co-opted the citizenship debate to assert a historical narrative that justified Japan's past colonial actions. However, lively public debate over alien suffrage was once again pushed to the back burner due to a historically contingent but catastrophic event.

Another seismic shift in the Japanese political power dynamic came after real seismic events in Japan. On March 11, 2011, triple disasters struck Japan—the Northeast Great Earthquake, followed by a massive tsunami and a nuclear disaster at Fukushima Dai'ichi Nuclear Power Plant. In the aftermath of these catastrophic events, the hawkish conservative LDP political leader Abe Shinzō seized the Japanese prime minister post again in 2012 and stayed in power until 2020, when he stepped down amid the global COVID-19 pandemic, citing

184   *Chapter 5*

health problems. In these contexts, public interest was no longer engaged with the issue of alien suffrage. In parallel to these changes in the configuration of the political, cultural, and economic fields within and outside Japan's national boundaries, the relationship between state and nonstate actors also shifted. The Japanese state introduced a series of significant immigration legal changes distinguishing between Special Permanent Residents—colonial migrants and their descendants—and other immigrant populations. The following section addresses how similar sets of external and internal forces in and outside Japanese society led to the emergence of a hierarchy of differentiated statuses for noncitizens, and what the implications are for subaltern social movements and for the concept of Japanese nationhood in the twenty-first century.

UNEVEN DECOUPLING BETWEEN NATIONHOOD AND CITIZENSHIP IN TWENTY-FIRST-CENTURY JAPAN

The heated public debate over alien suffrage was a significant development for contemporary Japanese society, especially considering its significantly smaller number of immigrants and refugees than other liberal democracies. In addition, a series of other citizenship rights has been extended to noncitizens that were previously reserved for Japanese citizens. As evident in the removal of ethnocentric requirements for naturalization (i.e., adopting Japanese names), the elimination of the fingerprinting requirement for registered aliens, and inclusion of registered aliens in public health insurance and national pension plans, national identification as Japanese is no longer a prerequisite for some critical citizenship rights in Japanese society. Although other resident aliens participated in and supported other social movements, the Korean social movement was one of the central forces in securing these policy changes for noncitizens. In other words, their movement, along with other minority movements in Japan, has spearheaded efforts to spread cosmopolitan norms of human rights and denationalized notions of citizenship rights for noncitizens across Japanese society (Shin and Tsutsui 2007; Tsutsui 2018).

Focusing on these positive movement outcomes alone may give the false impression that Japanese society is moving away from both a conception of a homogeneous nationhood and exclusive citizenship policies. But a closer look at these revisions reveals that this extension of rights is not evenly distributed to all noncitizens in Japan, nor is it decreasing inequality among noncitizens. In fact, the main beneficiaries of such liberalized immigration laws and extension of citizenship rights are Special Permanent Residents (colonial migrants and their descendants). Meanwhile, other immigrant groups with a different legal status do not receive the same benefits, even though the number of immigrants has been on the rise since the 1980s.

As we saw in chapter 4, the number of registered noncitizens in Japan increased in the 1980s, when Japan began to accept more labor immigrants from Latin America and Northeast and Southeast Asia (Douglass and Roberts [1999] 2003). The number of registered noncitizens continued to rise. The only exceptions to this trend were when the numbers of noncitizens in Japan temporarily decreased during the 2008 Great Recession and during the period of border restrictions due to the COVID-19 pandemic (see figure 5.1). In 2022, it reached over 2.9 million, or approximately 2.4 percent of the total population in Japan.[9] This is the highest recorded number of registered noncitizens in Japan since the 1950s. Before 1965, the total population of registered noncitizens was only available every five years. For a country that touted its homogeneity, this increase and its velocity is remarkable. The number of recently arrived immigrants now exceeds the total number

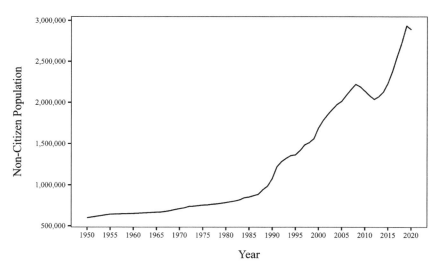

Figure 5.1. The registered noncitizen population in Japan, 1950–2020, based on data in table 10-1 from Kokuritsu Shakaihoshō Jinkō Mondai Kenkyūjo 2022, which includes data up to 2020. Before 1965, the total population of registered noncitizens was only available every five years.

of colonial migrants and their descendants (Special Permanent Residents). The number of Special Permanent Residents is now declining, which reflects the ongoing naturalization among colonial migrants and their descendants.[10]

Responding to demand from influential economic actors such as the Japanese Business Federation (Nippon Keidanren), the Japanese government introduced a series of immigration reforms in the late twentieth century (Brody 2002). As I discussed in the previous chapter, Japanese immigration law was amended in the 1980s when Japan signed the UN refugee treaty. This cluster of reforms from the late 1980s into the early 1990s is sometimes termed "the 1990s Immigration Reform" (Akashi 2010). The notable changes in these reforms from the 1990s include the introduction of several new statuses that delineate immigrant legal status categories based on the purpose of residency and familial ties to Japanese citizens. One of the new legal statuses was the Long-Term Resident status, reserved mostly for refugees and former Japanese citizens and their descendants. This new type of visa allowed the entry of coethnic Japanese Latin Americans (mostly the descendants of Japanese immigrants who had moved to Peru and Brazil decades earlier). This immigration policy change led to a rapid increase of Japanese Brazilians and Japanese Peruvians (which I will refer to henceforth as *nikkeijin* or *nikkei*). In 1990, the population of *nikkei* Brazilians in Japan was approximately 56,000, but by 2020 it had nearly quadrupled, to over 208,000.[11] The 1990 immigration law was based on the nepotistic preference of the LDP, the leading party at the time, for a coethnic population, as evident in the following statement by Katō Takenori, chair of LDP's special committee for foreign labor issue:

> If possible, I would like to have the younger generation of Japanese from Latin America come and work in Japan to learn Japanese high technology. However, most of the third generation already gave up their Japanese citizenship. . . . Consequently, even if they are coethnic, we would have to treat them just the same as other foreigners with our immigration laws. In other words, they would be subject to legal immigration restrictions in terms of type of occupation and residency, which would prevent them from doing manual labor. I would like to find some way to give special treatment to those third-generation coethnic Japanese from Latin America so that they can have the same legal status as the first and second generations [with Japanese citizenship].[12]

Conclusion

187

In parallel to admitting these *nikkeijin*, the Japanese government further changed its immigration laws in 1993, instituting a new training and internship visa program for foreign students. This new program allowed many unskilled, disposable laborers from China and other Southeast Asian countries to enter Japan on a temporary trainee/internship visa. As shown in figure 4.1, as of 2022, the largest population of noncitizens was from China. The second largest group was Vietnamese. Although Koreans comprised the third largest group in this figure, it is important to note that approximately two-thirds of these Koreans are Special Permanent Residents (colonial migrants and their descendants). Thus, if we take this into consideration, then the third largest recent immigrant group would be Filipinos, followed by Brazilians. However, the supposedly temporary labor immigrants did not leave Japan, nor did they become socially or culturally incorporated into Japanese society, as some lawmakers initially hoped. Instead, they were quickly marginalized as outsiders even as they prolonged their stay in Japan.[13]

While the *nikkeijin* and other holders of Long-Term Resident status could enjoy relatively stable immigration status with fewer restrictions, they are not always able to enjoy these rights fully, nor are their livelihoods secured. This is evident in the extremely low enrollment in school among *nikkei* children and the unstable living situations for many *nikkeijin* workers (Nakayasu 2007). Like Koreans in the postwar period, they are often seen as a source of social disturbance and crimes. Many *nikkeijins* are more likely to be isolated from mainstream communities, unable to access public benefits, and unaware of the law and their rights (Kajita, Tanno, and Higuchi 2005; Matsumiya 2010).[14] Furthermore, in contrast with Special Permanent Residents, whose residency status cannot be unilaterally revoked by the Japanese state, the residency of *nikkeijin* is far more vulnerable and insecure, as illustrated in the aftermath of the 2008 Great Recession, when the Japanese state paid *nikkeijin* to permanently leave Japan in order to get rid of unemployed foreign workers (Tabuchi 2009). It is obvious that both the Japanese state and private companies who hire them treat *nikkeijin* as importable and disposable laborers rather than fellow members of society, invoking the similarity with postwar Korean labor migrants' experiences.

The situation is even worse for other immigrant groups, as their allowable residency length and labor opportunities are restricted. As mentioned earlier, in 1993, the Japanese government introduced the

188   Chapter 5

trainee visa program to allow foreign unskilled laborers into Japan to work in the agriculture and manufacturing sectors (Yamanaka 1993). The program was intended to fill the labor shortage in job sectors avoided by the native-born population, including farming and manufacturing, with temporary, inexpensive labor. Trainees were supposed to learn skills in these sectors and return to their homeland after a short period of time. In theory the program was supposed to be mutually beneficial, but in reality it was highly exploitative. Numerous reports from immigrant advocacy groups in Japan, including the Japan Federation of Bar Associations (Nichibenren), documented disturbing cases of severe human rights violations against newly arrived immigrant workers in Japan (Gaikokujin Kenshūsei Mondai Network 2006; Nichibenren 2020, 2021). Because immigrant workers are underinformed about their legal rights in Japan, they are often not properly enrolled in health insurance or adequately compensated for their labor. In some cases, they are paid well below the legal minimum wage. Even if they are aware of their rights, they have little means to assert or protect themselves, as they are heavily dependent on brokers to find jobs (Gaikokujin Kenshūsei Mondai Network 2006). This situation supports British sociologist Kate Nash's observation about the proliferation of status groups among noncitizens (Nash 2009). Nash argued that European cosmopolitan citizenship created different types of status groups—including supercitizens, marginal citizens, quasi-citizens, subcitizens, and uncitizens—that concretized new forms of inequality. Nash's conceptualization of status groups revealed the limited reach of human rights norms and cosmopolitan citizenship to the most vulnerable populations in society. Despite the dissemination of human rights into domestic policies and laws in Japan, the actual application of these policies remains limited and fails to protect the most marginalized populations because of ethno-racial and socioeconomic discrimination. The Japanese case elaborates what Nash reported: the statuses of noncitizens are proliferating and becoming increasingly stratified.

Ebashi Takashi, a Japanese constitutional law scholar, is one of the scholars who, as early as the 1990s, expressed concern about the transfer of oppression from Special Permanent Resident Aliens (Korean and Taiwanese colonial migrants and their descendants) to new resident aliens (*nikkeijin*, short-term trainees and interns, and other unskilled labor workers).[15] Japan's leading news magazine, *Sekai,* featured a discussion of immigration in 1994 in which Ebashi (1994,

Conclusion 189

146) conveyed his concern: "There is no progress unless we fundamentally change Japanese society. Unless we do that, the discriminatory sentiments that Zainichi [Korean or Taiwanese] endured would be simply transferred to newly arrived immigrants. It would be a pity if elimination of anti-Zainichi discrimination meant [that society] found a new target of discrimination."

Ebashi's trepidation was prescient. A series of legal reforms passed in Parliament in 2009 further institutionalized the distinction between Special Permanent Resident Aliens and noncitizens with other legal statuses. Japanese lawmakers legally created a new identification system (Zairyū Kanri Seido) for all foreign residents in Japan as part of the national security measures and immigration control that was set to replace the Alien Registration System created in the postwar period. With the introduction of this new residency identification system, the Alien Registration Law and its systems were abolished on July 9, 2019. This punctuated the end of postwar immigration policies designed to control colonial migrants and marked the advent of new immigration policies in Japan.

In terms of requirements and regulations, the new system makes a sharp distinction between Special Permanent Resident Aliens and other categories of aliens. For example, while all other noncitizens are required to have a reentry permit whenever they travel and stay outside Japan for more than one year, Special Permanent Resident Aliens are largely exempt from such a requirement.[16] Furthermore, Special Permanent Resident Aliens are exempt from submitting fingerprints at immigration, a practice that was abolished for all aliens in 2000 but reintroduced as part of counterterrorist security measures, and that is enforced for all aliens entering Japan besides Special Permanent Resident Aliens. Special Permanent Resident Aliens are also exempt from the requirement to carry this identification at all times, while other foreign residents are legally required to carry this card to prove their legal status in Japan. As mentioned earlier, Special Permanent Alien Residents are also exempt from unilateral deportation by the state.

These facts from contemporary Japanese society have important implications for minorities' social movements, for the impact of the globalized norm of human rights, and for the ways citizenship is imagined and practiced in society. First, citizenship rights in Japan are no longer imagined as rights exclusively reserved for Japanese citizens. This finding reaffirms the claim by cosmopolitanists and postnationalists that cosmopolitan ideals increasingly blur the distinction between citizens and noncitizens. Second, the case presented here shows that the decoupling of citizenship and nationality also stems from grass-roots efforts among the subaltern activists. Minority activism in Japan, involving heavy transnational lobbying, has been an important medium for the cosmopolitanized notion of rights in Japanese society, confirming the cosmopolitanist observation about an association between cosmopolitan ideals and a rising global civil society.

However, the experiences of Korean social movements also reveal a very different outcome of citizenship from what cosmopolitanists and postnationalists have presumed because of the penetration of the globalized notion of human rights. Rather than universally equalizing rights between citizens and noncitizens, the Japanese case shows that specific historical backgrounds and transnational politics can become a filter that particularizes the effect of the globalized notion of human rights and that creates an uneven field of rights among noncitizens. This uneven field in turn results in new forms of inequality as well as violations of the human rights of society's most vulnerable populations.

Furthermore, this uneven extension of citizenship rights among different groups of noncitizens has a daunting effect on solidarity among marginalized populations in Japan. As I noted in chapter 4, Anthony Marx (1997) argued that exclusion from citizenship rights often allows the marginalized to see the boundaries of oppression clearly and concretely. This in turn enables them to construct a solid basis for collectively organizing actions against the state—their common target—for a shared goal. Yet when the state begins to assign different sets of rights and privileges by creating different categories of marginalized groups that overlap with ethno-racial and national origins, it facilitates a critical fragmentation among marginalized migrant groups, making it difficult for noncitizens to form solidarity among them.

The social movement of the previous generation of Koreans was able to overcome such heterogeneity and fraction among actors by effectively creating a coalition and solidarity across categorical differences via the unifying lexicon of human rights. But the circumstances are different now for Koreans and recent immigrants in Japan. Rising transnational attention and support for their claim-making has been a double-edged sword for Koreans. On the one hand, they were able to mobilize transnational support to create external pressure against the Japanese state to achieve their desired outcome in the 1990s; and in the backdrop of the transnational political struggle over representation in East Asia, Koreans' claims and interests began to carry valu-

Conclusion   191

able diplomatic capital for their homeland state and for nonstate actors. On the other hand, the regional tensions and standoff between their homeland states and the Japanese state added fuel to rising ethnoracial sentiments among ultranationalist groups such as Zaitokukai. The North Korean regime's provocative missile tests and refusal to release all Japanese abductees certainly played a significant role in demonizing those associated with the regime. In the post-9/11 context, security measures against terrorism were consciously placed into immigration legal reforms in Japan, even though the major terrorist attacks on Japan's soil in recent decades have been committed by domestic extremists such as religious cult group Ōmu Shinrikyō (or Aum Shinrikyō) and other Japanese individuals, including Abe Shinzō's assassin, Yamagami Tetsuya. This tendency to demonize foreigners is not unique to Japan; it can be seen also in the United States and Europe. In the twenty-first century, in a context of growing associations between homeland security and immigration around the world, the Japanese state introduced the aforementioned drastic immigration reform. These new immigration laws and policies were based on the false notion that immigrants and non-Japanese are a source of domestic disturbance and a national security threat, in much the same way that prewar and postwar Japanese policies were. But the forces that led to these policies in the twenty-first century were not driven by imperial and colonial sentiments or by the interests of the Cold War. Instead, they emerged in the nexus between globalization and colonial legacies.

The Future of Nationhood, Citizenship, and Immigration in Japan

In December 2020, six months after George Floyd's death sparked a global outcry against the violence that Black people experience, Nike launched an advertising campaign in Japan titled "The Future Isn't Waiting." The ad features three schoolgirl athletes, including one of mixed race and another who is a Korean girl, being bullied by their Japanese peers. The ad also includes an image of biracial tennis champion Naomi Osaka, a fierce advocate for the Black Lives Matter movement whose Japanese identity is often a subject of contention in Japan. The ad directly challenges Japan's homogeneous national self-image and its pervasive racial discrimination against its minority groups.

Nike Inc. has used politics as a theme of its US marketing strategy for some time. In 2018, it featured former NFL quarterback and

192　Chapter 5

vocal Black activist Colin Kaepernick for the thirtieth anniversary of the "Just Do It" campaign. This sparked controversy in the United States and prompted a call for boycotts of Nike's products. Despite this backlash, the campaign was a commercial success for Nike, resulting in strong revenue growth (Young 2018). Following this successful campaign in the United States, Nike brought its racial-justice-themed commercial to Japan in late 2020. This commercial turned out to be another success as an advertisement for Nike. However, the ad also triggered strong negative responses from the Japanese audience, who blamed Nike for exaggerating racial problems in Japan and threatened to boycott its products (Denyer and Kashiwagi 2020; McCurry 2020). Public responses to Nike's commercial were mixed: some responses showed people in Japan embracing increasingly globalized norms of diversity, equity, and inclusion, while other responses confirmed a stubborn tendency to prioritize the essentialized mythical homogeneity of Japanese identity over the reality of diversity.

Incidents of racial violence following the 2020 Nike commercial exemplify the later tendency. Six months after the Nike commercial was aired in Japan, a twenty-two-year-old Japanese man, Arimoto Takugo, committed arson at Korean residential properties in the Utoro district of Kyoto. He was arrested in December 2021 and was later found guilty and sentenced to four years in prison. The Utoro district is a site of Korean generational trauma of colonial oppression and the frontline of fighting against the colonial legacy. As referenced in chapter 3, many Korean colonial migrant workers were brought to this area to build a military airfield during the colonial period. The Utoro area was plagued with frequent flooding and lacked proper sewer and water lines, but these laborers lived near the construction site despite the terrible living conditions. After the war, the construction site was abandoned, and so were these Korean colonial migrant workers and their families. With nowhere to go, many continued to settle in the area. In the late 1980s, the owner of Utoro's land, Nissan Corporation—one of Japan's leading carmakers—sold the land to a developer, who issued eviction notices to Korean residents in the area, referring to them as illegal occupants. Korean activists and Japanese allies collectively fought against this eviction order. However, they have lost all the court battles to avert the eviction (Saitō 2022).

When they saw no path forward through domestic venues, Korean and Japanese activists for the Utoro community turned to a strategy used in other Korean social movements—mobilizing transnationally.

They successfully gained global attention and support from the UN and from their homeland, South Korea. In 2005, Doudou Dièn, a UN special rapporteur on racism and xenophobia, visited Utoro and expressed his grave concern about racism against Koreans in Japan. In the same year, the South Korean NGO Korean International Network also began investigating the Utoro issue. Thanks to all the attention both within and outside Japan, the Utoro community was able to receive international support and publicity (Saitō 2022). With the financial support from South Korean government in 2007, the residents were able to buy part of the land in the Utoro district from the developer. The activists and their supporters built a peace memorial museum to commemorate the history of colonialism and the generational trauma that Korean colonial migrants and their descendants have endured. The properties that Arimoto attacked were supposed to be displayed in this museum. This racially motivated brutal attack is a stark reminder to many Koreans and their allies that Koreans' fight for restorative justice is far from over.

In the spring of the same year that this racist arsonist attacked the Utoro community, the Japanese government proposed a bill to reform immigration law that aimed to eliminate prolonged detention. The Japan Federation of Bar Associations harshly criticized the proposed bill, as it would make deportation swift and easy for the state, while denying the due process rights of detained immigrants (Nichibenren 2021). One month after the bill was submitted to the parliamentary debate, a thirty-three-year-old Sri Lankan woman named Ratnayake Liyanage Wishma Sandamali—an alleged victim of domestic violence who was detained for overstaying her visa—died in the custody of Japan's infamous detention center in Aichi Prefecture. Immigration advocates and activists publicized her untimely death and alleged abusive treatment leading to her death. Her tragic death sparked public outcry against the bill. Opposition lawmakers seized on the moment and forcefully opposed the proposed bill. They argued that this reform made the deportation of asylum seekers far too easy because of a provision that would allow the state to deport asylum seekers after their third applications.

The Sri Lankan woman's unwarranted death was just the tip of the iceberg when it came to violations of human rights in Japan's dysfunctional detention system. Immigration advocate groups have reported numerous cases of physical and sexual violence against detainees by detention center workers. Detainees said the Japanese immigrant detention centers were worse than prisons because many people were locked up for an indefinite period of time (Hirano 2020; Yamada 2020). In 2019, a Nigerian man in his forties died after a long hunger strike to protest indefinite detention. This sparked a series of hunger strikes among detainees. The proposed bill was meant to force these defiant detainees out of Japan (*Mainichi Shinbun Digital* 2021). According to a nonprofit organization, the Japan Association for Refugees or Nanmin Shien Kyōkai (2022a), nearly 1,200 people were detained in these types of facilities in 2019, and about half of them have been detained for over six months. The number may seem small and thus insignificant to those in the countries where a larger number of immigrants are detained, but this number needs to be considered in the context of an extremely low number of asylum seekers who were actually granted refugee status in Japan—forty-four in 2019 (Hōmushō Shutsunyūkoku Zairyū Kanrichō 2019). Japan accepted only seventy-four refugees in 2021, significantly fewer than were accepted in the United States (20,590) or Germany (38,918) (Nanmin Shien Kyōkai 2022b). Considering how low Japan's immigration and refugee population is, it is striking how eager Japanese lawmakers in the ruling parties were to pass a bill that reinforced restrictive treatment of refugees.

But on May 18, 2021, when it was scheduled to be voted on in Parliament, the bill was suddenly pulled at the last minute. The next day, then–prime minister Suga Yoshihide stated that the government would not pursue this bill further in the current Diet session. This was a reactionary response to the fierce protest against the bill by immigration advocates, lawmakers, and activists, as well as ordinary citizens who spontaneously responded to and supported the organized efforts of activists and advocates for immigrants and refugees. Protesters were from all walks of life—Japanese immigrant advocates, progressive lawmakers, Japanese artists, celebrities, and Korean minorities. They organized sit-in protests even though COVID-19 cases were rising across Japan at that time. *Mainichi Newspaper Digital,* one of the leading newspapers in Japan, noted the presence of many young activists in sit-ins against the bill. The journalist wrote, "During a month-long reporting on this issue, we felt the power of young people" and "People's voice moves politics" (Kamihigashi 2021).

The heterogeneous group of people who protested this bill invoked memories of Park Jongseok's fight against Hitachi in the 1970s and Koreans' anti-fingerprinting efforts, a movement ignited by Han

Conclusion 195

Jongsok's defiance, in the 1980s. As in the movements of decades past, young people in Japan from various backgrounds in terms of gender, citizenship status, race, ethnicity, class, religion, and occupation broke their silence and physically and digitally showed up to protest the bill. As this case makes clear, there has been growing support for immigrants in Japan at the local and citizen level as immigrants steadily increase and become a permanent and critical part of Japanese society. Scholars in the United States and Japan have already analyzed this development in depth, so I did not cover it extensively in this book, but the growing trend is important and thus noteworthy (Komai 2004; Milly 2014; Tanno 2019).

Another noteworthy fact is that support for newly arrived immigrants in Japan emerged from the historical lessons that activists learned from their previous fights for Korean colonial migrants and their descendants. In fact, many actors who advocate for and support the growing number of immigrants in Japan have also been allies and advocates for Korean minorities in Japan. For example, Kawasaki City, a center stage of Park Jongseok's struggle against job discrimination by Hitachi, has been a model for municipal governance in its support for non-Japanese resident aliens in Japan (Katō 2008). One of his supporters, in fact, started working for the City Office of Kawasaki City. Kawasaki City has always had a sizable presence of Korean colonial labor migrants and continues to be a destination for more recent immigrants. Many public services for the non-Japanese population were made possible through the demands of Korean colonial migrants and their descendants in the 1960s and 1970s (i.e., demands for protections against discrimination and social welfare support). The gradual shift in the availability of public services allowed for multicultural community building, where noncitizens could politically and socially participate in local community affairs. Activists, their allies, and the municipal government often disagreed about the definition of multiculturalism and the ways it is practiced (Katō 2008). Nevertheless, Kawasaki City has been considered among the most progressive cities in Japan because of how they incorporated the minority population into their community.

Similar phenomena can be found in Yao City in the Osaka Prefecture, where there has been a high concentration of Korean colonial migrants and their descendants since the prewar period. Tokkabi Children's Group or Tokkabi Kodomokai, an after-school cultural program founded in the 1970s by student activists specifically for

Koreans in Yao City, was a backbone for Korean social activism for citizenship rights in the 1980s. By the 1990s, the organizers for the Tokkabi began to support Vietnamese refugees. In their twentieth-anniversary booklet, members of the Tokkabi (1995, 59) detailed the parallels between the needs of new immigrants and refugees and Korean minorities, and they described how they could use their experiences of working with Korean minorities to support newly arrived immigrants and refugees:

> There are already many children from Vietnam, China, and Brazil currently living in Japan and they will face many challenges as they grow up here. Going forward, the Tokkabi cannot focus and engage only with Korean minority children. We should educate Korean children in the Tokkabi to have the spirit [of mutual understanding and support for other marginalized immigrant children] and the Tokkabi must provide the opportunities and supports [to facilitate a mutual sense of community].

Like members of the Tokkabi, many descendants of Korean colonial migrants who grew up in Japan easily see parallels between the oppressive treatment of recent immigrants in the twenty-first century

Figure 5.2. The original building of Tokkabi Kodomokai in Yao City, Osaka. The sign reads "Together with Our Friends" in Korean, Vietnamese, and Japanese. Photo from NPO Tokkabi.

Conclusion   197

and the colonial oppression and institutionalized racism that their parents and grandparents endured in the twentieth century. After all, as shown in chapter 3, the Japanese state based its postwar immigration laws on its experiences with colonial migrants from Korea and Taiwan. For this reason, Korean colonial migrants and their descendants understood the colonial legacies and inequalities embedded and institutionalized in postwar Japan's citizenship and immigration laws better than other immigrants. To demonstrate this point, a group of people who self-identified as Zainichi Koreans created a website to issue a collective statement against the proposed immigration bills in May 2021 and to gather online signatures. On this website, they observed continuing colonial legacies in the treatment of recent immigrants and refugees: "Japan's immigration problems are tightly connected to the history of Zainichi Koreans. . . . Today's immigration reform, which worsens the treatment of immigrants and refugees, is linked to the actions the Japanese government had taken against Zainichi Korean. Both reflect ongoing Japanese colonialism and ethno-racism. . . . Thus, we as Zainichi Koreans oppose the bill that would worse the status of immigrants and refugees."[17] In the eyes of these young Koreans in Japan, colonial oppression has not yet ended. It morphed into the ethno-racial injustices that target the newly arrived immigrant population in Japan. Koreans in Japan went through the trials and tribulations of ethno-racial oppression originating in colonialism only to see the same injustices repeated in their society and targeting new immigrant groups from other parts of the world. Is it possible for Japan to completely sever the connection between a colonial legacy and its citizenship and immigration policies and move toward a more inclusive society whose members embrace its diversity? Although the dynamics that may answer this question are still underway, the final section of this book nevertheless ponders this question.

A DIALECTICAL, PENDULUM-SWING TRAJECTORY

Facing the irreversible trend of global migration, policymakers and scholars in industrial societies fiercely debate what type of immigration and citizenship policies the state should employ. They also ponder why a type of policy that works in one context fails in another. The heart of this debate rests on the common question of whether restrictive and nonrestrictive citizenship and immigration policies have a positive or negative effect on immigrant integration into a host

198   *Chapter 5*

society, an outcome that ultimately affects the quality of life for all residents in a society, regardless of legal status.

To better answer this question, we need to understand under which conditions, in what ways, and for what purposes a society chooses a certain type of nationhood, citizenship, and migration policy. We also need to understand under what conditions certain types of citizenship and migration policies integrate both newly arrived and permanently settled human begins without segregation or conflict. Moreover, we also need to understand what happens when state policies fail to integrate migrant groups from another nation-state. Also, what types of roles do immigrants play in modifying such policies so as to be better integrated into a society? Finally, and perhaps most significantly, what roles do the marginalized subaltern actors play in this process?

Japan has been seen as an unlikely country to offer useful and helpful empirical materials to answer these questions on citizenship and immigration in industrial societies, because of the notion that Japan is homogeneous. Nevertheless, the history of remaking nationhood, citizenship, and migration policies in twentieth- and twenty-first-century Japan provides us with a series of helpful and rich empirical material for answering questions relevant to contemporary debates about citizenship and immigration in many industrial societies.

The case of Koreans reminds us of the importance of including the colonial period and empire into sociological inquiries of citizenship and immigration policies, validating the argument by Julian Go summarized in chapter 1 (i.e., that sociologists' tendency to binarize social relations and to occlude empire in their accounts can minimize the influence of colonized people in the historical process). If we analyze the impact of empire and colonialism on the subsequent period's policies, we are forced to confront the pervasive analytical bifurcation in studies of citizenship and immigration—the binary of "citizen versus immigrant/noncitizen." Thus, this book introduced a third concept, "colonial migrant," into our analysis. This enabled us to avert the unnecessarily linear and simplistic conclusion that exclusive policies toward minorities and immigrants reflect national characteristics or an unbroken continuity of past colonialism. Transcending the occlusion of empire and analytical bifurcation also allowed us to incorporate subaltern perspectives into the analysis. This in turn empowered us to reveal a far more complex mechanism that produced and reproduced durable inequality and institutionalized racism. Subaltern perspec-

Conclusion   199

tives also let us understand how difficult yet important it is to continue to fight against both.

The historical trajectory of Japan's practices of making nationhood, citizenship, and migration is filled with moments of disjuncture created by both external and internal forces. The trajectory did not follow a steady, linear evolution, nor did it completely sever itself from the legacy of colonialism or exclusive policies. Instead, Japan's trajectory followed a dialectical, pendulum-swing pattern of changes in the twentieth and early twenty-first centuries. During this time, Japan's citizenship and migration policies and laws oscillated between inclusion and exclusion. In parallel to these policy changes, the collective sense of nationhood in Japan also shifted from a heterogeneous pan-Asian nation to a homogeneous nation and then to a diverse global nation. While nationhood, citizenship, and migration policies swung back and forth between seemingly two opposite spectrums, the Japanese state persistently practiced oppression against marginalized groups throughout all of the time periods discussed in this book.

Imperial Japan chose inclusive citizenship policies (expanding citizenship status to all subjects in its territory) and allowed colonial migrants to enter the metropole. They also deliberately constructed an expansive, multicultural national self-image. Unlike European empires that extended citizenship to the colonial population only conditionally, the Japanese Empire extended citizenship to all colonial subjects unconditionally. The choice of such inclusive and expansive citizenship and migration policies derived from its deliberate efforts to reconcile competing interests. Japanese policymakers in the late nineteenth and early twentieth centuries had to assert their presence and superiority to two separate audiences—the neighboring Asian countries that Japan was trying to colonize and the Western powers trying to dominate Japan. Hence, Imperial Japan intentionally created a Janus-faced citizenship and migration policy that was externally inclusive but internally exclusive. Japan attempted to present itself to Western powers as an inclusive and civilized imperialist nation by granting the colonial population the status of Japanese citizen to integrate them into the boundaries of the empire. With such a citizenship policy, they also cemented their ownership of the newly acquired territory, and the population that inhabited these territories, so that Western powers would not be able to claim influence over these territories, as was done after the Sino-Japanese War.

One distinctive feature of Japanese colonial policy during its early phase was that Japan established these inclusive institutional arrangements and national self-image without a sufficient cultural assimilation policy. Japanese policymakers were aware that cultural assimilation was necessary to tame the rebellious colonial population and transform them into obedient royal imperial subjects. Yet a lack of material and economic resources prevented the Japanese colonial government from implementing a rigorous assimilation policy. Nevertheless, Japanese colonialists retained their optimism at least initially, resting on the idea that the Japanese and the colonial population shared relative proximity in terms of culture, level of civilization, and racial phenotypes. Japanese policymakers originally hoped that inclusive policies—the extension of Japanese citizenship to Koreans, freedom to travel to the metropole, and the absence of any clear legal prohibition of interracial marriage between the colonizers and the colonized—would gradually facilitate an affinity between the Japanese and the colonized population.

Inside the empire, however, Japan did not hide its exclusionist face. The concept of pan-Asian unity remained mere rhetoric rather than an official policy guideline to be translated into actual practice among Japanese officials toward the colonial population. Everyday discrimination and prejudice against the colonial population persisted throughout the imperial era and further widened the conceptual and emotional gaps between the colonizers and the colonized. In addition to everyday oppression, the fact that the internal distinction between Korean and Japanese peoples was maintained through separate family registry systems served as a concrete example that Koreans were not fully integrated as equal citizens of the empire. In short, Japanese inclusive citizenship was not based on an egalitarian principle.

These facts combined indicate the important role that political, material, and cultural conditions play in a state's policymaking process. They also suggest that the extent to which these conditions matter to the repertoire of policies that the state and power elites could consider and ultimately choose varies depending on the country's position within the larger world society. For that reason, endogenous and exogenous factors need to be examined simultaneously, as FitzGerald and Cook-Martín (2014) demonstrated in their studies on immigration policies in the Americas. European empires that occupied the dominant position within world society have relatively abundant symbolic,

Conclusion 201

military, and economic resources. Hence, they exerted their racial superiority and justified their colonial acts as *mission civilisatrice* to fortify the inferior races. However, under the menace of Western imperial powers and with relatively little symbolic, material, and military resources, Japanese colonialists could not emulate Western colonial strategies without modification. Instead, they justified their colonialism toward their neighboring countries as a mission of constructing a hybrid ethnic-nation based on the idea of racial proximity manifested through the ideologies of *isshi dōjin* (imperial impartiality and equal favor for all imperial citizens) and *kunmin dōso* (same origin, same race).

Contrary to the policymakers' initial hopes and expectations, however, racial and cultural affinity did not emerge between the Japanese and the colonized population, as proven by the March First Movement in 1919 as well as the massacre of Koreans after the Great Kantō Earthquake in 1923. The disparity between the rhetoric of a hybrid Asian unity and the actual practice of colonialism and the Koreans' dual status—de jure Japanese and de facto alien—had an unintentional effect on self-identification among the colonized populace. That is, it transformed the national consciousness among Koreans. Prior to the advent of Japanese colonialism, national solidarity among Koreans had been fragmented, and the nationalist movement was largely an elite-reformist movement. However, the Japanese invasion and subsequent oppression invoked the collective consciousness of Koreans and solidified unity between the elite groups who had previously competed with one another for power and between the elites and the mass populace. This eventually led to large-scale mass protests in 1919 against colonial rule among Koreans across the Korean peninsula, as well as among political exiles abroad. This suggests that mere extension of citizenship status and civil rights, no matter how inclusive it is, will not necessarily facilitate a sense of belonging and affinity among the newly incorporated groups. What matters to people on the ground is not just how laws are written but also how they are applied and practiced. Thus, the Japanese experience tells us that just looking at the surface or the language of laws alone can't enable us to understand why marginalization continues when laws are changed or abolished. After all, actions matter more than words.

Stripping away Japanese citizenship status from the colonial population after World War II did not, of course, facilitate a sense of gratitude toward Japan among Koreans in Japan. The bitter defeat and ensuing occupation by the United States motivated both conservative rightists and radical leftists to collectively negate the nation's dark military past with its ambitious construction of a multiethnic empire and to look for a new foundation for a postwar Japanese sense of nationhood. In their search for a new foundation, intellectuals from both ends of the political spectrum found the notion of a mono-ethnic/racial origin of Japan the most appealing self-image for the suddenly shrunken country. This new national self-image as a homogeneous nation, celebrated among postwar intellectuals, was later used to justify the ongoing oppression of colonial migrants and their descendants and restrictive immigration policies in postwar Japan.

The emergence of a large-scale and steady collaboration between Japanese and Koreans had to wait until the 1970s. Although it was beyond the scope of this research to single out the most decisive factor for collaboration between the Japanese and Koreans beginning in the 1970s, the empirical materials analyzed in previous chapters allow us to identify a few key factors and mechanisms that facilitated this emergent collaboration in the global context. One factor was a shift in Koreans' conceptualization about their rights and self-understanding. Having settled in Japan since the early twentieth century, many Koreans today—who are mostly second-, third-, and fourth-generation Koreans—became culturally assimilated into Japanese culture. Most Koreans born and raised in Japan today do not speak the Korean language. Many have never been to either North or South Korea. The naturalization of Koreans continues as intermarriage between Koreans and Japanese increases. Many Koreans view Japanese society as their permanent home and consider themselves members of ethnoracial minority groups whose rights are anchored in Japanese society.

However, one should not conclude that cultural assimilation and generational change have led Koreans to see themselves as Japanese, or that assimilation and generational shifts are the only forces that facilitate the alliance we've seen between Japanese and Korean activists since the 1980s. Although most Koreans in Japan speak little Korean language, use Japanese names to disguise their identities, and have not been to Korea, many still identify as "Korean" instead of "Japanese." It's clear that being Korean in Japan is a relatively stable, fixed identity. But will Koreans in Japan ever become Japanese or come to identify as Japanese? It depends on what one means by "becoming Japanese" and whether the dominant notion of "Japaneseness" ever changes.

Conclusion 203

As scholarly works on the identity issues of Koreans in Japan have suggested, self-identification among Koreans in Japan is neither simplistic nor uniform.[18] Many Koreans call themselves Zainichi (Korean residents in Japan) rather than using a "hyphenated" identification such as "Korean-Japanese" or "Japanese-Korean." Furthermore, although the naturalization and cultural assimilation of Koreans is ongoing, a significant number of Koreans still retain Korean citizenship despite the considerable disadvantages associated with it and the obvious advantages of Japanese citizenship (Lee 2021). Some Koreans' reluctance to become naturalized and take on Japanese citizenship shows, in itself, how citizenship has become and remained an identity signifier embedded in their self-understanding. And this situation arose because citizenship in Japan has been functioning not only as a bundle of rights and duties but also as a device of social closure.

The empirical materials analyzed in previous chapters suggest that the mechanisms involved to facilitate the emergence of cohesive social movements among Korean and Japanese activists are far more complex than existing theory anticipates, as reflected by the complexity of Korean identities. As we saw in chapter 4, the introduction and penetration of the globalized concept of human rights in recent decades has played an important role in building a bridge between previously disconnected and fragmented groups of people in Japan. This was a decisive difference in social movements between the Cold War and global contexts. And because of the history of colonial experience, Korean activists in the early Cold War context believed that to secure their rights in Japan, they would first and foremost have to specify their national belonging. In the postwar context, when all the international laws and treaties presupposed national belonging as a prerequisite for the protections of individual rights, Korean activists firmly believed that defining their self-identification as Koreans, and thus as "liberated people," would prompt the international community to protect their rights. This explains why so many Korean activists in the early Cold War context devoted energy to cultivating political affinity with their homelands and the regimes in North or South Korea. However, this effort was in vain, as those regimes utilized the interests and claims of Koreans in Japan as diplomatic tools to pursue their own political and economic gains from the Japanese and American governments.

The collective memory of the bitter colonial past and abandonment by the United States and two Korean homeland states during the Cold War era, combined with cultural assimilation and generational changes, diverted a new generation of Korean activists from continuing to affiliate with their homelands and instead led them to collaborate with sympathetic Japanese civil rights activists as a means of furthering their claims in Japanese society. As I discussed in chapter 4, it was the concept of human rights that allowed them to create common ground with the Japanese and to overcome the division between North and South Koreans. Unlike in the two previous historical contexts, Koreans in the global context considered their rights as belonging not to particular nationhood but, rather, to universal personhood. As Korean-minority intellectuals and activists introduced the concept of globalized human rights and as the Japanese government subscribed to the global norm of human rights by signing the UN human rights treaties, many Korean activists used the concept of human rights to frame their claims in order to obtain equal civil rights without modifying their national belonging. This penetration of globalized norms of human rights provided Koreans with legitimate vocabularies to frame the cognitive shifts in their self-understanding about their rights and to build bridges between themselves, the Japanese, and other transnational activist groups.

The importation and penetration of external ideologies and norms, however, was not limited to the latter part of the twentieth century. As we saw in chapter 2, Korean activists under Japanese colonialism also incorporated an external ideology to legitimize their claims and appeals to the international community. Marxist socialism prompted Koreans to find transnational allies in Russia and China, while the Wilsonian ideal of ethnic self-determinism granted Western legitimacy to their claims against Japanese colonial rule. Exogenous ideologies of ethnic independence and self-determinism and external events such as the Russian Revolution played a critical role in facilitating the mobilization against Japanese colonialism among Koreans during the imperial period. However, their efforts fell short and did not lead to the modification of Japanese policies in their favor. When we contrast this result during the imperial context with the Koreans' social movements in the global context, it is clear that external support from the international community has a large impact on the outcome of social movements among marginalized groups. The protection of colonized peoples' human rights was hardly an important issue to the international community, which was dominated by Western imperialists during the imperial and early Cold War contexts. Hence, the voices

Conclusion 205

of Koreans, no matter how fierce and loud, did not grab sufficient attention, nor did they receive adequate support from the international community.

The historical trajectory of Koreans' fight for justice in Japan reminds us that the transformation of citizenship and nationhood should not be regarded as an entirely internal political process. This point echoes arguments presented by other scholars, including David Scott FitzGerald and David Cook-Martín (2014). Although late twentieth-century legal reforms were driven by internal protest, the emergence of activism was a response to newly institutionalized norms of human rights that gradually penetrated the society and lent legitimacy to minority social movements. This fact demonstrates the significant role played by newly emergent normative properties: the concept of human rights, a globally sanctioned normative repertoire of demands for reparations from the colonial actions, and the increase of globalized economic transactions between nations. This distinct shift in the economic, political, and normative arrangements of the international community in the context of globalization created a new field where domestic minority groups could claim cultural currency to legitimize their claims against the state's policies.

This complex set of simultaneous pressures from within and outside national boundaries set into motion policy changes that favored nonstate and subaltern agents in the late twentieth century. Specifically, exogenous factors such as the penetration of the concept of human rights and external pressure from the UN and Japan's former colonies were more responsible for facilitating political mobilization and its successful outcomes than endogenous factors such as the institutional categorization of racial or ethnic lines by the state. This finding supports arguments made by scholars who have pointed to the global dimensions of social movements and identified factors that lie beyond national borders, claiming that global alliances of nongovernmental actors have created new modes of political activism in the contemporary world.[19] The case presented in this book elaborated this argument by demonstrating that such success depends on the degree to which internal and external support can mobilize movements. This is most evident when we compare their success in the global context, despite a smaller Korean population, to the failure of their social movement during the imperial context, when their numbers were greater and the social movement was on a larger scale.

206   *Chapter 5*

Furthermore, empirical evidence from the mid- and late twentieth century also makes clear how and why supranational organizations succeed or fail in recognizing the claims and interests of marginalized populations. In the 1980s and 1990s, the UN Human Rights Committee was able to pay attention to claims made by minority activists from Japan. Given that the Japanese government signed various international human rights treaties in order to meet the standards of other industrial nations, the committee was also able to put pressure on representatives of the Japanese government, prompting the Japanese government to further revise its restrictive policies against Koreans in Japan. However, the fact that during the early Cold War context another supranational institution, the International Committee of the Red Cross Society (ICRC), failed to rescue the remaining Koreans in Japan from poverty and risky repatriation to North Korea makes it clear how the political interests of the state in power prevented a well-intended global organization from helping the vulnerable groups. The Japanese Red Cross Society, which supposedly worked on behalf of the ICRC, instead served the Japanese government in attempting to send Koreans back to North Korea, knowing that these Koreans' well-being would not be guaranteed. Although the ICRC suspected this effort was problematic, it could not exert enough pressure to constrain the Japanese government's treatment of Koreans in Japan. As these cases from two different time periods illustrate, the extent to which supranational institutions have influence over the domestic sphere within national boundaries has a significant—negative or positive—effect on the domestic treatment of marginalized groups.

Another negative impact on the marginalization of Koreans in postwar Japan also derived from the influence of the United States. American Cold War interests in postwar reconstruction in Far East Asia played a decisive role in worsening the living conditions and legal status of Koreans in postwar Japan. American authorities further marginalized Koreans in Japan because they feared Korean communist inclinations, and this gave the Japanese state free rein to exclude Koreans from various socioeconomic privileges. The decline of well-organized social movements that uniformly represented the needs and interests of Koreans to supranational organizations also did not help the circumstances of Koreans in Japan. These empirical facts have important implications for current situations in various parts of the world where the United States' involvement has played a significant

Conclusion

negative role in further complicating intergroup relationships. As the case of Koreans in Japan during the early Cold War context has shown us, the presence and political interests of a hegemonic foreign power influences how a marginalized population will be treated in a society and what kinds of immigrant and citizenship policies a state will adopt. Furthermore, the involvement of a hegemonic foreign power also has had an impact on subsequent bilateral relationships between Japan and its former colonies. As discussed in chapter 4, many of the diplomatic problems (i.e., island disputes and colonial reparations) between Japan and its former colonies were issues that the United States did not resolve during the occupation period. The political footprint that the United States has left and forgotten has significant lingering effects on international relationships between Japan and its former colonies, even over half a century later.

In summary, this book has demonstrated that nationhood, citizenship, and migration policies are not simply emergent properties of an evolving system; rather, they result from a clash of forces—the state's policymaking process, subaltern resistance to the state's policies, and the position of the nation-state within world society—that interface in new ways at different historical moments. But by closely examining discourse among policymakers, intellectuals, and journalists as well as the dissonant voices of minorities, we can identify the forces that will be part of the mix at each critical juncture. Citizenship restrictions, immigration policies, and the collective sense of nationhood change when the configuration of political, cultural, and economic fields in and outside the nation synthesize renewed contentious relationships between the state and nonstate actors.

These findings echo the arguments of other scholars in theories of nationhood, citizenship, and immigration policies: that is, a departure from authoritarian empire and the establishment of democratic government do not necessarily cultivate a path toward nondiscriminatory immigration policies or citizenship laws. The end of World War II certainly prompted many countries, including Japan, to reconfigure their citizenship and nationality. However, the same timing does not guarantee the same trajectory. As the Japanese case shows, the ways citizenship and nationality were reimagined and rearranged were largely contingent on the position of the country in world society, internal economic and demographic conditions, endogenous dynamics between the state and nonstate actors, and international relationships with other countries, particularly former colonies. The Japanese experiences allow us to imagine an alternative understanding, one where the process is contingent on geopolitical and economic conditions at a given period in history. We cannot simply associate the mode of citizenship in a society with its regime type or its national self-image or characteristics; nor can we anticipate the shape or strength of subaltern opposition. While regime type, a collective sense of nationhood, and subaltern political mobilization are major forces behind the transformation of citizenship and migration policies, they interact with economic and geopolitical imperatives and complex global processes. Only when we examine all these factors and assess the connections among them can we understand the malleable and contingent nature of the relationship between nationhood, citizenship, and migration policies.

A number of unresolved issues between Japan and Koreans in Japan remain, including the fact that not all of Koreans' demands were met sufficiently. Will Japan continue to respond to the demands of Koreans in Japan? Will Japan open its gates and accept a substantial number of immigrants in the near future? And if it does, will it embrace the cultural diversity and develop yet another hybrid national self-image and become inclusive toward non-Japanese members of its society? What roles do Koreans in Japan play in current and future debate over citizenship and immigration policies? Will the meaning of "being Japanese" change in the foreseeable future? Will Koreans in Japan ever see themselves as Japanese? We cannot fully answer these questions yet because the struggles to influence the direction of Japan's policies and collective sense of nationhood are underway. Nonetheless, recent developments—policy changes and the historical trajectories leading to them—give us insights into the ongoing transformation of Japanese nationhood, citizenship, and immigration. It is hard to imagine the future of Japan's nationhood, citizenship, and immigration without the involvement of the Koreans there.

As seen in the collective protests by Koreans in Japan against the anti-immigration bill, they could easily see parallels between their families' past struggles and the state's oppressive treatment of newly arrived immigrants who are heavily exploited, criminalized, and detained and whose human rights are violated. To them, it does not matter whether or not colonialism is continuing. Seeing the repeated history of oppressive experiences at the hands of Japanese bureaucrats and public servants is enough to make many Korean activists break their silence. They know that silence would make them complicit in the ethno-racial oppression in Japan that they themselves continue to face today. If they remain vigilant against continuing racial injustice in Japanese society, they will be, without a doubt, one of the most powerful forces fighting for social injustice and building an inclusive Japanese society. They can also cultivate meaningful spaces for other noncitizens and non-Japanese peoples in a collectively imagined nationhood in twenty-first-century Japan.

Notes

CHAPTER 1: INTRODUCTION

1. "Coupling" and "decoupling," as used in this book, are sociological concepts in neo-institutional theory (Meyer and Rowan 1977). The terms generally refer to the gap between formal policies and actual practice in organizational settings. In this book, "coupling" means there is no or little gap between nationhood and citizenship policies, while "decoupling" means there is a notable gap between them.

2. The UN's data set presents estimates of international migrants based on official statistics published by each nation-state. The definition of international migrants or foreigner varies from one country to another.

3. Some notable scholars who live and work outside Japan but specialize in minority issues in the country and challenged the notion of Japan as a homogeneous nation include but are not limited to Amos (2011), Howell (2005), Mitchell (1967), Neary (2003), Lie (2001), Wagatsuma and De Vos (1966), and Weiner (1994, 1997).

4. See works by Befu (2001), Mouer (1982, 1995), Olson (1992), Sugimoto (1999), Sugimoto and Mouer (1990), and Yoshino (1999) for early critiques against Nihonjinron, a very popular discourse on the distinctive uniqueness of the society, culture, and national character of the Japanese.

5. This book also draws on the sociology of human rights, which understands the power of human rights to be a normative claim-making repertoire in an imagined world where all humans share equally in the vulnerabilities and consequences of wars, terrorism, health crises, and natural disasters (Levy and Sznaider 2006; Turner 2006).

6. Transcending this binary framing and the conceptualization of Koreans as colonial migrants allows us to challenge an artificial severance between the colonial past and Japan's current immigration policies in contemporary scholarship. For example, Sassen (1994, 62) alleged that "Japan has never had immigration, although it has a history, even if at times brief, of forced labor recruitment, colonization and emigration. . . . The concept of 'immigration' did not exist in its

211

212   *Notes to Pages 14–34*

law on the entry and exit of alien." This type of argument unintentionally minimizes the lasting legacy of colonialism in Japan's current immigration policies.

7. Other notable scholars who have dealt with the same questions include but are not limited to Brubaker (1992, 1996), Cesarini and Fulbrook (1996), Gellner (1983), Greenfeld (1992), Hansen and Weil (2002), Hobsbawm and Ranger (1983), Joppke (2005b), Lamont (1995), Mann (1987), Marshall (1950), Marx (1997), Noiriel (1996), Pfaff (1993), and Smith (1986).

8. Brubaker (1996, 2004) offers a very different analysis of nationalism in his subsequent works on nationalism and ethnicity.

9. The impact of globalization on citizenship and migration policies have been contested, and this debate is ongoing among scholars in citizenship and immigration studies (Joppke 1998; Koopmans et al. 2005).

10. Finnemore (1996), Jacobson (1996), Joppke (1998), Kymlicka (1995), Sassen (1998), Shafir (1998), and Soysal (1994) are among the scholars who studied the impact of globalization on the nation-state and contributed to the debate about citizenship in the late twentieth century.

11. Many notable scholars who focus on social movements have also argued that social movements cannot be fully understood without considering international and global influence. See, e.g., Della Porta, Rucht, and Kriesi 1999; Della Porta and Tarrow 2004; McAdam 1998; McAdam, Tarrow, and Tilly 2001; McCarthy 1997; Meyer and Jepperson 2000; Smith, Chatfield, and Pagnucco 1997; Smith and Johnston 2002; Tarrow 2005; Tsutsui 2004, 2006; and Tsutsui and Wotipka 2004.

12. While my book is not directly engaging with the literature on social movements, I am greatly inspired by this scholarship, including but not limited to works by Della Porta and Tarrow (2004), Earl (2000), Giugni (1998), McAdam, Tarrow, and Tilly (2001), Risse, Ropp, and Sikkink (1999), and Smith (2002, 2008).

13. This book also found great inspiration in works by Albrow (1997), Bendix (1964), Bloemraad (2006), Brubaker (1992, 1996), Ikegami (1995), Marshall (1950), Meyer, Boli et al. (1997), Meyer and Jepperson (2000), Sassen (1998, 2002), Somers (1993), Tilly (1996, 2005, 2007), Torpey (1999), and Turner (1990, 2006).

14. It is also important to note that in Japanese there has not been a clear distinction between "migrant" and "immigrant." Both are expressed through the same term, *imin* or *ijyūsha*. The former is a more commonly used term that the Japanese state and public began to use more frequently in the late nineteenth century, when a number of Japanese citizens immigrated to other countries, including the United States. By the twentieth century, the term *imin* typically referred to "immigrants."

Chapter 2: Pan-Asian Empire

1. For more detailed scholarly work on Japanese colonial history, see Ching 2001; Dudden 2005; Duus 1995; Myers and Peattie 1984; and Young 1998.

Notes to Pages 35–44

2. Jurist Kiyomiya (1944) has played an important role in defining the legal boundaries between the metropole and the colonies. See Ishikawa 2014 for analyses of the role that Kiyomiya played in these legal constructs.

3. See Endō 2017 for a comprehensive explanation for a premodern and modern history of Japan's *koseki*.

4. See Itō [1936] 1970, 226–233, for a complete list of suggestions by Denison regarding citizenship in *Hisho Ruisan*, vol. 18: *Taiwan Shiryō* (Classified Documents, vol. 18: Materials on Taiwan), ed. Itō Hirobumi ([1936] 1970).

5. See Asano 2000, which describes this issue in depth.

6. The quotation at the beginning of the chapter is from Yamada Saburō's (1909) written opinion submitted to Terauchi Masatake with his signature and dated July 15, 1909. I am using the word "citizenship" to translate the Japanese word *kokuseki*. Citizenship is often translated into Japanese using the term *shiminken*, which usually refers to rights and duties. Centering what the actors in this book were referring to and conceptualizing, I decided that it was more appropriate to use the word "citizenship" in this chapter. Under my analysis, both state and nonstate actors are consciously decoupling and coupling the concept of nationhood/nationality and the concepts of rights and duties. For example, jurist Yamada was certainly mindful of what the concept of *kokuseki* refers to—not only national belonging or nationality but also rights and duties. Thus, the term "nationality" is too one-dimensional to capture what these actors were referring to in this historical context.

7. See *Shinryōchi Shinmin no chi'i* [The status of imperial subjects in the colonial territories] (Yamada 1896, 778–788).

8. In the United States, the Naturalization Act of 1790 legislated that foreign-born non-Caucasians were not allowed to become naturalized. Thus, Japanese immigrants in the United States were not able to become American citizens.

9. "Yamada Hakase Sōfu Kokuseki Mondai Hoka 3-ken" [Regarding the issue of citizenship and three other matters sent by Dr. Yamada], in Ōtsuka Tsunesaburō Bunsho 108-7 (Ōtsuka Tsunesaburō Documents) at the National Diet Library. No page number is imprinted in the original archive. The exact year of this document's creation (or production) was also not imprinted in the original, but historian Mizuno (2001) speculates that based on the content, it was probably produced around 1912. See the Ministry of Foreign Affairs (Gaimushō) historical archives for more information regarding the Japanese government's concerns about the naturalization of Koreans living overseas (Gaimushō 1915, 1916).

10. Oguma (1998) also discussed the role of Yamada Saburō in defining the citizenship of Koreans in his historical work on Japan in the colonial period.

11. The author of these reports is unknown because they were not listed. The quote is from the section appearing on 180–181 in *Sōtokufu Shisetu Rekishi Chōsa Shorui*, dated on *Taishō 4nen 11 gatsu* [Colonial government historical research reports, November 1915] in *Terauchi Masatake Kankei Bunsho: Shushō*

214 *Notes to Pages 44–50*

izen [Terauchi Masatake documents: Before Prime Ministry], where they discuss the rationale behind this policy (Yamamoto 1984).

12. *Chōsen tōchi shiryō* (Korean colonial governance archives), edited and compiled by Kim Jeong Myeong (1971), contains numerous confidential documents created and archived by the Japanese government concerning Korean insurgents living abroad, including the Gando region.

13. *Koseki* is a family registry system that requires all households to report births, deaths, marriages, adoptions, and even criminal convictions to their local authority. It serves in place of birth, death, and marriage certificates. Korea has its own family registry system that contains similar information, but its organizing format is different from that of the Japanese family registry system, reflecting Koreans' distinctive cultural concept of kinship. During the colonial period, the Japanese government deliberately kept Korean and Japanese family registry systems separate in order to delineate genealogical lines in the event of intermarriage between Koreans and Japanese, ultimately allowing the Japanese authorities to identify ethnic Koreans (Miyata, Kim, and Yang 1992). See Sakamoto 1997 and Mizuno 2004b for detailed analysis on the *koseki* system during the colonial period.

14. "Yamada Hakusi Sōfu Kokuseki Mondai Hoka San-ken" [Regarding the issue of citizenship and three other matters sent by Dr. Yamada], in Ōtsuka Tsunesaburō Bunsho 108-7 (Ōtsuka Tsunesaburō Documents) at the National Diet Library. Neither the page number nor the exact date is imprinted in the original archive.

15. As mentioned earlier, the Japanese government maintained separate jurisdictions between their colonies (*gaichi*) and the mainland (*naichi*). The laws in the *gaichi* were called "colonial laws" or "colonial ordinance" (*seirei* in Korea and *ritsurei* in Taiwan), which were directly announced and executed by the colonial generals. Thus, the colonial laws did not have to be approved by the mainland Cabinet. On the other hand, laws in the mainland had to be passed by the Cabinet.

16. Korean women who married Japanese men could "technically" become a part of the Japanese family registry. For that reason, this issue was problematized by some of the policymakers who wished to rigorously separate the family registries between the colonies and the mainland. However, due to the increasing prejudice against the colonized population among the general Japanese population, the number of intermarriages did not increase enough to pose a serious concern for the Japanese government (Miyata, Kim, and Yang 1992; Suzuki 1992).

17. The original archive contains the date, but no page numbers that can be used for in-text citation. The original archive can be found in *Gaimushō kiroku* B-9-2-02. See the bibliography for more information.

18. Silberman and Harootunian's *Japan in Crisis* (1999) is an excellent collection that details the cultural, political, social, and economic changes that transpired in the Taishō period. See Takenaka 2014 for more on democracy in prewar Japan.

Notes to Pages 51–65   215

19. Gotō Shinpei Bunsho (1898) in the National Diet Library contains the Kirkwood opinion report titled "Kirkwood shi Taiwan ni kansuru oboegaki setumei hikki." Oguma 1998 provides an elaborate analysis on Kirkwood's influence.

20. This list is a part of "Confidential 1-542: Materials concerning Korean Identification," sent by Keihokyokuchō (Director of Policy Department) to Chō-fu-ken Chōkan (Municipal Governors) on October 28, 1913 (Naimushō Keihokyokuchō 1913), which was reprinted in Park Gyeongsik's archival collection, *Zainichi Chōsenjin Kankei Shiryō Shūsei,* vol. 1 (Park 1979, 27–29). This memo also refers to linguistic, ceremonial, dietary, clothing, and customary characteristic of Koreans. For more historical evidence about Japanese attitudes, treatments, and policies toward Koreans, see Park 1975, 1979, 1981, 1989, and 2000.

21. Terauchi's quote is from Oguma 1998, 196. Oguma extracted the quote from Matsuoka Shizuo's "Chisensaku Yōshi," in *Saitō Makoto Monjo 104-48.* See Oguma 1998, 195–197, for an in-depth analysis of Terauchi's colonial policies.

22. Japanese newspapers and other media outlets also legitimize these academic theories and justify Japanese colonialism in Taiwan and Korea (Kang 1984). Scholars who influenced the concept of nationhood in prewar Japan include but are not limited to Aoyanagi ([1928], 1995) and Tori'i (1976). See Imanishi's (1999) work on Aoyanagi's thesis about the assimilation of Koreans in the 1920s.

23. *Kesareta Genron,* edited by Korea Kenkyūjo (1990), reprinted the deleted and censored articles in Korean newspapers. These deleted articles give us a sense of what kind of speeches the Japanese colonial government were trying to suppress.

24. One notable historical source that provides perspectives of Japanese colonial officers at the time of the March First Movement is the diary of the commander in Korea, Utsunomiya Tarō. His diary detailed how Utsunomiya perceived that the March First Movement was inevitable and a natural consequence of the misguided annexation policy, which he compared to a daughter being forced to marry to a man against her will. His diary also suggests the Japanese army's brutal methods of suppression and critiques against military governance, or *budan tōchi* (Utsunomiya Tarō kankei shiryō kenkyūkai 2007).

25. Japanese colonialists established a series of news publications in Korea as a means to propagate their official ideology to the colonized population (Ko 1976).

26. Scholars such as Baldwin (1979), Cumings (1997), Robinson (1988), G. Shin (1996, 2006), Y. Shin (1989, 1990, and 2000), G. Shin and Robinson (1999), and Wells (1989) have detailed the collective resistance among elites and ordinary people in colonial Korea. More recently, Fujitani (2013) studied young Korean men who volunteered to participate in Japanese military mobilization, exposing the complex and diverse responses among the colonized population in the Japanese Empire.

27. It is important to note that historian Iwamura (1972) extensively studied the relationship between Japanese laborers and Korean laborers and argued

216 *Notes to Pages 65–87*

that the Korean labor class greatly contributed to the development of Japanese labor activists.

28. The true death toll is unknown. According to official Korean sources, it is estimated as 6,400, while the Japanese Ministry of Justice reported only 243, which is, as many historians argue, "unquestionably far too low" (Cumings 1997; Kang 2003; Katō 2014; Nakajima 1973; Yamada 2003).

29. This ordinance could be considered the first officially codified immigration law in modern Japan. Although the Japanese state previously had regulations for foreign residents in Japan, they were never codified as an official law (Miyazaki 1973a, 1973b).

30. See Matsuda 1988, 1995, for more historical analysis of Koreans' suffrage in prewar Japan.

31. Chōsen Sōtokufu Teikokugikai Setsumei Shiryō, vols. 1–17 (Chōsen Sōtokufu [1933] 1994), compiled and reprinted by Fujishuppan, is a valuable source for understanding the Japanese colonial government's perspective on Koreans between the 1910s and the 1940s.

32. Park (1965), Higuchi (2015), and Yamada (1987) have produced historical evidence and analyses about the issue of Korean labor conscription. In recent years, some conservative scholars alleged that there was no organized labor conscription of Koreans. Yamada, Koshō, and Higuchi (2005) challenge this allegation with historical evidence.

Chapter 3: The Birth of a Homogeneous Nation-State

1. It is important to note that even if Japan claimed these territories as part of its empire, many parts of these geographical areas were also a part of Western empires, including the empires of the United States, the United Kingdom, and the Netherlands.

2. It should be noted that atomic bomb victims were not only Japanese but also Koreans. However, many Koreans were excluded from the medical benefits extended to the victims of atomic bombs by Japanese states.

3. Most of the English-language literature in the humanities and social sciences on postwar Japanese history and the US occupation in Japan has been silent on this issue (Allinson 1993, 2004; Dower 1999; Gordon 1993).

4. The *chokusen gi'in,* or Imperial Councilor of the House of Peers, was selected by the imperial command instead of through a general election, based on their contribution to the nation. They usually had a lifetime tenure. Sekiya's quote can be found in the digital transcript data at the National Diet Library, 89th session of the House of Peers, Imperial Diet: Plenary Session 11, Dec. 14, 1945.

5. The original archival document refers to nonconscripted laborers as *shūdan inyū rōmusha,* which means "collectively imported Korean laborers."

6. Ogasawara's quote can be found in the digital transcript data at the National Diet Library, 89th session of the House of Peers, Imperial Diet: Budget Committee 2, Dec. 14, 1945.

Notes to Pages 87–99   217

7. Koizumi's quote can be found in the digital transcript data at National Diet Library, 89th session of the House of Peers, Imperial Diet: Budget Committee 2, Dec. 14, 1945.

8. It is important to note that just as the determination of Koreans' status was influenced by their homeland's civil war and international politics, the status of Taiwanese colonial migrants and their descendants was also influenced by complicated homeland politics, including the division between the Republic of China and the People's Republic of China. See Tsuruzono 2020; He 2015.

9. The quotation is from the memorandum prepared by Kiyose Ichirō himself; he distributed it to lawmakers at the time that suffrage for colonial immigrants was being considered. See Mizuno Naoki's (1996, 1997) work to understand the influence of Kiyose's memorandum.

10. See Tonomura 2004 work for a more detailed analysis of demographic changes during this time period.

11. See Takahashi Masami 1954 for a more detailed analysis of the Koreans' crimes in postwar Japan. Takahashi (1954, 259–268) noted that Koreans were treated less leniently than Japanese in the Japanese judicial system.

12. "Third-country national," *sangokujin,* is a term that refers to the former colonial population from Taiwan, China, and Korea. It is often used in a derogatory sense (Mizuno 2000).

13. Kendō later became a part of Mindan, a pro–South Korea organization in Japan.

14. "Chongryon" is an abbreviation for Chae Ilbon Chosonin Chong Yonhaphoe (General Association of Korean Residents in Japan). In Japanese it is often referred to as "Sōren" or "Chōsōren," an abbreviation for "Zai-Nihon Chōsenjin Sōrengōkai."

15. This quote is from Fuse Tatsuji Shiryō 1948. Mizuno (2005, 229–230) reprinted this archival document, "Zainichi chōsenjin mondai ni tsuite" [Roundtable discussion on the issue of Koreans in Japan], in their work.

16. The original archive that recorded this meeting, "Zainichi Chōsenjin Mondai ni tsuite," can be found in "Fuse Tatsuji Shiryō" at Ishinomaki Culture Center, Miyagi Prefecture, archival number 3-040. Mizuno (2005) has introduced this archive in verbatim in his essay.

17. Mindan was established in 1946, the same year that Kendō was established, while Chōren was established in 1947.

18. See the report from Headquarter 1 Corps to Commanding General Eighth Army, "Staff Study on Korean School Problems" (SCAPIN n.d.), as well as "Status Treatment of Koreans in Japan" and "Foreign Nationals in Japan" (SCAPIN 1949a, 1949b).

19. See the report in the *Washington Post* (Schmidt et al. 2020).

20. This quote was reprinted in *Zainichi chōsenjin kyōiku kankei Shiryōshū* (Nakayama 1995) and *Zainichi chōsenjin kyōikuron rekishi-hen* (Ozawa 1973).

218   *Notes to Pages 100–112*

21. This quote was published in Japanese on the first page of *Asahi Shinbun* on April 27, 1948 (Jones 1948).

22. Before Nyūkoku kanribu changed its name to Nyukoku kanrikyoku in 1952, it was briefly called Shutsu-nyūkoku kanrichō. In 2019, it was replaced by Shutsu-nyūkoku zairyū kanrichō (Immigration Services Agency of Japan, also known as ISA).

23. Suzuki Hajime was the son of the forty-second prime minister of Japan, Suzuki Kantarō. He served as a public servant, including as Imperial Chamberlain and his father's secretary, before his appointment to the first director of the Immigration Bureau (Nyūkoku kanrichō). He devoted much of his career and life to helping Korean migrants in Japan.

24. The immigration agency was established in 1918 prewar Japan under the Ministry of Internal Affairs (Naimushō). Per the order "On Foreigners' Entry, Stay, and Deportation" [Gaikokujin no nyūkoku taizai oyobi taikyo ni kansuru ken] by the Ministry of Internal Affairs, local officials were put in charge of controlling foreign populations in Japan (Miyazaki 1973b).

25. The journal *Shinwa* is a valuable source of information to learn about the issue of Korean detainees in postwar Japan and how some Japanese politicians and former bureaucrats played a prominent role as guarantors and supporters of detained Korean colonial migrants. *Shinwa* was created by Nikkan Shinwakai (Japan-Korean Affinity Association), and Suzuki Hajime was also a leading figure for this association (see Ri 2016).

26. The journal *Gaijin Tōroku* [The alien registration] changed its name to *Gaikokujin Tōroku* in 1996.

27. The transcript of this meeting appeared across three issues of the journal *Alien Registration* (*Gaikokujin Tōroku Jimu-kyōkai Zenkoku Rengōkai* 1964a, 1964b, 1964c).

28. This was reflected in the following remark by Minematsu during this meeting: "For the revision of [immigration] laws, [Mr. Hida] incorporated our opinions" (*Gaikokujin Tōroku Jimu-kyōkai Zenkoku Rengōkai* 1964a, 9).

29. Here I am using the term "nationality" (*kokuseki*) instead of "citizenship" because in this context both the South Korean and Japanese governments were trying to discern Koreans' "national belonging."

30. The exact figure was 17,429,362,305 yen, which is approximately US $48.4 million, using 360 yen per dollar, a fixed exchange rate used between 1949 and 1971.

31. The Ōmura Detention Center has become a detention center for immigrants in Japan today.

32. Chongryon is called Chōsōren in Japanese-language publications.

33. See Morris-Suzuki 2005, 2007; Kim and Takayanagi 1995.

34. The quote is from the written record of the board of directors at the Japanese Red Cross Society. This record was titled "Zainichi chōsenjin no

Notes to Pages 114–133   219

kikokumondai wa naze jindōmondai de ari kinkyū shori o yōsurunoka?" and was written by Inoue ([1959] 1995). The copy of the original record was reprinted in *Kita chōsen kikokujigyō kankei shiryōshū,* edited by Kim and Takayanagi (1995, 29–36).

35. This quotation from Takagi was reprinted in *Kenshō Nicchō-kankei 60 nenshi* (Wada and Takasaki 2005, 119). Takagi (1970) also wrote a book on Korean repatriation.

36. It is beyond the scope of this book to discuss the role of the emperor in preserving the legacy of colonialism in postwar Japan. For notable studies on the emperor Hirohito and his legacy, see Bix 2000; Nakamura 1992; Dower 1999.

37. For more detailed discussions of postwar intellectual discourse, see Oguma's (1995) analysis of the myth of the homogeneous nation.

38. Ueda Shinkichi's remark appeared in the transcribed record of the forty-eighth session of the House of Representatives on April 20, 1965.

39. Takahashi Mamoru's quote is also from the forty-eighth session of the House of Representatives on April 20, 1965.

Chapter 4: The Fight for Social Justice and Human Rights

1. When he was a bureaucrat of the Japan Immigration Bureau in 1975, Sakanaka ([1975] 1989) wrote a controversial essay arguing that Koreans in Japan would naturally go extinct (*shizen shōshitsu*) due to assimilation and naturalization. He later argued that his intention was misunderstood and produced a series of works advocating for immigration reform in Japan and pushed the ideals of plural nationhood (Sakanaka 2005, 2011).

2. It is important to note that some sympathetic Japanese allies and educators supported Korean students in Japanese schools. Uchiyama's scholarship detailed Koreans' challenges and efforts to maintain their Korean cultural identity during their pursuit of ethnic education in Japan (Uchiyama 1995; see also Uchiyama and Cho 1989).

3. See Hōmushō Nyūkoku Kanrikyoku 2010; Hōmushō Shutsunyūkoku Zairyū Kanrichō 2022a.

4. See Hōmushō Shutsunyūkoku Zairyū Kanrichō 2022a; Sōmushō Tōkeikyoku 2022.

5. Taiwanese colonial migrants and descendants were also subject to Act No. 126. See He 2015, 24.

6. Because the timing of the renewal for one's residency is determined by one's birthday, each member of the family had to renew their residency at a different time, which caused a cumbersome burden and made it easier for one to forget. If one failed to renew one's residency in a timely manner, it was not renewed, resulting in deportation (Osaka Zainichi Chōsenjin no Jinken o Mamorukai 1978).

7. Koreans could qualify for this Treaty-Based Permanent Residency in Japan up to the second generation. Whether or not a third generation would qualify for

this status was to be determined twenty-five years later per the agreement between the Republic of Korea and Japan.

8. Chinese immigrants from mainland China were not included in this resolution. Thus, they retained the status of Regular Permanent Residency, or *ippan eijyū*. See Tsuruzono 2020 for more details on how Chinese colonial migrants' legal status was determined between Chinese and Japanese governments in the postwar period.

9. Many historians and jurists have produced in-depth analyses about Koreans in Japan, but until the 1990s there were very few sociological studies about Koreans in Japan that were written in Japanese languages.

10. Ryang's (1997) pioneering work about North Koreans in Japan vividly shows a heterogeneity among Koreans in Japan.

11. Barth ([1969] 1998) argued that there were at least two consequences of group interaction: boundary specification and boundary eradication.

12. This quote is from *Shimon ōnatsu kyohisha eno kyōhakujyo o yomu*, which in the 1980s printed numerous threatening letters that Japanese citizens sent to fingerprint objectors (Minzoku Sabetsu to Tatakau Kantō Kōryūshūkai Jikko I'inkai 1985, 101).

13. Kang's opinion was published on May 15, 1995, in the Korean minority's newspaper in Japan, *Tōitsu Nippo*.

14. Park Jongseok's legal battle against Hitachi was a well-studied case. See the research on this case by Tsukajima (2016) and Tsutsui (2018).

15. Date unknown. He recalled this fact on his personal website (http://jk-solidarity.com/).

16. This quote is from Mintōren's newsletter (Minzoku Sabetsu to Tatakau Renraku Kyōgikai 1975, 3).

17. To understand what kind of reforms were proposed between the 1950s and the 1980s, I reviewed governmental archives about immigration policy reforms by the Immigration Bureau (Nyūkoku Kanrikyoku) in the Ministry of Justice (Hōmushō Nyūkoku Kanrikyoku 1957, 1959, 1964, 1971, 1976, and 1987).

18. Kiyoteru Tsutsui and I previously published our analysis on the impact of global norms on social movement outcomes among Koreans in Japan (Shin and Tsutsui 2007; Tsutsui and Shin 2008).

19. For example, see the following debates in the Diet that show the government's reluctance in the 1980s: (1) House of Councilors, Committee on Account Settlement, 98th Diet, May 11, 1983, No. 11; (2) House of Representatives, Committee on Account Settlement, 98th Diet, July 7, 1983, No. 8; and (3) House of Representatives, Committee on Account Settlement, 101st Diet, April 19, 1984, No. 8.

20. The documentary film *1985nen Hana de aru koto* featured her fight against this fingerprinting requirement (Kim 2010). She vividly recounted the

humiliating experience of being strip-searched and serving ten days in jail as a result of her activism as an objector.

21. Tsutui and Shin (2008) have analyzed the impact of globalized human rights on Korean's claim-making in depth.

22. Ogata does not specify how she calculated these percentages in her article published in 1987, but given Ogata's expertise in the UN, it is reasonable to assume that she used the UN budget formula to calculate the percentages of contributions made by member states.

23. See Zainichi Chōsenjin no Jinken o Mamorukai 1977.

24. Kim's supporting group, Zainichi Kankoku Chōsenjin no Kokumin Nenkin o Motomerukai (1984), detailed his lengthy and agonizing legal fight for justice over his national pension. See also Yoshioka (1978) 1995; and Sorano and Ko 1995.

25. Tanaka (2013), a scholar and longtime advocate for foreign residents in Japan, also referred to the Indochinese refugees as "black ships."

26. My work supports Hafner-Burton and Tsutsui's (2005) analysis about "the paradox of [the] empty promise" in which the authors argued that relying exclusively on ratifying human rights treaties in the UN system does not improve human rights practices. The growing legitimacy of this idea helped provide leverage to nonstate actors who pressured to change the government's response to human rights violations.

27. These victims have filed a series of lawsuits against the Japanese and South Korean governments claiming that inadequate medical benefits were extended to the victims. Sociologist Kobayashi Sōmei (2022) analyzes the issue of Korean atomic bomb victims in South Korea.

28. Rice's quote is from her interview transcript with internet journalists on March 20, 2005, in Seoul (US Department of State 2005).

Chapter 5: Conclusion: Toward Diverse and Inclusive Japan

1. The quotes are from Kyoto District Court Statement on hate speech on October 7, 2013 (Kyoto Chihō Saibansho 2013).

2. J. Mark Ramseyer is a law professor at Harvard University who specializes in law and economics in Japan. There was a public outcry in response to his 2019 discussion paper. The paper was later extensively revised and was published in *The Cambridge Handbook of Privatization,* edited by Avihay Dorfman and Alon Harel, in 2021 (Ramseyer 2021a).

3. Higuchi (2011) and Kimura (2006) analyzed the discourse over alien suffrage in depth.

4. This observation is based on my review of nearly all the publications in popular magazines that the National Diet Library search engine identified with the keywords *gaikokujin sanseiken* or "alien suffrage."

222   *Notes to Pages 182–203*

5. For example, applicants are required to maintain, among other criteria, (1) an address in Japan for five consecutive years; (2) good behavior and a clean criminal history record; and (3) financial stability. Furthermore, the ultimate decision rests on the discretionary power of the minister of justice, which was cited as problematic due to the lack of transparency and clear criteria.

6. This quotation is from the article "Zainichi Shakai: Nihon kokuseki todokede kyoka Zainichi shakaini hamon hirogaru" (*Tōyō Keizai Nippō* 2001).

7. Higuchi (2011) quantitatively showed the three peaks when the alien suffrage debate became heated in Japanese public discourse.

8. The exchange between Ozawa Ichirō and Koizumi Junichirō can be found in the digital archive of the parliamentary record at the National Diet Library of Japan (Ozawa 2003).

9. See Hōmushō Shutsunyūkoku Zairyū Kanrichō 2022a; Sōmushō Tōkeikyoku 2022.

10. See Hōmushō Shutsunyūkoku Zairyū Kanrichō 2023.

11. These numbers are from data published by Kokuritsu Shakaihoshō Jinkō Mondai Kenkyūjo, or National Institute of Population and Social Security Research (2022).

12. Katō's quote is from an article published in the LDP's monthly journal (Nojima 1989, 98).

13. For detailed analyses on Nikkei Brazilian's experience, see Tsuda 1999, 2003.

14. The central government leaves responsibility for noncitizen residents to municipal governments. Despite the municipal offices' efforts, there remains a lack of practical expertise or experience, especially language skills and cultural knowledge, to effectively incorporate non-Japanese-speaking residents into their local communities.

15. Ebashi (1995) emphatically supports alien suffrage in Japan, and he wrote extensively on the topic.

16. Special Permanent Resident Aliens do not need a reentry permit so long as they return to Japan from abroad within two years of their initial departure. Other registered alien residents, on the other hand, must return to Japan within only one year of their initial departure without a reentry permit. The validity period for their reentry permit for multiple reentry for Special Permanent Resident Aliens is six years, whereas it is only five years for other registered aliens in Japan.

17. The Zainichi Korean Statement against Proposed Revision to Immigration Law was circulated online in 2021.

18. American social scientists Lee and De Vos (1981) analyzed the identities of Koreans in Japan before Japanese social scientists, such as Fukuoka (1993), began to treat this topic as worthy of scholarly attention. Park (1999) and Ryang (1997, 2000) provide uniquely valuable and important insights about Korean minority identity in Japan in part because they are among the few scholars who have analyzed this topic who have also experienced marginalization because of

their Korean minority status in Japan. See also Sasaki 2001, 2006 and Tai 2002 for more recent analyses of Korean identity and its relation to citizenship in Japan.

19. Della Porta and Tarrow (2004), Finnemore and Sikkink (1998), McCarthy (1997), Smith (2002), Smith, Chatfield, and Pagnucco (1997), and Tsutsui and Wotipka (2004) are among the scholars who have highlighted the significance of global alliances of nongovernmental actors in the contemporary world.

Bibliography

Akashi Junichi. 2010. *Nyūkoku kanri seisaku: 1990 nen taisei no seiritsu to tenkai*. Tokyo: Nakanishiya Shuppan.

Albrow, Martin. 1997. *The Global Age: State and Society beyond Modernity*. Stanford, CA: Stanford University Press.

Allinson, Gary D. 1993. "The Structure and Transformation of Conservative Rule." In *Postwar Japan as History*, edited by Andrew Gordon, 123–144. Berkeley: University of California Press.

———. 2004. *Japan's Postwar History*. 2nd ed. Ithaca, NY: Cornell University Press.

Amos, Timothy. 2011. *Embodying Difference: The Making of Burakumin in Modern Japan*. Honolulu: University of Hawai'i Press.

Anderson, Benedict. 1983. *Imagined Communities: Reflections on the Origin and Spread of Nationalism*. London: Verso.

Aoyanagi Tsunatarō. (1928) 1995. *Sōtokufu seijiron jyō*. Tokyo: Ryūkei Shosha.

Asahi Shinbun. 2007. "3.1 dokuritsu undō no chin'atsu o shojitsu: Chōsengun shireikan no shiryō hakken." *Asahi.com*, February 28, 2007. http://www.asahi.com/national/update/0228/TKY200702270448.html.

Asano Toyomi. 2000. "Nihon teikoku ni okeru taiwan hontōjin to sinkokujin no hazama: Kokuseki sentakuken to Taiwan hōsei." *Gendai taiwan kenkyū* 19: 70–86.

Asano Toyomi and Matsuda Toshihiko, eds. 2004. *Shokuminchi teikoku nihon no hōteki tenkai*. Tokyo: Shinzansha Shuppan.

Augustine, Matthew. 2017. "The Limits of Decolonization: American Occupiers and the 'Korean Problem' in Japan, 1945–1948." *International Journal of Korean History* 22 (1): 43–75.

Auslin, Michael. 2005. "Japan and South Korea: The New East Asian Core." *Journal of World Affairs* 49 (3): 459–473.

Baldwin, Frank. 1979. "Participatory Anti-imperialism: The 1919 Independence Movement." *Journal of Korean Studies* 1: 123–162.

Balibar, Etienne, and Immanuel Wallerstein. 1991. *Race, Nation, Class: Ambiguous Identities*. New York: Verso.

Bibliography

Barahona de Brito, Alexandra, Carmen González Enríquez, and Paloma Aguilar. 2001. *The Politics of Memory: Transitional Justice in Democratizing Societies.* Oxford: Oxford University Press.

Barnds, William J. 1976. "Japan and Its Mainland Neighbors: An End to Equidistance?" *International Affairs* 52 (1): 27–38.

Barth, Fredrik. (1969) 1998. "Introduction." In *Ethnic Groups and Boundaries: The Social Organization of Cultural Differences,* edited by Fredrik Barth, 9–28. Prospect Heights, IL: Waveland Press.

Befu, Harumi. 2001. *Hegemony of Homogeneity: An Anthropological Analysis of "Nihonjinron."* Melbourne: Trans Pacific Press.

Beiner, Ronald. 1995. *Theorizing Citizenship.* Albany: State University of New York Press.

Bendix, Reinhard. 1964. *Nation-Building and Citizenship: Studies of Our Changing Social Order.* New York: John Wiley.

Benford, Robert D., and David A. Snow. 2000. "Framing Processes and Social Movements: An Overview and Assessment." *Annual Review of Sociology* 26: 611–639.

Benhabib, Seyla. 1996. *Democracy and Difference: Contesting the Boundaries of the Political.* Princeton, NJ: Princeton University Press.

Bennett, Martin Toscan. 1948. "Japanese Reparations: Fact or Fantasy?" *Pacific Affairs* 21 (2): 185–194.

Bix, Herbert P. 2000. *Hirohito and the Making of Modern Japan.* New York: HarperCollins.

Blee, Kathleen M. 2012. *Democracy in the Making: How Activist Groups Form.* New York: Oxford University Press.

Bloemraad, Irene. 2006. *Becoming a Citizen: Incorporating Immigrants and Refugees in the United States and Canada.* Berkeley: University of California Press.

Brass, Paul. 1985. "Ethnic Groups and the State." In *Ethnic Groups and the State,* edited by Paul Brass, 1–56. Totowa, NJ: Barnes & Noble Books.

Brody, Betsy. 2002. *Opening the Door: Immigration, Ethnicity, and Globalization in Japan.* New York: Routledge.

Brubaker, Rogers. 1992. *Citizenship and Nationhood in France and Germany.* Cambridge, MA: Harvard University Press.

———. 1996. *Nationalism Reframed: Nationhood and the National Question in the New Europe.* Cambridge: Cambridge University Press.

———. 2004. *Ethnicity without Groups.* Cambridge, MA: Harvard University Press.

Brubaker, Rogers, and Fredrick Cooper. 2000. "Beyond 'Identity.'" *Theory and Society* 29 (1): 1–47.

Bruner, Jerome. 1991. "The Narrative Construction of Reality." *Critical Inquiry* 18 (November): 1–21.

Bibliography

Buraku kaihō jinken kenkyūjo. 1989. "Kokusai jinken kiyaku ni motozuku jōyaku tōjikoku no hōkokusho no shingi." *Buraku kaihō kenkyū* 67: 111–158.

Buruma, Ian. 1994. *The Wages of Guilt: Memories of War in Germany and in Japan.* New York: Farrar, Straus and Giroux.

Calder, Kent. 1988. "Japanese Foreign Economic Policy Formation." *World Politics* 40 (4): 517–541.

Calhoun, Craig. 1997. *Nationalism.* Minneapolis: University of Minnesota Press.

Caprio, Mark E. 2009. *Japanese Assimilation Policies in Colonial Korea, 1910–1945.* Seattle: University of Washington Press.

Cesarini, David, and Mary Fulbrook, eds. 1996. *Citizenship, Nationality and Migration in Europe.* London: Routledge.

Chang, Iris. 1997. *The Rape of Nanking: The Forgotten Holocaust of World War II.* London: Basic Books.

Chang Myong-Sue. 1991. *Uragirareta rakudo.* Tokyo: Kōdansha.

Chapman, David. 2008. *Zainichi Korean Identity and Ethnicity.* New York: Routledge.

Ching, Leo T. S. 2001. *Becoming "Japanese": Colonial Taiwan and the Politics of Identity Formation.* Berkeley: University of California Press.

Choi Seungkoo. 2006. "Hitachi tōsō towa nan dattanoka." In *Nihon ni okeru tabunka kyōsei towa nanika: Zainichi no keikenkara,* edited by Choi Seungkoo and Katō Chikako, 34–73. Tokyo: Shinyōsha.

Choi Sun-ae Lois. 2000. "'Jibun no kuni' o toitsuzukete: Aru shimon ōnatsu kyohi no hamon." *Iwanami Booklet* No. 525. Tokyo: Iwanashi shoten.

Chōsen Minshū Shinbun, ed. 1994. *Shashin-shū: Chōsen kaihō ichinen.* Tokyo: Shinkansha.

Chōsen Sinbō. 2008. "'4.24' kara rokujyū-nen, tsuioku no park jubeom sensei." May 9, 2008. http://korea-np.co.jp/j-2008/03/0803j0509-00001.html.

Chōsen Sōtokufu, ed. (1933) 1994. *Teikoku Gikai Setsumei Shiryō.* Vols. 1–17. Tokyo: Fuji Shuppan.

Chung, Erin A. 2010. *Immigration and Citizenship in Japan.* New York: Cambridge University Press.

Conklin, Alice L. 1997. *A Mission to Civilize: The Republican Idea of Empire in France and West Africa, 1895–1930.* Stanford, CA: Stanford University Press.

———. 1998. "Colonialism and Human Rights, a Contradiction in Terms? The Case of France and West Africa, 1895–1914." *American Historical Review* 103 (2): 419–442.

Cooney, Kevin. 2007. *Japan's Foreign Policy since 1945.* London: M. E. Sharpe.

Cooper, Frederick, and Ann Laura Stoler, eds. 1997. *Tensions of Empire: Colonial Cultures in a Bourgeois World.* Berkeley: University of California Press.

Cox, Jeffrey. 2002. *Imperial Fault Lines: Christianity and Colonial Power in India, 1818–1940.* Stanford, CA: Stanford University Press.

Crenshaw, Kimberlé, Luke Charles Harris, Daniel Martinez HoSang, and George Lipsitz, eds. 2019. *Seeing Race Again: Countering Colorblindness across the Disciplines*. Berkeley: University of California Press.

Croucher, Sheila L. 2003. "Perpetual Imagining: Nationhood in a Global Era." *International Studies Review* 5: 1–24.

Cumings, Bruce. 1997. *Korea's Place in the Sun: A Modern History*. New York: W. W. Norton.

Dale, Peter N. 1986. *The Myth of Japanese Uniqueness*. New York: St. Martin's.

Daughton, James P. 2006. *An Empire Divided: Religion, Republicanism, and the Making of French Colonialism, 1880–1914*. New York: Oxford University Press.

David, Eric John Ramos, ed. 2014. *Internalized Oppression: The Psychology of Marginalized Groups*. New York: Springer.

Della Porta, Donatella, Dieter Rucht, and Hanspeter Kriesi, eds. 1999. *Social Movements in a Globalising World*. London: Palgrave Macmillan.

Della Porta, Donatella, and Sidney Tarrow. 2004. *Transnational Protest and Global Activism*. Lanham, MD: Rowman & Littlefield.

Denyer, Simon, and Akiko Kashiwagi. 2020. "Nike Ad Showing Racial Discrimination Faced by Japanese Girls Provokes Backlash." *Washington Post,* December 1, 2020. https://www.washingtonpost.com/world/asia_pacific/nike-ad-japan-naomi-osaka/2020/12/01/cf310a2a-3387-11eb-9699-00d311f13d2d_story.html.

Dickinson, Frederick R. 1999. *War and National Reinvention: Japan in the Great War, 1914–1919*. Cambridge, MA: Harvard University Press.

Doak, Kevin M. 1997. "What Is a Nation and Who Belongs? National Narratives and the Ethnic Imagination in Twentieth-Century Japan." *American Historical Review* 102 (2): 283–309.

Douglass, Mike, and Glenda S. Roberts, eds. (1999) 2003. *Japan and Global Migration: Foreign Workers and the Advent of a Multicultural Society*. Honolulu: University of Hawai'i Press.

Dower, John W. 1999. *Embracing Defeat: Japan in the Wake of World War II*. New York: W. W. Norton.

Dudden, Alexis. 2005. *Japan's Colonization of Korea: Discourse and Power*. Honolulu: University of Hawai'i Press.

Dumont, Louis. 1994. *German Ideology: From France to Germany and Back*. Chicago: University of Chicago Press.

Duus, Peter. 1995. *The Abacus and the Sword: The Japanese Penetration of Korea, 1895–1910*. Berkeley: University of California Press.

Earl, Jennifer. 2000. "Methods, Movements, and Outcomes: Methodological Difficulties in the Study of Extra-movement Outcomes." *Research in Social Movements, Conflicts and Change* 22: 3–25.

Ebashi Takashi. 1994. "Gaikokujin no sanseiken: Zentei wa nanika? Ebashi Takashi and Bae Jung-do." *Sekai* 596: 143–152.

Bibliography

———. 1995. "Teijyū gaikokujin no sanseiken to minshushugi." In *Kyōsei shakai e no chihō sanseiken*, edited by So Yong-Dal, 65–86. Tokyo: Nihon Hyōronsha.

Endō Masataka. 2010. *Kindai nihon no shokuminchi tōchi ni okeru kokuseki to koseki: Manshū, Chōsen, Taiwan.* Tokyo: Akashi Shoten.

———. 2017. *Koseki to mukokusekisha: Nihonjin no rinkaku.* Tokyo: Jinmon Shoin.

Espiritu, Yen Le. 1992. *Asian American Panethnicity: Bridging Institutions and Identities.* Philadelphia: Temple University Press.

Eun Jong-Ki. 1983. *Zoku okasareru jinken.* Tokyo: Chōsen Seinensha.

Fackler, Martin. 2010. "New Dissent in Japan Is Loudly Anti-foreign." *New York Times,* August 28, 2010, Asia Pacific Section. https://www.nytimes.com/2010/08/29/world/asia/29japan.html.

Farnsworth, Lee W. 1972. "Japan: The Year of the Shock." *Asian Survey* 12 (1): 46–55.

Finnemore, Martha. 1996. *National Interests in International Society.* Ithaca, NY: Cornell University Press.

Finnemore, Martha, and Kathryn Sikkink. 1998. "International Norm Dynamics and Political Change." *International Organization* 52 (4): 887–917.

FitzGerald, David Scott, and David Cook-Martín. 2014. *Culling the Masses: The Democratic Origins of Racist Immigration Policy in the Americas.* Cambridge, MA: Harvard University Press.

———. 2015. "Culling the Masses: A Rejoinder." *Ethnic and Racial Studies* 38 (8): 1319–1327.

Fox, Cybelle. 2015. "What Counts as Racist Immigration Policy?" *Ethnic and Racial Studies* 38 (8): 1286–1291.

Fujioka, Mieko. 2003. "Japan's Human Rights Policy at Domestic and International Levels: Disconnecting Human Rights from Human Security?" *Japan Forum* 15 (2): 287–305.

Fujitani, Takashi. 2013. *Race for Empire: Koreans as Japanese and Japanese as Americans during World War II.* Berkeley: University of California Press.

Fukuchi Kōzō and Nishino Hideaki. 1970. *Zainichi chōsenjin seinen no shōgen.* Tokyo: Sanseidō.

Fukuoka Yasunori. 1993. *Zainichi kankoku chōsenjin: Wakai sedai no identity.* Tokyo: Chuōkoronsha.

Fukuoka Yasunori and Kim Myung-Soo. 1997. *Zainichi kankokujin seinen no seikatsu to ishiki.* Tokyo: Tokyo Daigaku Shuppankai.

Furukawa Noriko. 2006. "Shokuminchi chōsen ni okeru gakkō fukyū jittai to kyōiku sentaku: Kyongsang-do, Yong-Il gun ni kansuru ichi kōsatu." *Daito Bunka Daigaku Kiyo* 41: 105–131.

Fuse Tatsuji Shiryō. 1948. *Zainichi chōsenjin mondai ni tsuite.* 3-040. Miyazaki Prefecture: Ishinomaki Bunka Center.

Fuyushiba Tetsuzō. 1998. *142th Session of the House Representatives: National Diet Joint Committee 15.* February 27.

Bibliography

Gaikokujin Kenshūsei Mondai Network. 2006. *Gaikokujin kenshūsei jikyū 300yen no rōdōsha kowareru jinken to rōdōkijyun.* Tokyo: Akashi Shoten.

Gaikokujin Tōroku Jimu-kyōkai Zenkoku Rengōkai, eds. 1964a. "Zadankai: Ano tōji no gaikokujin-tōroku o kaerimite (I)." *Gaijin Tōroku* 83: 1–8.

———. 1964b. "Zadankai: Ano tōji no gaikokujin-tōroku o kaerimite (II)." *Gaijin Tōroku* 84: 4–9.

———. 1964c. "Zadankai: Ano tōji no gaikokujin-tōroku o kaerimite (III)." *Gaijin Tōroku* 85: 12–17.

Gaimushō. 1915. "Shina ni kika-shitaru chōsenjin no toriatsukaikatani kansuru ken." September 9, 1915, from Zaikantō sōryōji dairi Suzuki Yōtarō to Gaimudaijin Ōkuma Shigenobu. In "Chōsenjin no kika narabi kikajin ni taisuru kakkoku no taigūburi kankei zassan," *Gaimushō kiroku* 3-8-7-35.

———. 1916. "Zaikantō chōsenjin ni taishi pekin naimubu hakkyū kika kyokashokōfu no ken." August 10, 1916, from Zaishina rinji dairi kōshi Otaru Torikichi to gaimudaijin Ishi'i. In "Chōsenjin no kika narabi kikajin ni taisuru kakkoku no taigūburi kankei zassan," *Gaimushō kiroku* 3-8-7-35.

———. 1930a. "Kokusai hōten hensan kaigi chōsenjin no kokuseki sōshitsu nitsuite." February 1930, from Kokusai renmei kankei kokusai hōten hensan kaigi 1 ken, dai 3 kan. In *Gaimushō kiroku* B-9-2-02.

———. 1930b. "1930nen 4gatsu 10nichi zai hāgu kokusai hōten hensan kaigi daihyō yori Shidehara gaimudaijin ate 'kaigi no tōgi jyōkyō ni tsuite.'" In *Nihon Gaikō Bunsho: Shōwa-ki 1, dai 1 kan, 2bu.* Tokyo: Gannando Shoten.

Gaimushō Seimukyoku Tokubetu Shiryōka, eds. 1950. *Zainichi chōsenjin kanri jyūyō bunshoshū.* Tokyo: Kohokusha fukkokuban.

Gellner, Ernest. 1983. *Nations and Nationalism.* Ithaca, NY: Cornell University Press.

Ghadimi, Amin. 2018. "Shot Through with Democracy: Japan's Postwar Myths and the 1948 Hanshin Education Incident." *Social Science Japan Journal* 21 (2): 259–283.

Gibney, Mark, and Erik Roxstrom. 2001. "The Status of State Apologies." *Human Rights Quarterly* 23 (4): 911–939.

Giddens, Anthony. 1982. *Profiles and Critiques and Social Theory.* London: Macmillan.

Gilson, Julie, and Phillida Purvis. 2003. "Japan's Pursuit of Human Security: Humanitarian Agenda or Political Pragmatism?" *Japan Forum* 15 (2): 193–207.

Giugni, Marco G. 1998. "Was It Worth the Effort? The Outcomes and Consequences of Social Movements." *Annual Review of Sociology* 24: 371–393.

Go, Julian. 2016. *Postcolonial Thought and Social Theory.* New York: Oxford University Press.

Goodman, Roger, Ceri Peach, Ayumi Takenaka, and Paul White, eds. 2003. *Global Japan: The Experience of Japan's New Immigrants and Overseas Communities.* New York: Routledge Curzon.

Bibliography

Gordon, Andrew. 1991. *Labor and Imperial Democracy in Prewar Japan*. Berkeley: University of California Press.

———, ed. 1993. *Postwar Japan as History*. Berkeley: University of California Press.

Gotō Shinpei Bunsho. 1898. "Kirkwood shi Taiwan ni kansuru oboegaki setumei hikki." Kensei shiryō shitsu Kokkai Toshokan, Microfilm R7-33-3.

Greenfeld, Liah. 1992. *Nationalism: Five Roads to Modernity*. Cambridge, MA: Harvard University Press.

Guidry, John A., Michael D. Kennedy, and Mayer N. Zald, eds. 2000. *Globalization and Social Movements: Culture, Power, and the Transnational Public Sphere*. Ann Arbor: University of Michigan Press.

Gurowitz, Amy. 1999. "Mobilizing International Norms: Domestic Actors, Immigrants, and the Japanese State." *World Politics* 51: 413–445.

Habermas, Jürgen. 1995. "Citizenship and National Identity: Some Reflections on the Future of Europe." In *Theorizing Citizenship*, edited by Ronald Beiner, 255–281. Albany: State University of New York Press.

Hafner-Burton, Emilie, and Kiyoteru Tsutsui. 2005. "Human Rights in a Globalizing World: The Paradox of Empty Promises." *American Journal of Sociology* 110 (5): 1373–1411.

Hanagan, Michael. 1997. "Citizenship, Claim-Making, and the Right to Work: Britain, 1884–1911." *Theory and Society* 26 (4): 449–474.

Han-san no Shimon Ōnatsukyohi o Sasaerukai. 1990. *Shimon kyohisha ga sabaita nippon*. Tokyo: Shakai Hyōronsha.

Hansen, Randall, and Patrick Weil. 2002. *Dual Nationality, Social Rights and Federal Citizenship in the U.S. and Europe: The Reinvention of Citizenship*. Oxford: Berghahn Books.

Hata Ikuo. 1999. *Shōwa-shi no nazo o ou, jyo*. Tokyo: Bungei Shunshū.

———. 2006. *Yugame rareru nihon gendai-shi*. Tokyo: PHP Kenkyūjyo.

Hayashi Eidai, Park Gyeongsik, and Takasaki Sōji, eds. 1990. *Gurafikku ripōto: Seisan sarenai shōwa chōsenjin kyōsei renkō no kiroku*. Tokyo: Iwanami Shoten.

He Yilin. 2015. "Sengo nihon ni okeru Taiwanjin kakyō no kunō: Kokuseki mondai to sono identity no henyō wo chūshin toshite." *Ōhara shakaigaku mondai kenkyūjo zasshi* 679: 21–24.

Henry, Todd. 2014. *Assimilating Seoul: Japanese Rule and the Politics of Public Space in Colonial Korean, 1910–1945*. Berkeley: University of California Press.

Hicks, George. 1997. *Japan's Hidden Apartheid: The Korean Minority and the Japanese*. Farnham, UK: Ashgate.

Hida Yūichi. 1980. "San furanshisuko heiwa jyōyaku to zainichi chōsenjin." *Zainichi Chōsenjin-shi kenkyū* 6: 1–11.

———. 2004. "Zainichi korian no kokumin nenkin o meguru shōgai nenkin saiban, soshite rōrei nenkin saiban." *Mukuge Tsūshin* 202 (1): 1–7.

Bibliography

Higaki, Shinji, and Yūji Nasu, eds. 2021. *Hate Speech in Japan: The Possibility of a Non-regulatory Approach*. Cambridge: Cambridge University Press.

Higuchi Naoto. 2011. "Higashi ajia chiseigaku to gaikokujin sanseiken: Nihon ban denizunshippu o meguru aporia." *Shakai Shirin* 57 (4): 55–75.

———. 2017. "Gaikokujin sanseiken no mirai." *Éstrangeté* 1: 117–133.

———. 2019. "Tabunka kyōsei: Seisaku rinen tariurunoka." In *Imin seisaku towa nanika: Nihon no genjitsu kara kangaeru*, edited by Takaya Sachi, 129–144. Tokyo: Jinmon Shoin.

Higuchi Naoto and Oguma Eiji. 2020. *Nihon wa ukeika sitanoka*. Tokyo: Keio Daigaku Shuppankai.

Higuchi Yūichi. 2015. "Chōsenjin kyōsei dōin kenkyū no genjyō to kadai." *Ōhara Shakai Mondai Kenkyūjo Zasshi* 686: 5–16.

Hiraga Kenta. 1951. *Kokusekihō*. Tokyo: Teikoku Hanrei Hōki Shuppansha.

Hirano Yūgo. 2020. *Rupo nyūkan: Zetsubō no gaikokujin shūyō shisetsu*. Tokyo: Chikuma Shobō.

Hitosashiyubi no Jiyū Henshū I'inkai. 1984. *Hitosashiyubi no jiyū*. Tokyo: Shakai Hyōronsha.

Hobsbawm, Eric. 1990. *Nations and Nationalism since 1780: Programme, Myth, Reality*. Cambridge: Cambridge University Press.

Hobsbawm, Eric, and Terence Ranger. 1983. *The Invention of Tradition*. Cambridge: Cambridge University Press.

Hōmushō Nyūkoku Kanrikyoku. 1957. *Shutsunyūkoku kanri hōrei no kaihai shūroku*.

———. 1959. *Shutsunyūkoku kanri to sono jittai*.

———. 1964. *Shutsunyūkoku kanri to sono jittai*.

———. 1971. *Shutsunyūkoku kanri to sono jittai*.

———. 1976. *Shutsunyūkoku kanri to sono jittai*.

———. 1987. *Shutsunyūkoku kanri: henbō suru kokusai kankyō no naka de*.

———. 2010. *Zairyū gaikokujin tōkei (kyū gaikokujin tōkei) todōfuken betsu zairyūshikaku (zairyūmokuteki) betsu gaikokujin tōrokusha (sōsū), hyōbangō 09-99-04-0. Chōsa-nen 2009nen*. Accessed March 17, 2023. https://www.e-stat.go.jp/stat-search/files?tclass=000001048666&cycle=7&year=20090.

Hōmushō Shutsunyūkoku Zairyū Kanrichō (formerly known as Hōmushō Nyūkoku Kanrikyoku). 2019. *Hōdōhappō shiryō reiwa gannen ni okeru nanmin ninteishasū ni tsuite. Reiwa 2nen 3gatsu 27 nichi*. Accessed June 30, 2021. http://www.moj.go.jp/isa/publications/press/nyuukokukanri03_00004.html.

———. 2022a. *Hōdōhappō shiryō reiwa 4nen 10gatsu 14nichi: Reiwa 4nen 6gatzu matsu genzai ni okeru Zairyū Gaikokujinsū nitsuite*. Accessed March 17, 2023. https://www.moj.go.jp/isa/publications/press/13_00028.html.

———. 2022b. *Zairyū Gaikokujin tōkei kokuseki/chi'iki betsu zaryūshikaku (zairyū mokuteki) betsu*. Hyō bangō 22-06-01-1. Chōsanen 2022nen 6gatsu. Accessed March 7, 2023. https://www.e-stat.go.jp/.

Bibliography 233

———. 2023. *Kikakyoka shinseishasū, kika kyokashasū oyobi kika fukyokashasū no sui'i.* Accessed March 18, 2023. https://www.moj.go.jp/MINJI/toukei_t _minj03.html.

Honda Katsuichi. 1987. *Nankin e no michi.* Osaka: Asahi Shinbunsha.

Howell, David L. 2005. *Geographies of Identity in Nineteenth-Century Japan.* Berkeley: University of California Press.

Hunt, Lynn. 2008. *Inventing Human Rights: A History.* New York: W. W. Norton.

Ichikawa Masaaki. 1983. *San ichi dokuritsu undō 1–4.* Tokyo: Hara Shobō.

Ignatieff, Michael. 1993. *Blood and Belonging: Journeys into the New Nationalism.* New York: Farrar, Straus and Giroux.

Ikegami, Eiko. 1995. "Citizenship and National Identity in Early Meiji Japan, 1886–1889: A Comparative Assessment." *International Review of Social History* 40 (3): 185–221.

Imanishi Hajime. 1999. "Teikoku 'nihon' no jigazō: 1920nendai no chosen 'dōka' ron." In *Seiki tenkanki no kokusai chitsujo to kokumin bunka keisei,* edited by Nishikawa Nagao and Watanabe Kōzō, 5–22. Tokyo: Kashiwa shobō.

Inoue Masutarō. (1959) 1995. "Nihon sekijyūjisha zainichi chōsenjin no kikokumondai wa naze jindō mondai de ari kinkyū shori o yōsurunoka?" In *Kitachōsen kikokujigyō kankei shiryōshū,* edited by Kim Yong-Dal and Takayanagi Toshio, 29–36. Tokyo: Shinkansha.

Irie Akira. 1966. *Nihon no gaikō: Meiji ishin kara gendai made.* Tokyo: Chuōkōronsha.

———. 1991. *Shin-nihon no gaikō: Chikyūjidai no nihon no sentaku.* Tokyo: Chuōkōronsha.

Ishay, Micheline. 2008. *The History of Human Rights: From Ancient Times to Globalization Era.* Berkeley: University of California Press.

Ishihara Shintarō. 1969. "Sokokuni tsuite." In *Kokka no shisō, sengo nihon shisō taikei dai 5kan,* edited by Yoshimoto Takaaki, 357–375. Tokyo: Tsukoma Shobō.

Ishihara Shintarō and Mahathir Mohamad. 1994. *"No" to ieru ajia.* Tokyo: Kōdansha.

Ishikawa Kenji. 2014. "Kenpō no naka no 'gaikoku.'" In *Nihonhō no naka no gaikokuhō: Kihonhō no hikakuhōteki kōsatsu,* edited by Waseda Daigaku Hikakuhō Kenkyūjo, 13–46. Tokyo: Waseda Daigaku Hikakuhō Kenkyūjo.

Ishimoda Sho. 1952. *Rekishi to minzoku no hakken.* Tokyo: Tokyo Daigaku Shuppankai.

Itō Hirobumi, ed. (1936) 1970. *Taiwan shiryō.* Tokyo: Hisho Ruisan Kankōkai.

Iwamura Toshio. 1972. *Zainichi chōsenjin to nihon rōdōsha kaikyū.* Tokyo: Azekura Shobō.

Iwasawa Yūji. 1998. *International Law, Human Rights and Japanese Law: The Impact of International Law on Japanese Law.* Oxford: Clarendon.

Jacobson, David. 1996. *Rights across Borders: Immigration and the Decline of Citizenship*. Baltimore: Johns Hopkins University Press.

Janoski, Thomas. 1998. *Citizenship and Civil Society: A Framework of Rights and Obligations in Liberal, Traditional, and Social Democratic Regimes*. Cambridge: Cambridge University Press.

———, ed. 2010. *The Ironies of Citizenship: Naturalization and Integration in Industrialized Countries*. Cambridge: Cambridge University Press.

Jenkins, Richard. 1994. "Rethinking Ethnicity: Identity, Categorization and Power." *Ethnic and Racial Studies* 17 (2): 197–223.

———. 1996. *Social Identity*. London: Routledge.

Jiyū Jinken Kyōkai. 1984. "Hirogaru shimon ōnatsu kyohi." *Jinken Shinbun*, February 25, 1984.

Jo Sui Chin. 2020. *Kakyō nisei Jo Sui Chin teki zainichi: Sono teikō no kiseki kara mieru nihon no sugata*. Osaka: Tohō Shuppan.

Jones, George. 1948. "Hatsuno senryōgun hijyōjitai sengen beigun tōkyoku dan, haigo ni kyōsantō ugoku." *Asahi Shinbun*, April 27, 1948.

Joppke, Christian, ed. 1998. *Challenge to the Nation-State: Immigration in Western Europe and the United States*. Oxford: Oxford University Press.

———. 2005a. "Exclusion in the Liberal State: The Case of Immigration and Citizenship Policy." *European Journal of Social Theory* 8 (1): 43–61.

———. 2005b. *Selecting by Origin: Ethnic Migration in the Liberal State*. Cambridge, MA: Harvard University Press.

Kajita Takamichi, Tanno Kiyoto, and Higuchi Naoto. 2005. *Kao no mienai teijyūka: Nikkei burajirujin to kokka, shijō, imin tettowāku*. Nagoya: Nagoya Shuppan.

Kam, Henry. 1977. "Japan Weighs Easing Curbs on Refugees: U.S. and U.N. Applying Pressure but Only Low Improvement Is Foreseen for Vietnamese." *New York Times*, August 26, 1977.

Kamihigashi Asako. 2021. "Kanojo ga ikite iketa shakai o. Ima wa mada. Wakamono ga ugokashita nyūkan mondai." *Digital Hōdō Center, Mainichi Shinbun*. May 20, 2021. https://mainichi.jp/articles/20210520/k00/00m/040/070000c.

Kang Chol. 1994. *Zainichi chōsenjin no jinken to nihon no hōritsu*. Tokyo: Yūzankaku.

Kang Dok-Sang. 2003. *Kantō daishinsai: Gyakusatsu no kioku*. Tokyo: Seikyūbunka-sha.

Kang, Hildi. 2001. *Under the Black Umbrella: Voice from Colonial Korea, 1910–1945*. Ithaca, NY: Cornell University Press.

Kang Jae-eun. 1995. "Zainichi dōho no miraizō." In *Tōitsu Nippō*, May 15, 1995.

Kang Man Gil, ed. 2005. *Chōsen minzoku kaihō undō no rekishi: Heiwateki tōitsu e no mosaku*. Translated by Ōta Osamu and Anzako Yuka. Tokyo: Hosei University Press.

Bibliography

Kang Tongjin. 1984. *Nihongenronkai to chosen*. Tokyo: Hōsei Daigaku Shuppan.

Kashiwazaki, Chikako. 1998. "Jus Sanguinis in Japan: The Origin of Citizenship in a Comparative Perspective." *International Journal of Comparative Sociology* 39 (3): 278–300.

Katō Chikako. 2008. "Tabunka kyōsei e no dōtei to shin jiyū shugi no jidai." In *Nihon ni okeru tabunka kyōsei towa nanika: Zainichi no keikenkara*, edited by Choi Seungkoo and Katō Chikako, 11–21. Tokyo: Shinyosha.

Katō Naoki. 2014. *Kugatsu tōkyō no rojō de. 1923 nen kantō daishinsai genocide no zankyō*. Tokyo: Korokara.

Keck, Margaret E., and Kathryn Sikkink. 1998. *Activists beyond Borders: Advocacy Networks in International Politics*. Ithaca, NY: Cornell University Press.

Kim Dong-hoon. 1984. "Zainichi kankoku chōsenjin ni kansutu chinjutsu." *Buraku Kaihō Kenkyū* 42: 63–67.

———. 2003. *Kokusai jinkenhō to mainoritī no chi'i*. Tokyo: Toshindō.

Kim, Hong N. 1987. "Japanese-Korean Relations in the 1980s." *Asian Survey* 27 (5): 497–514.

Kim Il-Men. 1978. *Chōsenjin ga naze "nihonmei" o nanorunoka: Minzoku ishiki to sabetsu*. Tokyo: Sanichi Shobō.

Kim, Jaeeun. 2016. *Contested Embrace: Transborder Membership Politics in Twentieth-Century Korea*. Stanford, CA: Stanford University Press.

Kim Jeong Myeong, ed. 1971. *Chōsen tōchi shiryō dai 8 kan: Futei senjin*. Tokyo: Kankoku Shiryō Kenkyūjyo.

Kim Kyung-Duk. 1995. *Zainichi korian no identity to hōteki chi'i*. Tokyo: Akashi Shoten.

Kim Kyung Hae, ed. 1988. *Zainichi chōsenjin minzoku yōgo tōsō shiryō-shū 4.24 Hanshin kyōiku tōsō o chūshin ni*. Tokyo: Akashi Shoten.

Kim Puja and Nakano Toshio, ed. 2008. *Rekishi to Sekinin: Ianfu mondai to 1990nendai*. Tokyo: Seikyūsha.

Kim Seong Il. 2010. *1985nen hana de arukoto*. DVD. 75 mins. Self-produced.

Kim Tae-Gi. 1997. *Sengo hihon seiji to zainichi chōsenjin mondai: SCAP no taizainichi chōsenjin seisaku 1945–1952 nen*. Tokyo: Keiso-Shobō.

Kim Yong-Dal. 1987. "Zainichi chōsenjin no gaikokujin tōroku, 'kokuseki-ran' kisai ni kansuru gyōseijimu no henkan ni tsuite." *Zainichi Chōsenjin-shi kenkyū* 17 (9): 50–83.

———. (1980) 1990. *Nihon no kika gyōsei ni tsuite no kenkyū*. Tokyo: Akashi Shoten.

———. 1990. *Chōsenjin chūgokujin kyōsei renkō kyōsei rōdō shiryōshū*. Kobe: Kobe Daigaku Seinen Center.

———, ed. 1992a. *Chōsenjin jyūgun ianfu joshi teishintai shiryō*. Kobe: Kobe Gakusei Seinen Center.

———. 1992b. *Nicchō kokkō jyuritsu to zainichi chōsenjin no kokuseki*. Tokyo: Akashi Shoten.

———. 2003. *Chōsenjin kyōsei renkō no kenkyū*. Tokyo: Akashi Shoten.

Bibliography

Kim Yong-Dal and Takayanagi Toshio, eds. 1995. *Kitachōsen kikokujigyō kankei shiryōshū*. Tokyo: Shinkan-sha.

Kimura Kan. 2006. "Zainichi kankoku chōsenjin mondai to gaikokujin sanseiken: Sakugo suru rironteki konkyo to sono gei'in." In *Gaikokujin sanseiken mondai no kokusai hikaku,* edited by Kawahara Yūma and Uemura Kazuhide, 253–282. Tokyo: Shōwadō.

Kimura Kenji and Komatsu Hiroshi. 1998. *Shiryō to bunseki "kankoku heigō" chokugo no zainichi chōsenjin, chūgokujin: Higashi ajia no kindaika to hito no idō*. Kyoto: Akashi Shoten.

Kiyomiya Shirō. 1944. *Gaichihō Jyosetsu*. Tokyo: Yūhikaku.

Ko Junseok. 1976. *Kōnichi genron tosōshi*. Tokyo: Sinsen-sha.

Kobayashi Sōmei. 2022. "Zaikan hibakusha kyūgo o meguru nikkan kōshō 1960s–1970s: Mondai no 'hakken' kara nikkan kan no gōi seiritsu made." *Rekishikei Kentōkai Ronbun shū*. Accessed December 1, 2022. https://www.jiia.or.jp/JIC/pdf/2-4.pdf.

Kobayashi Tomoko. 1994. "GHQ no zainichi chōsenjin ninshiki ni kansuru ichi kōsatsu." *Chōsenshi Kenkyūkai Ronbunshū* 32: 165–192.

Kohn, Hans. (1944) 2005. *The Idea of Nationalism: A Study in Its Origins and Background*. New Brunswick, NJ: Transaction.

Koizumi Gorō. 1945. *89th Session of the House of Peers, Imperial Diet: Budget Committee 2*. December 14.

Kojima Kazushi. 1988. *Meiji tenken taisei no seiritsu: Kojima Kazushi kenpō ronshū I*. Tokyo: Bokutakusha.

Kokkai Toshokan Full-Text Database System for the Minutes of the Diet.

Kokuritsu Shakaihoshō Jinkō Mondai Kenkyūjo. 2022. *Hyō10–1 kokusekibetsu zaryū gaikokujin jinkō:1950–2020nen*. Accessed February 17, 2023. https://www.ipss.go.jp/syoushika/tohkei/Popular/Popular2022.asp?chap=10.

Komagome Takeshi. 1996. *Shokuminchi teikoku nihon no bunka tōgo*. Tokyo: Iwanami Shoten.

Komai Hiroshi, ed. 2004. *Imin o meguru jichitai no seisaku to shakai undō: Kōza, gurōbaru ka suru nihon to imin mondai. Dai II ki. Dai 5 kan*. Tokyo: Akashi Shoten.

Komatsuki Masao, ed. 2004. *Zainichi chōsenjin wa naze kikoku shitanoka: Zainichi to kitachōsen 50nen*. Tokyo: Gendai Jinmonsha.

Kondō, Atsushi. 2001. *Citizenship in a Global World: Comparing Citizenship Rights for Aliens*. New York: Palgrave Macmillan.

Koopmans, Ruud, Paul Statham, Marco Giugni, and Florence Passy. 2005. *Contested Citizenship: Immigration and Cultural Diversity in Europe*. Minneapolis: University of Minnesota Press.

Korea Kenkyūjo, ed. 1990. *Kesareta Genron: nihon tōchika no "chōsen nippō," "tōa nippō" ōshūkiji-shū*. Tokyo: Miraisha.

Koschmann, J. Victor. 1993. "Intellectuals and Politics." In *Postwar Japan as History,* edited by Andrew Gordon, 396–423. Berkeley: University of California Press.

Bibliography

Koseki, Shōichi. 1997. *The Birth of Japan's Postwar Constitution*. Translated by Ray A. Moore. Boulder, CO: Westview.

Kristof, Nicholas. 1995. "Japan's Invisible Minority: Better Off Than in Past, but Still Outcasts." *New York Times*, November 30, 1995.

Kuzio, Taras. 2002. "The Myth of the Civic State: A Critical Survey of Hans Kohn's Framework for Understanding Nationalism." *Ethnic and Racial Studies* 25 (1): 20–39.

Kymlicka, Will. 1995. *Multicultural Citizenship*. Oxford: Oxford University Press.

Kymlicka, Will, and Baogang He. 2005. *Multiculturalism in Asia*. Oxford: Clarendon.

Kymlicka, Will, and Wayne Norman, eds. 2000. *Citizenship in Diverse Societies: A Liberal Theory of Minority Rights*. Oxford: Oxford University Press.

Kyoto Chihō Saibansho. 2013. "Hanketsubun: Gaitōsenden sashidome seikyū jiken. Jiken bango (wa) 2655, on 2013nen 10gatsu 7nichi." Accessed October 14, 2021. https://www.courts.go.jp/app/hanrei_jp/detail4?id=83675.

Lamont, Michele. 1995. "National Identity and National Boundary Patterns in France and the United States." *French Historical Studies* 19 (2): 349–365.

Lee, Changsoo, and George De Vos. 1981. *Koreans in Japan: Ethnic Conflict and Accommodation*. Berkeley: University of California Press.

Lee Rika, ed. 2021. *Chōsenseki towa nanika: Transnational no shitenkara*. Tokyo: Akashi Shoten.

Lee Yonghwa. 1993. *Zainichi kankoku chōsenjin to sanseiken*. Tokyo: Akashi Shoten.

Lee Yoohwan. 1980. *Nihon no nakano sanjyū-hachi do sen: Mindan chōsōren no rekishi to genjitsu*. Tokyo: Yōyōsha.

Levy, Daniel, and Natan Sznaider. 2006. "Sovereignty Transformed: A Sociology of Human Rights." *British Journal of Sociology* 57 (4): 657–676.

Lie, John. 2001. *Multiethnic Japan*. Cambridge, MA: Harvard University Press.

Lie, John, and Sonia Ryang, eds. 2008. *Zainichi (Koreans in Japan): Diasporic Nationalism and Postcolonial Identity*. Berkeley: University of California Press.

Loveman, Mara. 1999. "Is 'Race' Essential? (Comment on Bonilla-Silva, ASR June 1997)." *American Sociological Review* 64 (4): 891–898.

———. 2014. *National Colors: Racial Classification and the State in Latin America*. New York: Oxford University Press.

Ludi, Regula. 2006. "The Vectors of Postwar Victim Reparations: Relief, Redress and Memory Politics." *Journal of Contemporary History* 41 (3): 421–450.

Mainichi Shinbun Digital. 2021. "Nyūkanhō kaisei, konkai kokkai dan'nen: Shiensha ando "Yoron no takamari mushi dekinai." May 18, 2021. https://mainichi.jp/articles/20210518/k00/00m/040/358000c.

Malcom, Andrew H. 1978. "Japan Decides to Keep Its Curbs on Vietnamese Refugees." *New York Times*, March 15, 1978.

Mann, Michael. 1987. "Ruling Class Strategies and Citizenship." *Sociology* 21 (3): 339–354.

———. 2005. *The Dark Side of Democracy: Explaining Ethnic Cleansing*. New York: Cambridge University Press.

Marinari, Maddalena. 2016. "Divided and Conquered: Immigration Reform Advocates and the Passage of the 1952 Immigration and Nationality Act." *Journal of American Ethnic History* 25 (3): 9–40.

Marshall, Thomas H. 1950. *Citizenship and Social Class and Other Essays*. Cambridge: Cambridge University Press.

Marx, Anthony W. 1997. *Making Race and Nation: A Comparison of the United States, South Africa and Brazil*. Cambridge: Cambridge University Press.

———. 2003. *Faith in Nation: Exclusionary Origins of Nationalism*. Oxford: Oxford University Press.

Matray, James I. 2001. *Japan's Emergence as a Global Power*. Westport, CT: Greenwood.

Matsuda Toshihiko. 1988. "Paku chun-gum ron: Sono senkyo undō to gikai katsudō o chūshin ni." *Zainichi Chōsenjinshi Kenkyū* 18: 13–49.

———. 1995. *Senzenki no zainichi korian to sanseiken*. Tokyo: Akashi Shoten.

Matsumiya Ashita. 2010. "Keizai fukyōka ni okeru burajirujin community no kanōsei: Aichiken nishioshi ken'ei jyūtaku no jireikara." *Social Welfare Studies* 12 (7): 33–40.

Matsumoto Narumi. 1996. *Kassōro to shōnen dokōfu: Chōsenjin kyōseirenkō no horiokoshi*. Tokyo: Kusanone Shuppankai.

Matsuo Takayoshi. 1968. "Yoshino Sakuzō to chosen: 3.1 undō o chūshin ni." *Jinmon Gakuhō* 25: 125–149.

McAdam, Doug. 1998. "On the International Origin of Domestic Political Opportunities." In *Social Movements and American Political Institutions*, edited by Anne N. Constain and Andrew S. McFarland, 251–267. Lanham, MD: Rowman & Littlefield.

McAdam, Doug, Sidney Tarrow, and Charles Tilly. 2001. *Dynamics of Contention*. Cambridge: Cambridge University Press.

McCarthy, John D. 1997. "The Globalization of Social Movement Theory." In *Transnational Social Movements and Global Politics: Solidarity beyond the State*, edited by Jackie Smith, Charles Chatfield, and Ron Pagnucco, 243–259. Syracuse: Syracuse University Press.

McCorquodale, Robert. 2003. "The Individual and the International Legal System." In *International Law*, edited by Malcolm D. Evans, 299–328. Oxford: Oxford University Press.

McCurry, Justin. 2020. "Nike Japan Ad on Teenage Bullying and Racism Sparks Debate." *The Guardian*, December 2, 2020. https://www.theguardian.com /world/2020/dec/02/nike-japan-ad-on-teenage-bullying-and-racism-sparks -debate.

McIntosh bokushi no zairyūken soshō o shien surukai, ed. 1987. *McIntosh bokushi no "zainichi" ni kakeru yume: Senkyō 25nen. Shimon ōnatsu o kyohi shite*. Tokyo: Kirisuto Shinbunsha.

Bibliography

Meyer, John W. 2010. "World Society, Institutional Theories, and the Actor." *Annual Review of Sociology* 36: 1–20.

Meyer, John W., John Boli, George M. Thomas, and Francisco O. Ramirez. 1997. "World Society and the Nation State." *American Journal of Sociology* 103 (1): 144–181.

Meyer, John W., David J. Frank, Ann Hironaka, Evan Schofer, and Nancy Brandon Tuma. 1997. "The Structuring of a World Environmental Regime, 1870–1990." *International Organization* 51 (4): 623–651.

Meyer, John W., and Ronald L. Jepperson. 2000. "The 'Actors' of Modern Society: The Cultural Construction of Social Agency." *Sociological Theory* 18 (1): 100–120.

Meyer, John W., and Brian Rowan. 1977. "Institutionalized Organizations: Formal Structure as Myth and Ceremony." *American Journal of Sociology* 83 (2): 340–363.

Mills, Charles W. 2017. *Black Rights / White Wrongs: The Critique of Racial Liberalism.* New York: Oxford University Press.

Milly, Deborah. 2014. *New Policies for New Residents: Immigrants, Advocacy, and Governance in Japan and Beyond.* Ithaca, NY: Cornell University Press.

Mindan Shinbun. 1998. "Eijyū gaikokujin no chihō sanseiken: Nihonkakukai ni kiku." *Mindan Shinbun,* August 15, 1998. https://www.mindan.org/old/shinbun/980815/topic/topic_h.html.

Minzoku Sabetsu to Tatakau Kantō Kōryūshūkai Jikko I'inkai. 1985. *Shimon ōnatsu kyohisha eno kyōhakujyo o yomu.* Tokyo: Akashi Shoten.

Minzoku Sabetsu to Tatakau Renraku Kyōgikai. 1975. *Mintōren nyūsu 6 gatsu sōkangō.*

———. 1975. *Mintōren nyūsu 7 gatsu go.*

Mitchell, Richard. 1967. *The Korean Minority in Japan.* Berkeley: University of California Press.

Miyashita, Akitoshi. 1999. "*Gaiatsu* and Japan's Foreign Aid: Rethinking the Reactive-Proactive Debate." *International Studies Quarterly* 43: 695–731.

Miyata Setsuko, Kim Yong-Dal, and Yang T'aeho. 1992. *Sōshi kaimei.* Tokyo: Akashi Shoten.

Miyazaki Shigeki. 1973a. "Senzen no wagakuni ni okeru gaikokujin no shogū." *Kokusaiho Gaiko Zasshi* 72 (2): 137–173.

———. 1973b. "Shutsunyūkoku kanri to kokusaiho." *Meiji Daigaku Shakaikagaku Kenkyū Nenpo* 13: 34.

Mizuno Naoki. 1992. "Chōsen sōtokufu no 'naichi' tokō kanri seisaku: 1910 nendai no rōdōsha boshyū torishimari." *Zainichi Chōsenjin-shi Kenkyū* 22: 23–40.

———. 1996. "Zainichi chōsenjin taiwanjin sanseiken 'teishi' jyōkō no seiritsu: Zainichi chōsenjin sanseiken mondai no rekisikentō 1." *Sekai Jinken Mondai Center Kenkyū Kiyō* 1 (3): 43–65.

—. 1997. "Zainichi chōsenjin taiwanjin sanseiken 'teishi' jyōkō no seiritsu: Zainichi chōsenjin sanseiken mondai no rekisikentō 2." *Sekai Jinken Mondai Center Kenkyū Kiyō* 2 (3): 59–82.

—. 1999. "Chōsenjin no kokugai ijyū to nihon teikoku." *Sekai Rekishi Iwanami Kōza* 18 (8): 255–275.

—. 2000. "Dai sangokujin no kigen to rufu ni tsuiteno kōsatsu." *Zainichi Chōsenjin-shi kenkyū* 30: 5–26.

—. 2001. "Kokuseki o meguru higashi ajia kankei: Shokuminchiki chōsenjin kokuseki mondai no isō." In *Kindai nihon ni okeru higashi ajia mondai*, edited by Furuya Tetsuya and Yamamuro Shinichi, 211–237. Tokyo: Yoshikawa Kōbunkan.

—. 2002. "Chōsen shokuminchi shihai to namae no 'saika': 'Naichijin ni magirawashiki seimei' no kinshi o megut'te." In *Shokuminchi shugi to jinruigaku*, edited by Yamaji Katsuhiko and Tanaka Masakazu, 143–164. Osaka: Kansei Gakuin Daigaku Shuppankai.

—, ed. 2004a. *Seikatsu no nakano shokuminchi-shugi*. Kyoto: Jinmon Shyoin.

—. 2004b. *"Sōshi kaimei" no jisshi katei nitsuite*. Kyoto: Jinmon Shyoin.

—. 2005. "Shiryō shokai zadankai 'zainichi chōsenjin mondai ni tsuite." *Sekai Jinken Mondai Center Kenkyū Kiyō* 10 (3): 203–225.

Moon, Katherine H. S. 1999. "South Korean Movements against Militarized Sexual Labor." *Asian Survey* 39 (2): 310–327.

Moore, Barrington. 1966. *Social Origins of Dictatorship and Democracy: Lord and Peasant in the Making of the Modern World*. Boston: Beacon.

Morita Yoshio. 1955. *Zainichi chōsenjin shogū no sui'i to genjyō: Hōmukenkyūhōkokusho dai 4shū 3gō*. Tokyo: Hōmukenkyūsho.

—. 1996. *Sūji ga kataru zainichi kankoku chōsenjin*. Tokyo: Akashi Shoten.

Morris-Suzuki, Tessa. 1998. *Re-inventing Japan: Time, Space, Nation*. New York: M. E. Sharpe.

—. 2005. "Japan's Hidden Role in the 'Return' of Zainichi Koreans to North Korea." *Asia-Pacific Journal*. Accessed on January 18, 2021. https://openresearch-repository.anu.edu.au/handle/1885/29083.

—. 2006. "Invisible Immigrants: Undocumented Migration and Border Controls in Early Postwar Japan." *Journal of Japanese Studies* 32 (1): 119–153.

—. 2007. *Exodus to North Korea: Shadows from Japan's Cold War*. New York: Rowman & Littlefield.

Mouer, Ross. 1982. *Nihonjin wa "nihonteki" ka: Tokushuron o koete, tagenteki bunseki e*. Tokyo: Tokyo Keizai Shinpōsha.

—. 1995. "Nihonjinron at the End of the Twentieth Century: A Multicultural Perspective." In *Japanese Encounters with Postmodernity,* edited by Yoshio Sugimoto and Johann P. Arnason, 237–269. London: Kegan Paul.

Mushanokōji Kindate, ed. 1994. *Kokuren to jinken NGO: Hansabetsu kokusai undō towa?* Osaka: Buraku Kaihō Kenkyūjo.

Bibliography

Myers, Ramon H., and Mark R. Peattie, eds. 1984. *The Japanese Colonial Empire, 1895–1945*. Princeton, NJ: Princeton University Press.

Naimushō Keihokyokuchō. 1913. "'Chōsenjin shikibetsu shiryō ni kansuru ken' Keihokyokuchō yori chō-fu-ken chōkan ate, naimushō maruhi dai 1, 542 go." In *Zainichi chōsenjin kankei shiryō shūsei dai 1 kan,* edited by Park Gyeongsik, 27–29. Tokyo: Sanichi Shobō.

Naimushō Keihokyoku Hoanka. 1945. "Sensō shūketsu ni kansuru byōgi kettei zengo ni okeru chian jyōkyō." In *Shiryo Nihon Gendaishi 2: Haisenchokugo no seiji to shakai I,* edited by Awaya Kentaro, 25–35. Tokyo: Ōtsuki shoten.

Nakahara Ryōji. 1993. *Zainichi kankoku/chōsenjin no shūshoku sabetsu to kokuseki jyōkō*. Tokyo: Akashi Shoten.

Nakajima Yōichirō. 1973. *Kantō daishinsai*. Tokyo: Yūzankaku Shuppan.

Nakamura, Masanori. 1992. *The Japanese Monarchy: Ambassador Joseph Grew and the Making of the "Symbol Emperor System," 1931–1991*. New York: M. E. Sharpe.

Nakayama Hideo, ed. 1995. *Zainichi chōsenjin kyōiku kankei shiryōshū*. Tokyo: Akashi Shoten.

Nakayasu Toshifumi. 2007. "Nikkei burazirujin rōdōsha no genjō to soshikika." *Keizai* 12 (147): 59–67.

Nanmin Shien Kyōkai. 2022a. *Kari-hōmenseido no unyō henkō niyoru shūyōmondai no akka: Kaizen ni mukete*. January 5, 2022. https://www.Refugee .or.jp/report/refugee/2022/01/prov-release/.

———. 2022b. *Nihon no nanmin nintei wa naze sukunaika: Seidomen no kadaikara*. February 19, 2022. https://www.refugee.or.jp/refugee/japan_recog/.

Nash, Kate. 2009. "Between Citizenship and Human Rights." *Sociology* 43 (6): 1067–1083.

Neary, Ian. 2003. "The Burakumin at the End of History." *Social Research: An International Quarterly* 70 (1): 269–294.

Ngai, Mae. 2004. *Impossible Subjects: Illegal Aliens and the Making of Modern America*. Princeton, NJ: Princeton University Press.

Nichibenren. 1999. *Nihon no jinken 21seiki e no kadai*. Tokyo: Gendai Jinmonsha.

———. 2020. *Opinion on the Reform of the Immigration Detention Facilities Visiting Committee*. August 20, 2020. https://www.nichibenren.or.jp/en /document/opinionpapers/200820.html.

———. 2021. *Opinion on the Bill for Amendments to the Immigration Control and Refugee Recognition Act*. Accessed March 21, 2021. https://www .nichibenren.or.jp/en/document/opinionpapers/210318.html.

Nishinarita Yutaka. 1997. *Zainichi chōsenjin no sekai to teikoku kokka*. Tokyo: Tokyo Daigaku Shuppan.

———. 2002. *Chūgokujin kyōsei renkō*. Tokyo: Tokyo Daigaku Shuppankai.

Nishio Kanji. 2005. *Nihon wa nachisu to dōzai ka?* Tokyo: Wac Bunko.

Noiriel, Gérard. 1996. *French Melting Pot: Immigration, Citizenship and National Identity*. Minneapolis: University of Minnesota Press.

Nojima Toshihiko. 1989. "Seisaku shūdan 10: Jiyū minshutō gaikokujin mondai tokubetsu i'inkai: susumetai nikkeijin no tokubetsu ukeire." *Gekkan Jiyū Minshū* 440 (11): 92–99.

Nonaka Hiromu and Shin Sugok. 2009. *Sabetsu to nihonjin*. Tokyo: Kadokawa Bunko.

Nozoe Kenji. 1999. *Akita no chōsenjin kyōseirenkō: Rekishi no yami o aruku*. Tokyo: Sairyūsha.

Nyūkanho Kaiaku ni Hantai suru Zainichi Korian. 2021. *Nyūkanhō kaiaku ni hantai suru zainichi korian*. Accessed on September 20, 2021. https://zainichistatement.myportfolio.com/seimei.

Ogasawara Sankurō. 1945. *89th Session of the House of Peers, Imperial Diet: Budget Committee 2*. December 14.

Ogata, Sadako. 1983. "The Changing Role of Japan in the United Nations." *Journal of International Affairs* 37 (1): 29–42.

———. 1987. "Japan's United Nations Policy in the 1980s." *Asian Survey* 27 (9): 957–972.

Oguma Eiji. 1995. *Tanitsu minzoku shinwa no kigen: Nihonjin no jigazō no keifu*. Tokyo: Shinyosha.

———. 1998. *Nihonjin no kyōkai: Okinawa, Ainu, Taiwan, chōsen shokuminchi shihai kara fukki undō made*. Tokyo: Shinyosha.

Okamoto Masataka. 1999. "Hōkokuseido to NGO no yakuwari." In *Uoc'chi, kiyaku jinken i'inkai*, edited by Kokusai Jinken NGO Network, 230–249. Tokyo: Nihon Hyōronsha.

Okamoto, Shunpei. 1970. *The Japanese Oligarchy and Russo-Japanese War*. New York: Columbia University Press.

Ōkuma Shigenobu. 1906. "Taikan iken." *Taiyō* 25 (4): 66–76.

Olson, Lawrence. 1992. *Ambivalent Moderns: Portraits of Japanese Cultural Identity*. Lanham, MD: Rowman & Littlefield.

Omi, Michael, and Howard Winant. (1986) 2014. *Racial Formation in the United States*. 3rd ed. New York: Routledge.

Ōmura Sei'ichi. 1946. "Daisangokujin no torishimari kyōka: Naisō, hōsō ra shoshin o hyōmei." *Asahi Shinbun*, September 3, 1946.

Ōnuma Yasuaki. 1978. "Shutsunyūkoku kanri hōsei no seiritsu katei: 1952nen taisei no zenshi." In *Kokusai Hōgaku no Saikōchiku (ge)*, edited by Terasawa Hajime, Yamamoto Kusaji, and Hatano Ribō, 257–328. Tokyo: Tokyo University Press.

———. 1993. *Tanitsu minzoku shakai no shinwa o koete: Zainichi kankoku chōsenjin to shutsunyūkoku kanri taisei*. Tokyo: Tōshindo

———. 2004. *Zainichi kankoku chōsenjin no kokuseki to jinken*. Tokyo: Tōshindō.

Orakhelashvili, Alexander. 2001. "The Position of the Individual in International Law." *California Western International Law Journal* 31: 241–276.

Bibliography 243

Osaka Zainichi Chōsenjin no Jinken o Mamorukai. 1978. *Zainichi chōsenjin no zairyūken: Kyōsei sōkan to ikani tatakauka.* Osaka: Osaka Zainichi Chōsenjin no Jinken o Mamorukai.

Ōta Osamu. 2003. *Nikkan Kōshō Seikyūken Mondai no Kenkyū.* Tokyo: Kurein.

Otsuka Tsunesaburō Bunsho. n.d. *"Yamada Hakushi Sōfu Kokuseki Mondaihoka Sanken"* at Kensei-shiryōshitsu in Kokkai Toshokan.

Ozawa Ichirō. 2003. *156th Session of the Both Houses of Representatives and Councilors: National Diet Joint Committee on Fundamental National Policies 4.* June 11.

Ozawa Yūsaku. 1973. *Zainichi chōsenjin kyōikuron rekishi-hen.* Tokyo: Akishobō.

Paku kun o Kakomukai. 1974. *Minzoku sabetsu.* Tokyo: Aki Shobō.

Park Gyeongsik. 1965. *Chōsenjin kyōsei renkō no kiroku.* Tokyo: Miraisha.

———. 1975. *Zainichi chōsenjin kankei shiryō shūsei dai 1kan–dai 6 kan.* Tokyo: San'ichi Shobō.

———. 1979. *Zainichi chōsenjin undōshi 8.15 kaihōmae.* Tokyo: San'ichi Shobō.

———. 1981. *Chōsen mondai shiryō sōsho.* Vols. 1–15. Tokyo: Ajia Mondai Kenkyūjo.

———. 1989. *Kaihōgo zainichi chōsenjin undōshi.* Tokyo: San'ichi Shobō.

———, ed. 2000. *Zainichi chōsenjin kankei shiryō shūsei sengohen dai 1kan–dai 6kan.* Tokyo: Fuji Shuppan.

Park Il. 1999. *"Zainichi" to iu ikikata.* Tokyo: Kōdansha.

Park Jong-myung, ed. 1995. *Zainichi chōsenjin rekishi genjō tenbō.* Akashi Tokyo: Shoten.

———. 2006. *Zainichi chōsenjin no rekishi to bunka.* Tokyo: Akashi Shoten.

Parkin, Frank. 1979. *Marxism and Class Theory: A Bourgeois Critique.* London: Tavistock.

Paul, Kathleen. 1997. *White Washing Britain: Race and Citizenship in the Postwar Era.* Ithaca, NY: Cornell University Press.

Peattie, Mark R. 1984. "Japanese Attitudes toward Colonialism, 1895–1945." In *The Japanese Colonial Empire, 1895–1945,* edited by Ramon H. Myers and Mark R. Peattie, 80–127. Princeton, NJ: Princeton University Press.

Peek, John M. 1992. "Japan, the United Nations, and Human Rights." *Asian Survey* 32 (3): 217–229.

Pfaff, William. 1993. *The Wrath of Nations: Civilizations and the Furies of Nationalism.* New York: Simon & Schuster.

Pitts, Jennifer. 2005. *A Turn to Empire: The Rise of Imperial Liberalism in Britain and France.* Princeton, NJ: Princeton University Press.

Polanyi, Karl. 1957. "The Economy as an Instituted Process." In *Trade and Market in the Early Empires,* edited by Karl Polanyi, Conrad M. Arensberg, and Harry W. Pearson, 243–270. New York: Free Press.

Ramakrishnan, S. Karthic, and Thomas J. Espenshade. 2001. "Immigrant Incorporation and Political Participation in the United States." *International Migration Review* 35 (3): 870–909.

Ramseyer, J. Mark. 2019. "Privatizing Police: Japanese Police, the Korean Massacre, and Private Security Firms." *Harvard John M. Olin Center for Law, Economics, and Business. Discussion Paper No. 1008 (June)* Accessed May 20, 2021. http://www.law.harvard.edu/programs/olin_center/.

———. 2021a. "On Privatizing Police, with Examples from Japan." In *The Cambridge Handbook of Privatization,* edited by Avihay Dorfman and Alon Harel, 195–205. Cambridge: Cambridge University Press.

———. 2021b. "Social Capital and the Problem of Opportunistic Leadership: The Example of Koreans in Japan." *European Journal of Law and Economics* 52: 1–32.

Reischauer, Edwin O. 1951. "Forewords." In *The Korean Minority in Japan 1904–1950,* edited by Edward W. Wagner, 1. New York: International Secretariat, Institute of Pacific Relations.

Ri Yongmi. 2016. "1950 nendai ni okeru nikkan shinwakai 'hogo jigyōbu no karihōmen jigyō: Shinwa' o tegakarini." *Korea Kenkyū* 3 (7): 89–96.

Risse, Thomas, Stephen C. Ropp, and Kathryn Sikkink, eds. 1999. *The Power of Human Rights: International Norms and Domestic Change.* Cambridge: Cambridge University Press.

Robillard-Martel, Xavier, and Christopher Laurent. 2019. "From Colonization to Zaitokukai: The Legacy of Racial Oppression in the Lives of Koreans in Japan." *Asian Ethnicity* 21 (3): 393–412.

Robinson, Michael E. 1988. *Cultural Nationalism in Colonial Korea, 1920–1925.* Seattle: University of Washington Press.

Ryang, Sonia. 1997. *North Koreans in Japan: Language, Ideology, and Identity.* New York: Avalon.

———. 2000. *Koreans in Japan: Critical Voices from the Margin.* London: Routledge.

Said, Edward. 1978. *Orientalism.* New York: Pantheon Books.

Saikō Saibansho Dai 3 Shō Hōtei. 1995. "Senkyonin meibo futōroku shobun ni taisuru igi no mōshide kyakka kettei torikeshi." *Heisei 7nen 2gatsu 28nichi* 49 (2): 639.

Saitō Masaki. 2022. *Utoro kyōsei tachinoki tono tatakai.* Tokyo: Tōshindō.

Sakamoto Shinichi. 1997. "Haisenmae nihonkoku ni okeru chōsen koseki no kenkyū." *Seikyū Bungakuronshyū* 10: 231–293.

Sakanaka Hidenori. (1975) 1989. *Kongo no nyūkan kanri gyōsei no arikatani tsuite.* Tokyo: Nihon Kajo Shuppan.

———. 2005. *Nyūkan senki: Zainichi sabetsu, nikkeijin mondai, gaikokujin hanzai to nihon no kinmirai.* Tokyo: Kōdansha.

———. 2011. *Nihongata imin kokka e nomichi.* Tokyo: Tōshindō.

Sakurai Yoshiko. 2000. "Gaikokujin sanseiken wa jindō mondai ni arazu: Shuken kokka no konkan o yuragasu kiki." *Seiron* 340 (12): 56–69.

Sano Michio. 1993. *Nihon Shokuminchi kyōiku no tenkai to chōsen minshū no taiō.* Tokyo: Shakaihyōronsha.

Bibliography

Saotome Katsumoto. 2000. *Ana kara ana e 13nen: Liu Lianren to kyōsei renkō.* Tokyo: Kusanone Shuppankai.

Sasaki Teru. 2001. "Kokuseki shutoku to esunikku identity: Nihon kokuseki o shutokushita zainichi kankoku chōsenjin eno chōsa kara." *Sociology Today* 12: 14–27.

———. 2006. *Nihon no kokuseki seido to koria-kei nihonjin.* Tokyo: Akashi Shoten.

Sasaki, Yuzuru, and Hiroshi Wagatsuma. 1981. "Negative Self-Identity in a Delinquent Korean Youth." In *Koreans in Japan: Ethnic Conflict and Accommodation,* edited by Changsoo Lee and George De Vos, 334–353. Berkeley: University of California Press.

Sassen, Saskia. 1994. "Economic Internationalization: The New Migration in Japan and the United States." *Social Justice* 21–22 (56): 62–82.

———. 1998. *Globalization and Its Discontents: Essays on the New Mobility of People and Money.* New York: New Press.

———. 2002. "Towards Post-national and Denationalized Citizenship." In *Handbook of Citizenship Studies,* edited by Brian Turner and Engin Isin, 277–291. Thousand Oaks, CA: Sage.

SCAPIN. n.d. Headquarter 1 Corps to Commanding General Eighth Army on "*Staff Study on Korean School Problems.*" GHP/SCAPIN Record. Tokyo: National Diet Library.

———. 1949a. Record Group 5, *Foreign Nationals in Japan,* May–August. Jean MacArthur Research Center (MacArthur Memorial), Norfolk, VA.

———. 1949b. Record Group 5, *Status and Treatment of Koreans in Japan,* May–August. Jean MacArthur Research Center (MacArthur Memorial), Norfolk, VA.

Schaller, Michael. 1985. *The American Occupation of Japan: The Origins of the Cold War in Asia.* Oxford: Oxford University Press.

———. 1997. *Altered States: United States and Japan since the Occupation.* Oxford: Oxford University Press.

Schlichtmann, Klaus. 2003. "Japan, Germany and the Idea of the Hague Peace Conferences." *Journal of Peace Research* 40 (4): 377–394.

Schmidt, Samantha, Jessica Contrera, Rebecca Tan, Hannah Natanson, and John Woodrow Cox. 2020. "Protesters Throng D.C., Vowing to Be Heard after George Floyd's Death." *Washington Post,* June 7, 2020. https://www.washingtonpost.com/local/protesters-gather-for-massive-day-of-rallies-in-dc/2020/06/06/92cd6838-a6cb-11ea-bb20-ebf0921f3bbd_story.html.

Scott, James C. 1998. *Seeing like a State: How Certain Schemes to Improve the Human Condition Have Failed.* New Haven, CT: Yale University Press.

Sekiya Teisaburō. 1945. *89th Session of the House of Peers, Imperial Diet: Plenary Session 11.* December 14.

Selinger, Vyjayanthi. 2019. "War without Blood? The Literary Uses of a Taboo Fluid." *Heike Monogatari: Monumenta Nipponica* 74 (1): 33–57.

Shafir, Gershon, ed. 1998. *The Citizenship Debates: A Reader.* Minneapolis: University of Minnesota Press.

Shibuichi, Daiki. 2015. "Zaitokukai and the Problem with Hate Groups in Japan." *Asian Survey* 55 (4): 715–738.

Shin, Gi-Wook. 1996. *Peasant Protest and Social Change in Colonial Korea.* Seattle: University of Washington Press.

———. 2006. *Ethnic Nationalism in Korea: Genealogy, Politics, and Legacy.* Stanford, CA: Stanford University Press.

Shin, Gi-Wook, and Michael Robinson, eds. 1999. *Colonial Modernity in Korea.* Cambridge, MA: Harvard University Press.

Shin, Hwaji. 2010. "Colonial Legacy of Ethno-Racial Inequality in Japan." *Theory and Society* 39: 327–342.

Shin, Hwaji, and Kiyoteru Tsutsui. 2007. "Constructing Social Movement Actorhood: Resident Koreans' Activism in Japan since 1945." *International Journal of Comparative Sociology* 48 (4): 317–335.

Shin, Yong-ha. 1989. "The Revolutionary Movement of the Tonghak Peasant Army of 1894: Seen vis-à-vis the French Revolution." *Korea Journal* 29 (10): 28–33.

———. 1990. *Formation and Development of Modern Korean Nationalism.* Seoul: Dae Kwang Munhwasa.

———. 2000. *Modern Korean History and Korean Nationalism.* Seoul: Jimoondang.

Shin Yong Hong. 1995. "Zainichi chōsenjin to shakai hoshō." In *Zainichi Chōsenjin, rekishi, genjō, tenbō,* edited by Park Jong-myung, 285–318. Tokyo: Akashi Shoten.

Shinozaki Heiji. 1952. "Saikin ni okeru zainichi chōsenjin no fuhōkōi no hassei jyōkyō ni tsuite." *Keisatsu Jiho* 7 (15): 91–92.

———. 1953. "Zainichi chōsenjin no seikatsu jittai." *Keisatsu Jiho* 8 (6): 27–31.

———. 1955. *Zainichi chōsenjin undō.* Tokyo: Reibunsha.

Shipper, Apichai. 2008. *Fighting for Foreigners: Immigration and Its Impact on Japanese Democracy.* Ithaca, NY: Cornell University Press.

Shulman, Stephen. 2002. "Challenging the Civic/Ethnic and West/East Dichotomies in the Study of Nationalism." *Comparative Political Studies* 35 (5): 554–585.

Silberman, Bernard S., and Harry D. Harootunian. 1999. *Japan in Crisis: Essays on Taisho Democracy.* Ann Arbor: University of Michigan Press.

Smith, Anthony. 1986. *The Ethnic Origins of Nations.* Oxford: Blackwell.

Smith, Jackie. 2002. "Bridging Global Divides? Strategic Framing and Solidarity in Transnational Social Movement Organizations." *International Sociology* 17: 505–528.

———. 2008. *Social Movement for Global Democracy.* Baltimore: Johns Hopkins University Press.

Smith, Jackie, Charles Chatfield, and Ron Pagnucco, eds. 1997. *Transnational Social Movements and Global Politics: Solidarity beyond the State.* Syracuse: Syracuse University Press.

Smith, Jackie, and Hank Johnston, eds. 2002. *Globalization and Resistance: Transnational Dimensions of Social Movements.* Lanham, MD: Rowman & Littlefield.

Snow, David A., E. Burke Rochford Jr., Steven K. Worden, and Robert D. Benford. 1986. "Frame Alignment Processes, Micromobilization, and Movement Participation." *American Sociological Review* 51 (4): 464–481.

Somers, Margaret R. 1993. "Citizenship and the Place of the Public Sphere: Law, Community, and Political Culture in the Transition to Democracy." *American Sociological Review* 58 (5): 587–620.

Sōmushō Tōkeikyoku. 2022. *Jinkō suikei. 2022nen (reiwa 4nen) 6gatsu-hō.* Accessed March 17, 2023. https://www.stat.go.jp/data/jinsui/pdf/202206 .pdf.

Sorano Yoshihiro and Ko Chanyu, eds. 1995. *Zainichi chōsenjin no seikatsu to jinken.* Tokyo: Akashi Shoten.

Soysal, Yasemin. 1994. *Limits of Citizenship: Migrants and Postnational Membership in Europe.* Chicago: University of Chicago Press.

———. 1997. "Changing Parameters of Citizenship and Claims-Making: Organized Islam in European Public Spheres." *Theory and Society* 26 (4): 509–527.

Stokes, Henry S. 1979. "Ships Bound for Japan Avoiding Seas Traversed by 'Boat People.'" *New York Times,* July 15, 1979.

Sugimoto, Yoshio. 1999. "Making Sense of Nihonjinron." *Thesis Eleven* 57 (1): 81–96.

Sugimoto, Yoshio, and Ross Mouer. 1990. *Images of Japanese Society: A Study in the Social Construction of Reality.* London: Kegan Paul.

Suzuki Hajime. 1966. "Nikkan shinwakai to watashi." *Shinwa* 157: 30–34.

Suzuki Yūko. 1992. *Jyūgun ianfu, naisen kekkon: Sei no sinryaku, sengo sekinin o kangaeru.* Tokyo: Miraisha.

Tabuchi, Hiroko. 2009. "Japan Pays Foreign Workers to Go Home." *New York Times,* April 23, 2009.

Tai Eika. 2002. "Zainichi nitotte 'minzoku' towa?" *Osaka City University Jinken Mondai Kenkyū* 2: 5–20.

Takagi Takesaburō. 1970. *Kikan mondai oboegaki.* Tokyo: Toyokan Shuppansha.

Takahashi Mamoru. 1965. *48th Session of the House of Representatives: Cabinet Committee 34.* April 20.

Takahashi Masami. 1954. "Gaikokujin (toku ni chōsenjin) no hanzai." *Hōmu shiryō honpō senji sengo no hanzai genshō dai 1 pen* 331: 255–285.

Takaichi Sanae and Momochi Akira. 2000. "Rippōfu ga okasu kenpō ihan no gu: Saikōsai no peten no yōna 'bōron' ni genwaku sarete 'kokuminkoyū no kenri o gaikoku ni uritobasunoka." *Shokun!* 32 (11): 48–55.

Takasaki Sōji and Park Jung. 2005. *Kikoku undō towa nandattanoka: Fūin sareta nicchō kankeishi.* Tokyo: Heibonsha.

Takaya Sachi. 2014. "Tsuihō to hōsetsu no shakaigaku: 1950nendai chōsenjin no zairyūtokubetsukyoka o megutte." *Osaka Keizai Hōka Daigaku Ajia Taiheiyō Kenkyū Center Nenpō* (11): 2–9.

———, ed. 2019. *Imin seisaku towa nanika: Nihon no genjitsu kara kangaeru.* Tokyo: Jinmon Shoin.

Takemae Eiji. 2002. *GHQ no hitobito: Keireki to seisaku.* Tokyo: Akashi Shoten.

———. 2003. *The Allied Occupation of Japan.* New York: Continuum.

Takenaka, Harukata. 2014. *Failed Democratization in Prewar Japan: Breakdown of a Hybrid Regime.* Stanford, CA: Stanford University Press.

Takubo Tadaē, ed. 2001. *"Kokka" o miushinatta nihonjin: Gaikokujin sanseiken mondai no honshitsu.* Tokyo: Shogakukan.

Tanaka Hiroshi. 2013. *Zainichi gaikokujin dai 3 pan: Hō no kabe, kokoro no kabe.* Tokyo: Iwanami Shoten.

Tanno Kiyoto. 2019. "Gaikokujin no Shichizunshippu: Gyōsei unyō to shakai undō no aidani umareru shiminken." *Fukushi Shakaigaku Kenkyū* 16: 13–31.

Tarrow, Sidney. 2005. *The New Transnational Activism.* Cambridge: Cambridge University Press.

Tashiro Aritsugu. 1974. *Kokusekihō Chikujo Kaisetsu.* Tokyo: Nihon Kajyo Shuppan.

Terao Gorō. 1959. *38 do sen no kita.* Tokyo: Shin Nihon Shuppan.

Terashima Mizuho. 1995. "Shimon ōnatsu kyohi no shisō to undō (1)." *Ōsaka Furitsu Daigaku Kiyō* 43: 17–29.

Thompson, Edward P. 1963. *The Making of the English Working Class.* London: Victor Gollancz.

Tilly, Charles, ed. 1996. *Citizenship, Identity and Social History.* Cambridge: Cambridge University Press.

———. 1998. *Durable Inequality.* Berkeley: University of California Press.

———. 2005. *Identities, Boundaries and Social Ties.* Boulder, CO: Paradigm Press.

———. 2006. *Regimes and Repertoires.* Chicago: University of Chicago Press.

———. 2007. *Democracy.* New York: Cambridge University Press.

Tokkabi Kodomokai. 1995. *Tokkabi kodomokai 20nen no ayumi: Tomo ni ikiru Yao, machi zukuri.* Osaka: Tokkabi Kodomokai.

Tōma Seita. 1951. *Nihon minzoku no keisei.* Tokyo: Iwanashi Shoten.

Tonomura Masaru. 2004. *Zainichi chōsenjin shakai no rekishigaku-teki kenkyū: Keisei, kōzō, henyō.* Tokyo: Ryokuin-shobō.

Tori'i Ryūzō. 1976. *Tori'i ryūzō zenshū dai 5 kan.* Tokyo: Asahi Shinbunsha.

Torpey, John. 1999. *The Invention of the Passport: Surveillance, Citizenship and the State.* Cambridge: Cambridge University Press.

Bibliography

Tōyō Keizai Nippō. 2001. "Zainichi shakai: Nihon kokuseki todokede kyōka zainichi shakaini hamon hirogaru." April 27, 2001. http://www.toyo-keizai .co.jp/news/society/2001/post_3246.php.

Trewartha, Glenn, and Wilbur Zelinsky. 1955. "Population Distribution and Change in Korea, 1935–1949." *Geographical Review* 45 (1): 1–26.

Tsuda Sōkichi. (1946) 1968. "Kenkoku no jijyō to mansei ikkeino shisō." In *Sengo Shisō no Shuppatsu,* edited by Hidaka Rokurō, 114–142. Tokyo: Chikuma Shobō.

Tsuda, Takeyuki. 1999. "The Permanence of 'Temporary' Migration: The 'Structural Embeddedness' of Japanese-Brazilian Immigrant Workers in Japan." *Journal of Asian Studies* 58 (3): 687–722.

———. 2003. *Strangers in the Ethnic Homeland: Japanese Brazilian Return Migration in Transnational Perspective.* New York: Columbia University Press.

———, ed. 2006. *Local Citizenship in Recent Countries of Immigration: Japan in Comparative Perspectives.* Oxford: Lexington Books.

Tsukajima Jyunichi. 2016. "Hitachi tōsō o hottantosuru kawasaki kyōkai seikyūsha ni atsumatta shimin ni yoru minkan kigyō ni taisuru minzoku sabetsu teppai undō." *Ibunka* 17 (4): 73–102.

Tsuruzono Yūki. 2020. "Nikka heiwa jyōyaku to nihon kakyō: Gojyū ninen taisei ka ni okeru 'chūgokujin' no kokuseki kizoku mondai (1951–1952)." *Nihon Taiwan Gakkaihō* 6: 41–64.

Tsutsui, Kiyoteru. 2004. "Global Civil Society and Ethnic Social Movements in the Contemporary World." *Sociological Forum* 19 (1): 63–87.

———. 2006. "Redressing Past Human Rights Violations: Global Dimension of Contemporary Social Movements." *Social Forces* 85 (1): 331–354.

———. 2018. *Rights Make Might: Global Human Rights and Minority Social Movements in Japan.* New York: Oxford University Press.

Tsutsui, Kiyoteru, and Christine M. Wotipka. 2004. "Global Civil Society and the International Human Rights Movement: Citizen Participation in International Human Rights Nongovernmental Organizations." *Social Forces* 83 (2): 587–620.

Tsutsui, Kiyoteru, and Hwaji Shin. 2008. "Global Norms, Local Activism, and Social Movement Outcomes: Global Human Rights and Resident Koreans in Japan." *Social Problems* 55 (3): 391–418.

Turner, Bryan S. 1990. "Outline of a Theory of Citizenship." *Sociology* 24 (2): 189–217.

———. 2006. *Vulnerability and Human Rights.* University Park: Penn State University Press.

Uchiyama, Kazuo. 1995. "The Present Problems of Education for Koreans in Japanese School: Especially about Systematic Support for 'Their Native Names and Post-graduate Life.'" *Japanese Journal of Education* 62 (3): 207–218.

Uchiyama Kazuo and Cho Bak, eds. 1989. *Zainichi chōsenjin minzoku yōgo tōsō shiryō-shū (II): 4.24 ikō osaka o chūshin ni.* Tokyo: Akashi Shoten.

Ueda Shinkichi. 1965. *48th Session of the House of Representatives: Cabinet Committee 34.* April 20, 1965.

UN Department of Economic and Social Affairs, Population Division. 2020. *International Migrant Stock 2020.* New York: United Nations. https://www.un.org/development/desa/pd/content/international-migrant-stock.

UN International Law Commission. 2017. *About the Commission: Origin and Background. League of Nation Codification Conference.* Last updated June 19, 2023. https://legal.un.org/ilc/league.shtml.

US Department of State. 2005. *Remarks in Dialogue with Internet Journalists.* March 20. Seoul, Korea. https://2001-2009.state.gov/secretary/rm/2005/43661.htm.

Utsunomiya Tarō kankei shiryō kenkyūkai. 2007. *Nihon rikugun to ajia seisaku—rikugun taishō Utsunomiya Tarō nikki.* Vols. 1–3. Tokyo: Iwanami Shoten.

Wada Haruki and Takasaki Soji. 2005. *Kenshō nicchō-kankei 60 nenshi.* Tokyo: Akashi Shoten.

Wagatsuma, Hiroshi, and George De Vos. 1966. *Japan's Invisible Race: Caste in Culture and Personality.* Berkeley: University of California Press.

Wagner, Edward W. 1951. *The Korean Minority in Japan 1904–1950.* New York: International Secretariat, Institute of Pacific Relations.

Waters, Mary. 1990. *Ethnic Options: Choosing Identities in America.* Berkeley: University of California Press.

Watsuji Tetsurō. (1948) 2019. *Kokumin tōgō no shōchō.* Tokyo: Chuōkōronsha.

Watt, Lori. 2009. *When Empire Comes Home: Repatriation and Reintegration in Postwar Japan.* Cambridge, MA: Harvard University Press.

Weber, Max. 1949. *The Methodology of the Social Sciences.* Translated and edited by Edward A. Shils and Henry A. Finch. Glencoe, IL: Free Press.

Weiner, Michael. 1994. *Race and Migration in Imperial Japan: The Limits of Assimilation.* New York: Routledge.

———. 1997. *The Illusion of Homogeneity.* London: Routledge.

Weinstein, Michael A. 2006. "South Korea's and Japan's Dokdo/Takeshima Dispute Escalates toward Confrontation." *Asia-Pacific Journal* 4 (5): 1–7.

Wells, Kenneth M. 1989. "Background to the March First Movement: Koreans in Japan, 1905–1919." *Korean Studies* 13: 5–21.

Wimmer, Andreas, and Nina Glick Schiller. 2003. "Methodological Nationalism, the Social Science, and the Study of Migration: An Essay in Historical Epistemology." *International Migration Review* 37 (3): 576–610.

Yack, Bernard. 1996. "The Myth of the Civic Nation." *Critical Review* 10 (2): 193–211.

Yamada Saburō. 1895. "Shinryōchi ni kansuru hōritsu kankei o ronzu." *Kokka Gakkai Zasshi* 102: 630–663.

Bibliography

———. 1896. "Shinryōchi shinmin no chi'i." *Kokka Gakkai Zasshi* 113: 778–789. Tokyo: Fuji Shuppan.

———. 1909. "Heigō go ni okeru kankokujin no kokuseki mondai." *Kokkai Toshokan Kensei Shiryōshitsu Terauchi Masatake Monjo* 439–444.

———. [1912?]. "Yamada hakase sōtokufu kokuseki mondai hoka 3ken." *Kokkai Toshokan Kensei Shiryōshitsu Ōtsuka Tsunesaburō Monjo* 108–107.

Yamada Shōji. 1987. "Chōsenjin kyōseirōdō no rekishiteki zentei: Chikuhō tanden no omona jirei to shite." *Zainichi Chōsenjin-shi Kenkyū* 17: 20–58.

———. 2003. *Kanto daishinsaiji no chōsen gyakusatsu: Sono kokka sekinin to minshū sekinin.* Tokyo: Soshisha.

Yamada Shōji, Koshō Tadashi, and Higuchi Yūichi. 2005. *Chōsenjin senji rōdō dōin.* Tokyo: Iwanami Shoten.

Yamada Terumi and Park Jong-myung, eds. 1991. *Zainichi chosenjin: Rekishi to genjō.* Tokyo: Akashi Shoten.

Yamada Tetsuya. 2020. "Fuhō nyūkokusha ga shūyō sareru genbano sōzetsuna jittai." *Tōyō Keizai,* January 18, 2020. https://toyokeizai.net/articles/-/325058.

Yamamoto Shiro, ed. 1984. *Terauchi Masatake kankei shiryō—shushō izen.* Kyoto: Kyoto Jyoshi Daigaku.

Yamanaka, Keiko. 1993. "New Immigration Policy and Unskilled Foreign Workers in Japan." *Pacific Affairs* 66 (1): 72–90.

Yamashita Yon'e. 2008. *Nashonarizumu no hazama kara—jyūgun ianfu mondai e no mō hitototsu no shiza.* Tokyo: Akashi Shoten.

Yamawaki Keizō. 1994. *Kindai nihon to gaikokujin rōdōsha—1890 nendai kōhan to 1920 nendai zenhan ni okeru chūgokujin chōsenjin rōdōsha mondai.* Tokyo: Akashi Shoten.

———. (1999) 2003. "Foreign Workers in Japan: A Historical Perspective." In *Japan and Global Migration: Foreign Workers and the Advent of a Multicultural Society,* edited by Mike Douglass and Glenda S. Roberts, 38–51. Honolulu: University of Hawai'i Press.

Yang Yeong-Hu. 1994a. "Osaka ni okeru 4.24 kyōiku tōsō no oboegaki." *Zainichi Chōsenjinshi Kenkyū* 6: 70–88.

———. 1994b. *Sengo Osaka no chōsenjin undō 1945–1965.* Tokyo: Miraisha.

Yasuda Kōichi. 2015. *Net to aikoku: Zaitokukai no yami o oikakete.* Tokyo: Kōdansha.

Yorozu Chōhō. 1910. *"Keizai jyō no eikyō."* Tokyo: Chōhōsha.

Yoshino, Kōsaku, ed. 1999. *Consuming Ethnicity and Nationalism: Asian Experiences.* Honolulu: University of Hawai'i Press.

Yoshioka Masuo, ed. (1978) 1995. *Zainichi chōsenjin to shakai hoshō: Sengo no nihon no mainoritei jyūmin no jinken.* Tokyo: Shakai Hyōronsha.

Young, Louise. 1998. *Japan's Total Empire: Manchuria and the Culture of Wartime Imperialism.* Berkeley: University of California Press.

Young, Soo. 2018. "Nike Sales Booming after Colin Kaepernick Ad, Invalidating Critics: Nike Blew Past Estimates for the Quarter It Released the

Kaepernick Ad." ABCNews.com, December 21, 2018. https://abcnews.go.com/Business/nike-sales-booming-kaepernick-ad-invalidating-critics/story?id=59957137.

Yun Koncha. 1997. *Nihon kokuminron: Kindai nihon no identity.* Tokyo: Chikuma Shobō.

Zainichi Chōsenjin no Jinken o Mamorukai. 1977. *Zainichi chōsenjin no kihonteki jinken.* Tokyo: Nigatsusha.

Zainichi Kankoku Chōsenjin no Kokumin Nenkin o Motomerukai. 1984. *Kokuseki sabetsu to no tatakai: Nenkin saiban shōri e no kiroku.* Tokyo: Gaifūsha.

Zainichi Korean Statement against Proposed Revision to Immigration Law. 2021. *Nyūkanhō kaiaku ni hantaisuru zainichi korian no seimei.* May 15, 2021. https://zainichistatement.myportfolio.com/home.

Zainihon Daikanminkoku Mindan Chuō Honbu. 1997. *Kankoku mindan 50nen no ayumi.* Tokyo: Satsuki Shobō.

Zhou, Min, and Anthony C. Ocampo. 2016. *Contemporary Asian America: A Multidisciplinary Reader.* New York: New York University Press.

Zubrzycki, Genevieve. 2001. "'We, the Polish Nation': Ethnic and Civic Visions of Nationhood in Post-Communist Constitutional Debates." *Theory and Society* 30 (5): 629–668.

Index

Note: Page numbers in *italics* refer to illustrative matter.

Abe Shinzō, 172, 183
ability, 7
Act No. 126 (Hōritsu 126 Gō), 132–133, *134*
"Act on Measures concerning Orders Related to the Ministry of Foreign Affairs Pursuant to the Imperial Ordinance on Orders Issued Incidental to Acceptance of the Potsdam Declaration No. 126-2-6" (Act No. 126), 132–133, *134*
agency: of citizenship, 8, 76–77, 81; colonial, 9
aikokushin, 172
Ainu, 5, 121, 142
Alien Registration (publication), 104
Alien Registration Law (formerly Alien Registration Ordinance), 93–94, 100–102, 103, 123, 149
alien status, 92–97, 100–102. *See also* citizenship; noncitizen status; Special Permanent Resident Aliens
alien suffrage, 157, 179–184, 222n15. *See also* suffrage
Allied Control Council, 79
Allied Powers, 79, 108
analytic bifurcation, 8
Anderson, Benedict, 13
anticommunism, 103–104. *See also* communism

anti-Japanese sentiments, 84–85
anti-Korean violence, 86, 176–177. *See also* Koreans in Japan; violence
Arai Shōji. *See* Park Jongseok (Arai Shōji)
Arimoto Takugo, 192
Arita Hachirō, 113
arson, 192–193
Asahi (publication), 92, 100
Asamura Inajirō, 113
Asano Toyomi, 41
Asia-Pacific War (1945), 78
assimilationism, 21, 50–51, 56–57, 70–73, 219n1
atomic bombings (1945), 78, 166, 216n2
Australia, 79
author's positionality, ix–xii, 24–25

Baldwin, Frank, 64
Barth, Fredrik, 137–138
belonging, 96
Bendix, Reinhard, 13
Black Lives Matter movement, 191. *See also* Floyd, George
black ships, 163, 221n25
Blee, Kathleen, 25
boundaries, national, 70–74
Brazil, 5, 63, 128, 186–187, 196
Brazilian immigrants in Japan, 5, *128*

253

254 *Index*

Britain, 9–10, 50–51, 79
Brubaker, Rogers, 23, 28, 212n8
Bruner, Jerome, 27
budan tōchi, 49, 64
bunka tōchi, 49, 65
Burakumin, 5, 50, 142, 144

Cairo Declaration (1943), 95
censorship, 215n23
change and oppression, 17–23
Chang Myon, 114
China: Allied Powers and, 79; family
  registry system in, 39; Gando
  region and, 44;—Japan relations,
  164; labor migration from, 187;
  military and warfare of, 37, 38, 72,
  73–74; political activism in, 63;
  political divisions in, 217n8;—US
  relations, 160
Chinese immigrants in Japan, 5, *128,*
  128–129
Choi Changhwa, 148, 154
Choi Seungkoo, 143, 144–145, 146
Choi Sun-ae Lois, 148, 154
chokusen gi'in, 216n4
Chongryon, 110–111, 144, 151,
  217n14, 218n32
Chōren (Zainihon Chōsenjin Renmei),
  92–93, 96–97, 100, 110, 217n17
Chōsen, as term, 107
Chōsenjin, as term, 27
Chōsen tōchi shiryō, 214n12
Chōsōren. *See* Chongryon
Christian activists, 148–151
citizen/immigrant binary, 8–11
Citizens Group against the Special
  Privileges of Resident Koreans in
  Japan. *See* Zaitokukai
citizenship: alien status and, 92–97,
  100–102; decoupling of nationhood
  and, 184–191; defined, 7, 39–42;
  future of, 191–197; identification
  labels and, 27–31; migration

policies and, 42–45, 74–77; postwar
  struggles of, 87–97; San Francisco
  Peace Treaty on, 88, 89, 97, 100;
  scholarly theories on, 13–17; of
  Taiwanese in Japan, 40, 88, 90; as
  term, 213n6; 38th parallel division
  and, 106–107. *See also* Koreans in
  Japan; membership; nationhood;
  Pan-Asian Empire
claim-making among noncitizens,
  11–13, 127, 142, 158, 173, 190,
  211n5. *See also* citizenship
Collaer, Nicholas D., 102
collective action, 59–65, 76, 82, 86,
  98–99, 127–131, 173–174, 215n27.
  See also *names of specific
  movements*
collective identification, 76–77,
  82–83. *See also* citizenship;
  identities; nationhood
colonial migrants, as term and
  concept, 9, 29, 211n6
colonial migration, defined, 8, 211n6
comfort women, 165
communism, 63–64, 103, 110,
  113–114, 118, 119–120, 125.
  See also anticommunism
Communist Party of Japan, 92, 100,
  110, 113
constitution, 79, 93
Cook-Martín, David, 16–17, 175,
  200, 205
cosmopolitanism, 184, 188–190
coupling, as concept, 211n1

Daikanminkoku, as term, 106–107
decoupling, as concept, 211n1
Democratic Liberal Party, 120
Democratic Party of Japan, 143, 183
democratic popular sovereignty, 79
Denison, Henry W., 40, 41
Department of Police (Japan), 52
detention system, 193–194

Dièn, Doudou, 193
The Discovery of the Ethnic Nation
(Ishimoda), 118
discrimination cases, 1, 2, 142–148,
166
dōka, 49
dōka seisaku, 49
Dokdo/Takeshima Islands, 168
dōso dōshu, 54
duress, 36–39
Duus, Peter, 36

Ebashi Takashi, 188–189
educational policies and practices, 56,
97–101, 177
"Emergency Treatment of Collectively
Imported Korean Laborers" (1945),
85
Empire. *See* Pan-Asian Empire
emulation, 49–53
entitlement, 7
ethnic nationalism, 116–121
ethno-racial, as term and concept, 30,
53–59, 83–84, 91, 116, 135–142.
See also homogeneity myth;
identities; racial formation;
self-identification
European colonial models, 50–53
Exclusive Economic Zone, 168

false consciousness, x
family registry. *See koseki* system
Far Eastern Commission, 108
fascist authoritarianism, 75
Filipinos in Japan, *128*
fingerprinting, activism against, 139,
146, 148–155, 166, 194–195
FitzGerald, David Scott, 16, 17, 200,
205
Floyd, George, xi, 27, 99, 191
forced labor conscription, 73–74.
See also labor immigrants
France, 51, 79

French language, 35
Fujioka Nobukatsu, 171
Fukuoka Yasunori, 135
Fukushima Dai'ichi Nuclear Power
Plant disaster (2011), 183–184
Fuse Tatsuji, 96
Fuyushiba Tetsuzō, 180

gaichi, 214n15
Gaijin Tōroku (publication), 218n26
Gando region, 44
General Election Law, 69
generational trauma, x, 10, 149, 154,
192
Germany, 5, 38, 79, 171, 194
globalization, 19, 21–23, 32, 164–
169, 178, 191, 205, 212nn9–10
Go, Julian, 8, 9, 198
Gotō Shinpei Bunsho, 215n19
Great Kantō Earthquake (1923), 20,
65, 66, 67, 201
Great Recession (2008), 185
guerrilla resistance movement, 60

Hague Conference (1930), 48
Han Duk-Su, 94, 95, 96, 97, 110,
156, 157
Han Jongsok, 148, 150, 151–152,
154, 173, 194–195
Hanshin Education Struggle, 97–101,
177
Hara Takashi, 64, 66
Hart-Celler Immigration Act (1965),
104, 175
hate speech, 5–6, 176–177
Hate Speech Act (2016), 6
Hatoyama Ichirō, 113
Hayashi Toshimasa, 105
Hida Kōhei, 105
Hida Yūichi, 162–163
Hirohito (emperor), 154, 219n36
Hiroshima bombing (1945), 78, 166
Hitachi Inc., 1–2, 142–148, 194

Hobsbawm, Eric, 13
hojeok system, 72
homogeneity myth, 5–6, 116. *See also* ethno-racial, as term and concept
Hōritsu 126 Gō (Act No. 126), 132–133, *134*
human rights, 7–8, 147–151, 158, 173, 178–184, 211n5. *See also* personhood
hunger strikes, 194
Hunt, Lynn, 8

ICRC (International Committee of Red Cross), 111, 112–113, 123, 206
identification system, 189
identities: collective identification, 76–77, 82–83; ethno-racial, as concept, 30, 53–59, 83–84, 91, 116, 135–142; self-identification, 75–76, 82, 169–172, 203. *See also* Koreans in Japan
ijyūsha, as term, 212n14
imin, as term, 212n14
immigrant/citizen binary, 8–11
immigration, defined, 8
Immigration Bureau (Nyūkoku Kanrikyoku), 102, 123, 220n17
Imperial Ordinance No. 352, 66
inclusive citizenship, 56–57
informal imperialism, 36–37
Inoue Tetsujirō, 66, 113
intellectualism, 116–121
internalized oppression, as term, 172
internalized other, 45–49
International Committee of Red Cross (ICRC), 111, 112–113, 123, 206
International Covenant on Civil and Political Rights (ICCPR), 150, 155–156, 161
International Covenant on Economic, Social and Cultural Rights (ICESCR), 162

International Japanese Cultural Research Center, 170
invisibility, 6
Ippan Eijyūken (Regular Permanent Residency), 133. *See also* Special Permanent Resident Aliens
Ishay, Micheline, 8
Ishihara Shintarō, 170
Ishimoda Shō, 118
Is Japan as Guilty as Nazi(s)? (Nishio), 171
isshi dōjin, 54, 57, 58, 61, 201
Itō Hirobumi, 54, 73
Iwamoto Nobuyuki, 113
Iwasawa Yuji, 150

Japan: colonial empire and postwar transition of, 78–81; pendulum-swing pattern of change in, 17–23, 197–209; place in global society of, 158–163; unresolved colonial past of, 164–169
Japan Association for Refugees, 194
Japan Civil Liberties Union, 153
Japanese Communist Party, 92, 100, 110, 113
Japanese Federation of Bar Associations, 193
Japanese Institute for Orthodox History Education, 171
Japanese language, 29, 56, 65, 92, 107, 127, 220n9, 222n14
Japanese Red Cross, 111–114, 123, 206
Japan Federation of Bar Associations, 153, 188
Japan-Korea Normalization Treaty (1965), 114–115
Japan-Korea Treaty (1876), 66
Japan–South Korean Memorandum (1991), 166
Jenkins, Richard, 31, 137–138
jinken ishiki. *See* human rights
jinmeiyō kanji, 181

Index

job discrimination case, 1, 2, 142–148
Jones, George, 99–100
jus sanguinis, 14, 139
jus soli, 14, 28, 137

Kaepernick, Colin, 192
Kaifu Toshiki, 155
Kang Jae-eun, 141–142
Kankoku, as term, 106–107
Kankokujin, as term, 27
Kan Naoto, 143
Kantō Army, 71
Kantō Massacre (1923), 69
kazoku kokka, 72
Kendō, 92–93, 217n13. *See also* Mindan (Zainihon Chōsen Kyoryū Mindan)
kika, as term, 181
kikajin, as term, 181
Kim Dae-Jung, 180
Kim Hyeon Gyun, 161–162
Kim Il-sung, 44, 93, 97, 106
Kim Kyung-Duk, 140
Kim Puja, 165
Kim Tae-Gi, 90
Kim Tae-il, 99, 177
Kim Yong-Dal, 107
Kirkwood, William M. H., 50–51
Kissinger, Henry, 159
Kita Chōsen, as term, 107
Kiyose Ichirō, 88, 217n9
Kiyoteru Tsutsui, 12, 220n18
Koizumi Gorō, 87
Koizumi Junichirō, 172, 183, 222n8
kokuseki, as term, 213n6
Komagome Takeshi, 49
Kōmeitō, 180, 181
kōminka seisaku, 49
kōminka undō, 72
Korea: colonization of, 42–43; economy of, 92; 38th parallel division of, 106–116. *See also* North Korea; South Korea

Korean Independence Movement, 96
Korean language, 97, 136, 202
The Korean Minority in Japan (Wagner), 80–81
Koreans in Japan, 11–13, 198–209; alien status of, 92–97, 100–102; citizenship and migration policies on, 42–45, 74–77; educational policies and practices for, 56, 97–101, 177; as ethnic minority, 5; legal statuses of, *134, 185;* names and classifications of, 27–31; population statistics on, *68, 91, 128, 185;* in postwar period, 80–91; protest movements of, *59–65, 127–131;* Reischauer on, 80–81, 90. *See also* Special Permanent Resident Aliens; suffrage
koseki system, 35, 39, 46, 49, 72, 75, 138, 214n13
kunmin dōso, 54, 57, 61, 201
Kwantung Army, 71
Kyōiku Chokugo, 55
Kyōtei Eijyūken (Treaty-Based Permanent Residency), 133. *See also* Special Permanent Resident Aliens

labor immigrants, 2, 65, 73–74, 129, 216n5. *See also* forced labor conscription
language. See *names of specific languages*
Last Imperial Ordinance of Alien Registration, 93–94
League of Nations, 64
League of Nations Codification Conference (1930), 48
Lee Inha, 143, 145–146
Lee Yonghwa, 156–157
Lenin, Vladimir, 63
Liberal Democratic Party (LDP), 180, 183, 186

liberalism, 15–17
Liberal View of History Study Group, 171
Lie, John, 27
Liu Lianren, 165
Loveman, Mara, 30

MacArthur, Douglas, 79
Mainichi Newspaper Digital (publication), 194
Manchukuo, 71
Manchuria, 44, 64, 70–72, 78, 84, 93
Manchuria Incident (1934), 71
Mao Zedong, 63
March First Movement (1919), 59–65, 67, 69, 167, 201
marriage, 139, 214n16
Marshall, T. H., 15
Marx, Anthony, 138, 139–140, 190
Marxist socialism, 63, 118
"Materials concerning Korean Identification" (1913), 52–53
May Fourth Movement, 63
McCarran, Pat, 103
medical discrimination, 165–166, 216n2
Meiji Restoration, 39, 117
membership, 7, 14–16, 19, 157–159. *See also* citizenship
methodology, 3–4, 23–26
Meyer, John, 3, 26, 167, 173
migration, defined, 8
migration control, 65–70, 128–130
Migration Control Ordinance, 102
Mills, Charles, 15
Mindan (Zainihon Chōsen Kyoryū Mindan), 96–97, 110–111, 115, 151, 179–180, 182, 217n13, 217n17
Minematsu Tamesaku, 105
Ministry of Agriculture and Forestry, 87
Ministry of Education, 97

Ministry of Foreign Affairs, 102–103
Ministry of Health and Welfare, 85, 111
Ministry of Internal Affairs, 85, 218n24
Ministry of Justice, 103, 107
Minsei, 100
Minshutō (DPJ), 183
Mintōren, 146–147
mission civilisatrice, 51, 57
Miyamoto Keiji, 113
Mizuno Naoki, 49, 73, 87, 217n9
Mochiji Rokusaburō, 66
modernization under duress, 36–39
mono-ethnicity. *See* ethno-racial, as term and concept; homogeneity myth
Morris-Suzuki, Tessa, 102, 112
Mutual Love or Brotherhood Association, 70

Nagaoka Harukazu, 48
Nagasaki bombing (1945), 78, 166
naichi, as term, 214n15
naisen yūwa, 68
Nakasone Yasuhiro, 170
names and classification, 27–31
Nanjing Massacre, 171
Nanmin Shien Kyōkai, 194
Nash, Kate, 188
national boundaries, 70–74
National Committee of Lawsuits against Fingerprinting, 153
National Councils of Alien Registration Offices, 104
National Health Insurance Plan, 115
nationality, as term, 218n29
National Levelers Association, 50
national sovereignty, 16
nationhood: assimilation and, 56–57; colonialism and postwar of, 84–91, 101–106; decoupling of citizenship and, 184–191; defined, 6–7; effects

of globalization and migration on, 16; future of, 191–197; nonstate *vs.* state agents, 76–77; scholarly theories on, 13–17; to universal personhood, 142–158. *See also* citizenship; collective identification
nation-state, 78–84, 121–126
naturalization, 137, 181–182, 186, 202–203, 219n1
Naturalization Act (1790), 213n8
naturalization law, 16, 43–44, 181
new "patriotism," 172
New Zealand, 79
Nichibenren, 153
nihonjinron, 169
Nike, 191–192
nikkei, 186, 187
nikkeijin, 186–187
1985nen Hana de aru koto (film), 220n20
Nishimura Hitoshi, 176
Nishino Hideaki, 144
Nishio Kanji, 171
Nissan Corporation, 192
Nixon, Richard, 159, 160
Nonaka Hiromu, 180
noncitizen status, 1, 2, 7–13, 18, 21, 88, 128–132, 140–142, *185. See also* alien status
nonstate agents, 76–77, 81
nopperi gao, 52
Northeast Great Earthquake (2011), 183
North Korea, 106–116, 129. *See also* Korea
Nyūkoku Kanribu (later Nyūkoku Kanrikyoku), 102, 218n22, 220n17

Obuchi Keizō, 180
Office of Immigration (Nyūkoku Kanribu), 102, 218n22
Ogasawara Sankurō, 86–87
Ogata Sadako, 161, 221n22

Okinawans, 5, 142
Ōkuma Shigenobu, 54
Ōmura Detention Center, 110, 218n31
Ōmura Sei'ichi, 92
Ōmu Shinrikyō, 191
"On the Suffrage of Taiwanese and Koreans Living in Japan" (Kiyose), 88
"On the Treatment of Korean Schools" (1948 directive), 97–98
oppression and change, 17–23
Osaka, Naomi, 191
othering, 12–13, 45–49
Ōtsuka Tsunesaburō, 66
Ozawa Ichirō, 181, 183, 222n8

Pachinko (Lee), xi
Paku kun o Kakomukai, 143–144
Pan-Asian Empire, 34–36, 74–77; citizenship undermined in, 59–65; ethno-racial contradiction in, 53–59; internalized othering in, 45–49; limits of emulation in, 49–53; migration control in, 65–70; modernization under duress, 36–39; national boundaries and, 70–74; trapping Koreans within citizenship, 42–45. *See also* citizenship
Paris Peace Conference (1919), 167
Park Chungeum, 1, 2, 69, 70, 105
Park Chunghee, 114
Park Jongseok (Arai Shōji), 1, 2, 142–148, 173, 194
Park Jubeom, 1, 100
Park Yul, 92–93, 110, 111
Peattie, Mark, 59
pendulum-swing pattern of change, 17–23, 197–209
Perry, Matthew, 37
personhood, 95, 142–158. *See also* human rights; rights, defined
Peru, 186

260   *Index*

Philippines, 5
physical characteristics, 52–53
police brutality, xi, 27, 99, 191
population statistics, 68, 91, 128, 129, 185
postnationalism, 128, 157–158, 190
postnational membership, 14–15
postwar policies and colonialism, 84–91, 101–106
Potsdam Declaration (1945), 95. See also Act No. 126 (Hōritsu 126 Gō)
prison violence, 193–194
privilege, 7
"Proposal to Grant Special Permanent Residents Japanese Citizenship by Exception," 181
protests. See collective action

racial formation, 139–140. See also ethno-racial, as term and concept
racial violence, xi, 27, 99, 191–192
racism, 5–6, 15–17
radical leftism, 116–121
Ramseyer, J. Mark, 177
Red Cross, 111–114, 123, 206
redress, 166–167, 169, 179–180
Reischauer, Edwin, 80, 90
reparations, 64, 106, 108–109, 114, 122, 166, 178–184
repatriation, 111–112, 114
research methodology, 3–4, 23–26
Resident Aliens. See Special Permanent Resident Aliens
restorative justice, 10, 74, 86, 130, 165, 193
Rhee Syngman, 106, 108, 111, 114
Rice, Condoleezza, 168
Righteous Army, 60
rights, defined, 7–8, 95–96. See also citizenship; human rights; personhood; suffrage
Roh Moo-hyun, 180

Russia, 63
Russian Revolution, 62
Russo-Japanese War (1904–1905), 38
Ryang, Sonia, 23, 27, 220n10, 222n18
ryokō shōmei seido, 67
Ryūkyūans, 5

Said, Edward, 177
Sakurai Yoshiko, 180
Sandamali, Ratnayake Liyanage Wishma, 193
San Francisco Peace Treaty (1952), 88, 89, 97, 100
sangokujin, as term, 217n12
SCAP. See Supreme Commander for the Allied Powers (SCAP)
schools. See educational policies and practices
Seiron (publication), 180–181
Sekai (publication), 188–189
Sekiya Teisaburō, 84–85, 86–87, 216n4
self-determination, 63
self-identification, 75–76, 82, 169–172, 203. See also identities
Sengoku Yoshito, 143
sex slaves, 165
sexual violence, 193–194
Shidehara Cabinet, 87–88
shiminken, as term, 213n6
Shinwa (publication), 218n25
shizen shoshitsu, 219n1
Sino-Japanese War (1894–1895), 38, 40
Sōaikai, 70
social closure, 138
socialist-communist movements, 63–64, 110, 113–114, 118–120
Socialist Party of Japan, 110, 113, 120
social movements. See collective action
Soka Gakkai, 180

Index

South Korea, 106–116, 165. *See also* Korea
Soviet Union, 79, 106
Soysal, Yasemin, 14
Special Committee for Social Policy, 69
Special Permanent Resident Aliens, 2, 130–135, 136, 181, 185–189, 222n16. *See also* alien status
Special Permanent Residents. *See* Special Permanent Resident Aliens
Stalin, Joseph, 63, 119
statelessness, 1, 2. *See also* noncitizen status
Strike, Clifford, 108
suffrage: alien suffrage, 157, 179–184, 222n15; during colonial era, 9, 20, 35; Kiyose on, 217n9; of Park Chungeum, 1, 2; postwar, 87–88, 95–97; voting on, 69. *See also* Koreans in Japan
Suga Yoshihide, 194
Supreme Commander for the Allied Powers (SCAP), 79–80, 85, 97, 99, 124
Suzuki Hajime, 102–103, 104, 218n23, 218n25

Taishō Democracy, 50
Taiwan, 42, 217n8
Taiwanese in Japan, 5, 40, 88
Taiyō (publication), 54
Takahashi Mamoru, 120
Takeshima, 168
Tanaka-Nixon Communique (1973), 159
Terao Gorō, 119
Terauchi Masatake, 46, 54, 213n6
38th parallel division of Korea, 106–116
"Tightened Control toward the Third Country National" *(Asahi),* 92
Tilly, Charles, 138
Tōjō Hideki, 88

Tokkabi Children's Group, 195–196
Tokkabi Kodomokai, 195–196
Tokubetsu Eijyūken. *See* Special Permanent Resident Aliens
Tokurei Eijyūken (Special Case Permanent Residency), 133. *See also* Special Permanent Resident Aliens
Tokyo Trial, 88
Tōma Seita, 118
Tōyō Keizai Nippō, 182
trainee visa program, 187–188
transborder membership, 19
Triple Intervention, 38
Truman, Harry, 103
Trump, Donald J., 17
Tsuda Sōkichi, 118

Ueda Shinkichi, 120
Uibyong, 60
Umehara Takeshi, 170
UN Commission on Human Rights, 165
UN Human Rights Committee, 155, 158, 174, 206
United Kingdom. *See* Britain
United Nations, 80, 160, 530
United Nations High Commissioner for Refugees (UNHCR), 160
United States: immigration policies in, 17, 103–104, 175; internal migration of, 8; on Korean and Taiwanese citizenship in Japan, 90–91; on Korean reparations, 108–109; police brutality in, xi, 27, 99, 191; political and social unrest in, xi, 27, 99, 191; postwar occupation of Japan by, 79–81; 38th parallel division and, 106
universal human rights. *See* human rights
universal personhood, 7, 15, 95, 142–158, 173, 204

Index

Utoro community, Kyoto, 86, 192–193

Versailles Peace Conference (1919), 63, 64
Vietnamese immigrants in Japan, 5, *128*, 160–161, 187, 196
violence, 5–6, 86, 176–177, 193–194, 201
voting rights. *See* suffrage

Wagner, Edward, 80–81
Walter, Francis, 103
Washington Naval Conference (1920), 167
Watsuji Tetsurō, 118
Weber, Max, 23
Western imperialism, 36–37
White supremacy, 35
Wilson, Woodrow, 62
world society, as term, 3

xenophobia, 5–6

Yachimata school, *98*
Yamada Saburō, 34, 41–42, 43, 46–47, 213n6, 213n10
Yamagami Tetsuya, 191
yangban, 60
Yasemin Soysal, 157–158
Yasukuni Shrine, 172
Yi dynasty, 47
Yorozu Chōhō (publication), 45
Yoshino Sakuzō, 66

Zainichi, as term, 27, 136
Zainichi Koreans, as term, 27, 197
Zainichi Tokken o Yurusanai Shimin no Kai. *See* Zaitokukai
Zainihon Chōsenjin Renmei. *See* Chōren
Zainihon Chōsen Kyoryū Mindan. *See* Mindan
Zairyū Kanri Seido, 189
Zaitokukai, 176–177, 191
Zenkoku Suiheisha, 50

About the Author

Hwaji Shin is associate professor in the Department of Sociology at the University of San Francisco.